MW01174118

CREATING
PLACES

THE ART OF WORLD BUILDING

VOLUME II

RANDY ELLEFSON

Evermore Press
GAITHERSBURG, MARYLAND

Evermore Press, LLC
Gaithersburg, Maryland
www.evermorepress.org

Publisher's Cataloging-In-Publication Data
(Prepared by The Donohue Group, Inc.)

Names: Ellefson, Randy, author.
Title: Creating places / Randy Ellefson.
Description: [Gaithersburg, Maryland] : Evermore Press,
    [2017] | Series: The art of world building ; volume 2 |
    Includes bibliographical references.
Identifiers: ISBN 9781946995032 (CreateSpace paperback)
    | ISBN 9781946995100 (IngramSpark paperback)
    | ISBN 9781946995094 (IngramSpark hardcover)
Subjects: LCSH: Fantasy fiction--Authorship. | Imaginary
    places. | Creative writing. | Storytelling.
Classification: LCC PN3377.5.F34 E452 2017 |
    DDC 808.38766--dc23

This volume...is exhaustive. It also has advice along the way on writing that I'm sure novice writers and perhaps some established ones too can profit from. I recommend this book as a basic reference; at worst it is a review of necessary concepts, and at best it will upgrade you from a mediocre speculative fiction writer to a superior one.

—BESTSELLING AUTHOR PIERS ANTHONY

Like Ellefson's preceding book, Creating Places is one of that rare breed: an essential reference work. Unlike most references, this one is fun to read. Not to mention a goad and spark for the imagination!

—ED GREENWOOD INVENTOR OF THE FORGOTTEN REALMS® AND DOZENS OF IMAGINARY WORLDS

Contents

TABLE OF FIGURES

ACKNOWLEDGEMENTS

Special thanks to Raoul Miller, Rachel Hoff, and Margarita Martinez for their input

Edited by JJ Henke

Cover design by Deranged Doctor Design

Figures 1-11, 34-47, 62: Copyright Randy Ellefson 2017
All other figures are public domain and used with permission, and if needed, credited below:

Figure 16: KDVP (Wikipedia User)
Figures 20-22: domdomegg (Wikipedia User)
Figure 24: Dustin M. Ramsey
Figure 28: P199 (Wikipedia User)
Figure 29: Ivo Kruusamägi (Wikipedia User)
Figure 48: Stan Shebs
Figure 51: Rama
Figure 53: Lance Woodworth

Introduction

I f we've created gods, species, plants, animals, monsters, and more such as in *Creating Life (The Art of World Building, #1)*, we need somewhere for everyone to live. Creating the world can help us envision conflicts, alliances, and struggles our characters might endure while traveling across mountains, through forests, or over the sea.

In this volume, we'll discuss:

• Solar systems, planets, moons, stars, constellations
• Continents, oceans, seas, and other water bodies
• Land features such as forests, mountains, and deserts
• Sovereign powers like kingdoms
• Settlements such as cities, towns, villages, and more
• Travel on land, sea, and in space by various means of locomotion (horse, wagon, dragons, ships) and how to consistently calculate travel times
• Places of interest
• History
• Drawing maps for continents, settlements, and more

The examples included in the text were created specifically for this guide and are not drawn from any setting

I've created, except in rare instances and in Chapter One, "Case Studies" (drawing new maps for that is too time consuming).

The series has a website where you can find additional resources, information on other volumes in this series, and other items as they are added.

http://www.artofworldbuilding.com

WHERE TO START

The series and chapters within each volume can be read in any order but are arranged according to what might come first in a world's timeline. A planet precedes continents, which precede land features, et al. But our creations can be invented in any order. Only you can decide where to begin, but it's recommended to take any idea and run with it, writing down whatever occurs to you. If there are problems with it, they can be fixed later as you update and improve upon it. If you haven't read a chapter in this book and have an idea for something that's covered here, you can adjust your work later.

So where do you start? Where your heart lies.

ABOUT ME

By profession I'm a software developer, but I've been writing fantasy fiction since 1988 and building worlds just as long, mostly one planet called Llurien. Yes, I am crazy. But I love what I do. I didn't intend to work on it for so long, but when life has prevented me from writing, I've worked on Llurien. I've done everything in these chapters and authored two hundred thousand words of world building in my files. Llurien even has its own website now at http://www.llurien.com. I've written six novels and over a dozen short stories over the years, and have just begun my publishing career with a novella that you can read for free (see below).

I'm also a musician with a degree in classical guitar; I've released three albums of instrumental rock, one classical guitar CD, and a disc of acoustic guitar instrumentals. You can learn more, hear songs, and see videos at my main website, http://www.randyellefson.com.

FREE BOOK

If you'd like to see a free sample of my own world building efforts in action, anyone who joins my fiction newsletter receives a free eBook of *The Ever Fiend (Talon Stormbringer)*. Please note there's also a newsletter for *The Art of World Building* that is separate, though both can be joined on the same signup form. Just check the box for each at http://www.randyellefson.com/newsletter.

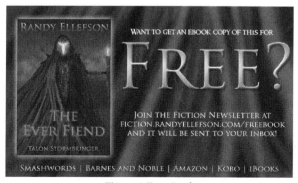

Figure 1 Free Book

DISCLAIMERS

World building is defined as the act of creating an imaginary world. While that suggests an entire planet, the result is often one continent or less. By world building, I don't mean using pre-existing ideas and putting your own spin on them, such as reimagining Greek gods in modern or ancient times, or writing an alternate reality of Earth. While such approaches are fine, that's not what this series is about, though such creators may find the series useful.

I've omitted the science behind any real or imagined technology (like the warp drive from *Star Trek*) because other books on these subjects exist. Something like plate tectonics is discussed in this volume because it impacts the formation of mountains, but the details of subduction zones are seldom relevant for us when drawing mountain ranges, for example.

While some authors prefer the term "races" to "species," I've used the latter term throughout most of the series. This book uses "SF" to abbreviate science fiction. SF is broadly defined herein as a setting with technology far in excess of current capabilities. Fantasy is loosely defined in this book as a setting using magic, knights, and lacking modern technology. As a stylistic point, to avoid writing "he/she," I've also opted for "he" when discussing someone who could be either gender.

Since I am an author, and primarily write fantasy, the series is admittedly weighted in this direction, but whether you're in the gaming industry, a screenwriter, a hobbyist, or write science fiction, much of the three volumes can help you anyway. I just don't claim to have covered every element despite my attempts to be reasonably comprehensive. If you have suggested topics you feel should be covered, feel free to contact me at mail@randyellefson.com about updates for later editions.

THE CHAPTERS

What follows is a summary of what's included in each chapter in volume two, *Creating Places*.

CHAPTER 1—CASE STUDIES

Three case studies show how the contents of this volume can aid in creating relationships we can use in our work. They discuss the effects of prevailing winds, climate, land features, rain shadows, and the impact of passages to travel through troubling areas. Each affects the sort of sovereign power suggested by a region and how alliances and enemies can be forged, some changing with time. Each power will have different ideologies and geographical features and needs, which can help us determine relationships between different powers.

CHAPTER 2—CREATING A PLANET

This chapter focuses on creating an Earth-like planet. World builders should understand the role of the moon and its effects on tides, seasons, and more if we intend to have a moon different from our own or multiple moons. Mention of other planets, constellations, and comets can make our world seem like it's not an island. The equator, climate zones, prevailing winds, and rain shadows all affect how much precipitation falls in an area, which in turn affects all life there, including vegetation or the lack thereof. Understanding these basics will help us create believable landscapes.

CHAPTER 3—CREATING A CONTINENT

Which hemisphere our continent lies in affects the seasons and might impact where we place constellations. Understanding plate tectonics can help us build believable mountain ranges and place volcanoes where they might occur. This can also determine where deep areas of the sea are, giving our sea monsters somewhere to call home. We have some liberty to name bodies of water what we want, but this chapter includes details on when to use which name, including seas, bays, inlets, and more.

CHAPTER 4—CREATING LAND FEATURES

A continent will have mountains, volcanoes, lakes, rivers, forests, woodlands, savannahs, jungles, prairies, wetlands, and deserts, but world builders should understand each to place them in believable locations. While some aspects are obvious, minor details can change our decisions and augment our resulting stories. Why say characters have entered a run-of-the-mill forest when we can say it's a savannah instead, describing how it looks and what life is like for inhabitants and those traversing it? This chapter aids world builders in making a more varied landscape— one that is accurately depicted.

CHAPTER 5—CREATING A SOVEREIGN POWER

Kingdoms, empires, dictatorships and more are types of sovereign powers that world builders can create. Before we do, a high-level understanding of the differences m is crucial. Many variations to government types exist, which gives us freedom to tweak details for our needs, but we should know the rules before we break them. The role of sovereignty, including how it is gained and lost, is examined in this chapter along with the "divine right of kings." We also look at the head of state and head of government roles, the differences between them, and the conflicts that can arise. The nature of each branch of government is examined along with parliamentary systems. Democracies, federations, theocracies, monarchies, autocracies and more are examined for their key differences.

Inventing a sovereign power should include friends and enemies who shape policy, lifestyle, and culture. The form of government has significant impact on inhabitants and results from world view. History affects this as well, and while creating a history is optional, it enriches the dynamics of relationships and can create heroes, villains, and attitudes in the population. We should consider which species are present and in how great a percentage, and what languages are spoken or forbidden. Our power's location and climate will impact lifestyles and vegetation, which also influences what natural resources it has or lacks, and what the power does as a result. These can all lead to tensions both with other powers or the residents. Symbols, colors, flags, and slogans will be a source of pride and even fear for both foreigners and the population.

CHAPTER 6—CREATING A SETTLEMENT

Location impacts a settlement more than many world builders realize, from climate to terrain and water supply, but our neighbors also determine how much fortification is needed and the number of armed forces, including their skill sets. Ancient and recent history can bring lasting change and cause attitudes that enrich our setting. Our population's diversity is also critical for determining what life is like for the majority and minorities alike, but first we need to decide who is who (and why), how much power they have, and whether they can subvert those who are supposedly in power. Whether outposts, castles, villages, towns, or cities, or even an orbiting station, a settlement will have secrets, a reputation, colors, symbols, and local lore that characterize it in the minds of inhabitants, friends and enemies.

CHAPTER 7—TRAVEL OVER LAND

In settings without automobiles, world builders may struggle to determine how long it really takes people to traverse a distance, whether that's between settlements or land features. Mountains, hills, desert, and vegetation all impact speed and endurance, whether one is walking, riding a steed (even flying on one), or hauling freight like a wagon. The presence and quality of roads alter this, as do life forms that might cause wariness and therefore slower travel. A methodology is presented to assist with organizing distance measurements and scale, determining the base miles per day (BMPD) for various mode of travel, and terrain modifiers to BMPD. Using both miles and kilometers, formulas are provided for making calculations, which can also be estimated for overall land area in sovereign powers. Newsletter subscribers receive an Excel spreadsheet that can be used to alter scale and modifiers so that all calculations are automatically updated, reducing the need for manual calculations.

CHAPTER 8—TRAVEL BY WATER

Landlubbers have difficulty determining how long it takes for any ship, whether powered by oars or sails, to traverse a distance. This chapter explores the factors affecting sailing speeds and what vessels are most likely to be used during an Age of Sail period. Calculations are provided for realistic estimates. Both long and round ships are discussed, including the galley, brig, frigate, galleon, sloop-of-war, and ship-of-the-line. In fantasy, we have species and warrior types who might be part of our crew. We might also rule out gunpowder and cannon, which means having ships with no real fire power or which use alternative weapons, some of which are examined. Subscribers to *The Art of World Building* newsletter receive an Excel spreadsheet that performs calculations in kilometers, miles, and nautical miles.

CHAPTER 9—TRAVEL IN SPACE

Science fiction features invented technologies for traveling the cosmos, but that doesn't free us from attempts to be realistic about life in space or how to maneuver. Modern engines operate on the principle of thrust, which requires rear-facing engines, and we'll need this for slower-than-light travel within a solar system. Imaginary propulsions, like warp, hyper, or jump drives can benefit from believable limitations. We should remember that locations in space are ever changing positions so that how long it takes to travel between two points is seldom the same—or convenient for characters. The need to enter a planet's atmosphere affects the ship's structure, but world builders will be most interested in the internal organization and the effect we can make this have on people and story.

CHAPTER 10—CREATING TIME AND HISTORY

History can enrich a world and provide us with cultural clashes, famous items, and world figures to which our stories and characters can refer or cite as inspiration. To save time, we can create a master history file with short entries that are invented in a few minutes and which do not need long explanations. Some could be turned into stand-alone stories if we stumble upon a great idea. Historic entries can be created at any time and can include events involving the gods, technology, supernatural, wars, the rise and fall of sovereign powers, artifacts, and famous missions by groups or individuals.

We also need a universal way to measure time because each sovereign power might have its own calendar, making the correlation of events across kingdoms harder. The merits of keeping timeframes similar to Earth's are discussed; this includes the reasons why minutes and hours benefit from little alteration, while the number of days, weeks, and months can experience greater variation without disrupting the audience's sense of time.

CHAPTER 11—CREATING PLACES OF INTEREST

Even seemingly ordinary locations can acquire significance due to scale, features, or people associated with them. These include monuments, graves, catacombs and hidden passages, and unusual buildings, whether built in stone, flying in the air, or floating on water like Venice. Ruins offer places for treasure to be found or horrors unleashed, including magical or technological items. Event sites and shipwrecks also give inhabitants places to reference, seek, or avoid, and can be where items of our invention originated.

BONUS CHAPTER 12—DRAWING MAPS

While drawing maps is optional, they can help us visualize where everything's taking place, and if done well, can even be included in published works. Drawing skill isn't really needed, as modern map making programs allow us to place pre-existing shapes onto a map and move them around. Continent maps help us decide on the location and quality of land features like mountains, forests, and deserts so that we create a realistic ecosystem. The location of settlements, rivers, and bodies of water will also impact the stories and lives of characters we create. We can also draw settlement, dungeon, and ship maps to solidify our decisions and find new inspiration in our layouts.

CREATING LIFE
(VOLUME ONE)

Everything we need to know about how to create gods, species/races, plants, animals, monsters, heroes, villains, and undead is included in *Creating Life (The Art of World Building, #1)*. Some basic techniques are also discussed, such as using analogies and deciding how many worlds to build in a career. As with every volume, it includes reusable templates that can help you build better, faster.

CULTURES AND BEYOND
(VOLUME THREE)

Everything not covered in the first two volumes lies within the finale, *Cultures and Beyond (The Art of World Building, #3)*. This includes creating culture, organizations, armed forces, religions, the supernatural, magic systems, technological and supernatural items, languages, names, and various systems our world will have, from health, educational, legal, commerce, to information systems. Finally, we look at how to manage our world building projects. Without these subjects, no world building project is complete.

TEMPLATES AND NEWSLETTER

Effective world building requires having written down details about the created world. To help you organize and jumpstart your efforts, each volume in this series includes templates in the appendices. This volume includes three: solar systems, sovereign powers and settlements.

Rather than typing these up yourself, you can download these templates for free by joining the newsletter for *The Art of World Building*. As each volume is published, whether you've bought the book or not, subscribers will automatically receive an email with links to download the templates as Microsoft Word files.

In addition, this volume provides two Microsoft Excel files for calculating moon orbits and travel times on land, sea, and air. While the formulas are discussed in the book, the files come set with the needed calculations. I recommend that interested world builders download them rather than try to create them.

http://www.artofworldbuilding.com/newsletter

THE PODCAST

The Art of World Building podcast expands on the material within the series. The additional examples offer world builders more insight into ramifications of decisions. You can hear the podcast, read transcripts, and learn more about the episodes at

http://www.artofworldbuilding.com/podcasts.

IMAGES

This book includes a number of images, which are greyscale in the print copy and color in the eBook. Larger, full color copies can be viewed for free online at http://www.artofworldbuilding.com/creatingplaces/imag

es. They are organized by chapter and will provide more detail that make it easier to learn from.

CHAPTER ONE

CASE STUDIES

Whether we're new to world building or a pro, the following case studies can give insight into how the material in this volume can help our efforts. They demonstrate what can result from learning the contents of this book: how land features and map making can lead to decisions on allies and enemies, trade routes, and what types of sovereign powers could exist. Concepts are alluded to here but not explained; world builders can revisit these case studies as knowledge of this book's content is assimilated. The maps are also available online at http://www.llurien.com/continents/llorus/, where it might be easier to see what's being referred to.

Each case study will use my setting, Llurien, because I know what I was thinking while creating it, as opposed to someone else's world. It's a fantasy world with knights, magic, gods, and seven species of my invention instead of the staples—elves, dwarves, and dragons.

Case Study 1—Two Straits and a Sea of Enemies

The first case is the effect two narrow straits have on access to a sea and how this affects the relationships of several sovereign powers. If following along with the maps online (instead of the one below), expand the following sovereign powers sections to see the maps: Erizon, Kysh, Marula, Niora, Pell, and Rone.

The Sea of Fire and Straits

Figure 2 Sea of Fire

On the western coast of this continent lies the Sea of Fire, which is accessible from the ocean to the west via two straits (two narrow channels) that flow north or south of the large island there (see the map below). The northern Strait of Erizon is not particularly treacherous due to its width. Technically, it's too broad to be considered a strait; even on Earth we sometimes use the wrong word, so world builders can, too. The southern Strait of Niora is narrow enough to fit the definition of "strait" better due to being narrow, so I decided it is treacherous to differentiate it from the northern strait (variety is good).

THE EQUATOR

The equator runs through the center of the sea, which means almost all the woods near the sea are rainforests. The equator's location also means the prevailing winds are from the east (i.e., blowing east-to-west). When drawing a map, we should know where land lies in relation to the equator, as this impacts forest types, skin color of inhabitants, wind direction, and where rainfall occurs, which in turn affects vegetation or the lack thereof.

ERIZON

Above the Strait of Erizon lies Erizon, a wizard-centric oligarchy, where personal liberties are fewer. It lies on the northwestern corner of the continent by the ocean, which suggests that Erizon is a seafaring power. Given its naval might and the proximity to the Strait of Erizon, it seems obvious that Erizon would want to control access to the Sea of Fire via the strait. This becomes the dominant factor in its relationships with every sovereign power to the east.

Figure 3 Erizon

KYSH

The Kingdom of Kysh is the heart of the Empire of Kysh. An empire requires stability, which suggested power not rest with a single person, so I decided the Kingdom of Kysh is a constitutional monarchy ruled by parliament. The king/emperor is a ceremonial head-of-state, not head of government. In other words, this is not an absolute monarchy where the leader is all powerful.

Kysh and Erizon have philosophically different forms of government, setting them up as potential ideological enemies, so I made this true. Erizon has resisted annexation by the Empire of Kysh partly because powerful wizards are in charge.

Kysh controls the difficult Strait of Niora just north of its capital. Since no one gets through there without Kysh's cooperation, powers adjacent to the Sea of Fire might want to be on friendly terms with Kysh. Otherwise, to reach the ocean, their only option is the Strait of Erizon and Erizon's ships. With Kysh respecting personal rights far more than Erizon, it is a potentially better ally. Both powers clash on the sea, whether in the Strait of Erizon or open ocean.

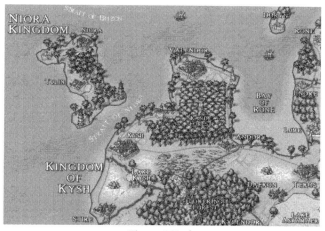

Figure 4 Kysh

NIORA

The island Kingdom of Niora separates the straits and influences both. The larger Erizon and Kysh have each conquered Niora more than once over the centuries. Both have left a lasting impact on culture and architecture.

Niora seldom had time to develop a constitutional monarchy (i.e., a bigger government) that lasted very long. I therefore decided it's an absolute monarchy, partly because it's small enough for one extended family to remain in power when independent. It is currently part of the Empire of Kysh, giving the latter more control over the Strait of Erizon. This is another reason that a sovereign power inside the Sea of Fire might prefer an alliance with Kysh over Erizon.

RONE

Figure 5 Rone

That brings us to Rone Kingdom, which lies on the right of the Sea of Fire, across the Bay of Rone from Kysh. For reasons explained in "Case Study 2—Stopping an Empire's Expansion," Rone prevented the Kingdom/Empire of Kysh from expanding farther north and is therefore

Kysh's enemy. That leaves Erizon as Rone's only ally regarding these straits, but what's in it for Erizon? For one, enmity with Kysh implies friendship with Erizon, so Erizon will help Rone for a price, such as escort fees or high taxes on goods. Rone has access to lands and resources to the east and south that Erizon doesn't, causing some mutual benefits to an alliance. This tense partnership has fallen apart more than once. Finally, I made Rone a constitutional monarchy to distinguish it from Marula, its neighbor.

MARULA

To the northeast of Rone is the very hot Marula Kingdom, located at the equator and with some of the darkest skinned peoples (see the next map). The Marula Mountains to the east block the westerly prevailing winds, causing a rainforest on the eastern side of them and a rain shadow and desert on the western side where Marula stands. A desert normally can't form near the equator due to heavy rains, but the tropical climate in Marula is really a temperate one due to high elevation, and this combination allows for a desert. Its people worship the sun and life-giving Alura River. Lacking many resources (like forests) and surrounded by enemies, it feels vulnerable, hence the ruling family's insistence on holding onto power, resulting in a brutal, absolute monarchy. Marula has a small stretch of coastline and can be easily cut off from the sea and everything beyond, so it became Rone's reluctant ally to gain aid on the sea and to prevent Kysh from conquering it next if Rone fell. The alliance is tense.

Marula and Erizon surround a common enemy (the Pell Republic) and are also philosophically compatible, making them allies. This gives Marula two allies on the Sea of Fire (Erizon and Rone) and two enemies (Pell and, Kysh).

Figure 6 Marula

PELL

Between Marula and Erizon stands Pell, a federal republic with great freedom for its citizens, putting it at philosophical odds with those neighbors (see next map). Pell became an ally of Kysh for protection and access to the ocean. Pell has another ally to the north, a larger federal republic called Siara, who has encouraged Pell's transition from constitutional monarchy to republic. Siara and Erizon are enemies—they share a border—and Siara is another seafaring superpower with a small fleet stationed at Pell, its ally. Erizon tries to thwart Siara from sailing around it and entering the Sea of Fire, so Siara responds, in part, by just building ships *at* Pell. See "Case Study 3—Mountains and

Murder," for more about this relationship and how geography suggested it.

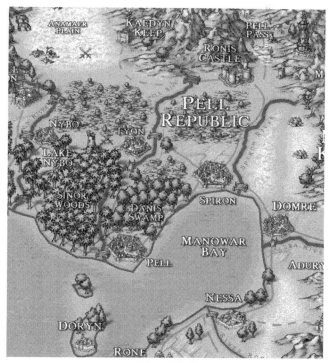

Figure 7 Pell

NAMING CONSIDERATIONS

The sea's location at the equator and the often-heard command to "fire" during the frequent ship battles on its waters suggested a name: the Sea of Fire. Manowar Bay also received its name from the ships-of-the-line that sometimes blockade access to the sea.

CASE STUDY 2—
STOPPING AN EMPIRE'S EXPANSION

In this case study, we look at how one sovereign power's position earned it enemies and allies, and how a way could be found to stop an empire from consuming an entire continent. If following along with the maps online, expand the following sovereign powers sections: Erizon, Kysh, Marula, Pell and Rone.

Figure 8 Controlling Territory

In the lower right on the map below, we see Rone Kingdom. The Empire of Kysh, to the southwest, must conquer Rone to expand northeast. When it tried, other powers came to Rone's aid for fear that if Rone fell, they'd be next. This included Marula farther to the northeast. Erizon joined forces with Rone because Kysh is their mutual enemy and Erizon doesn't want a stronger Empire of Kysh. Erizon believes it saved Rone, leading to some continued tension between these reluctant allies.

The Republic of Pell is an ally of Kysh but helped Rone instead, because if Kysh conquered Rone, then Marula, Pell assumed it would be absorbed next; the country's enmity with Erizon meant that Erizon would not come to its aid. Since then, Pell and Kysh have had strained relations. To the north of Pell is Pell's ally, Siara, which also aided the war against Kysh on principle; Siara, a federal republic, is opposed to sovereign powers conquering each other.

These relationships can impact stories and characters, such as someone from Erizon being haughty toward someone from Rone, a supposedly weak nation that needed so much help. A character from Rone might be bitter at the contemptuous way those of Erizon view him. This sort of dynamic is something world builders can create by drawing maps and creating different government types.

It can't be seen on the map above, but to the right are north-to-south running mountain ranges that cause rain shadows and deserts to their west. The rain forest in Rone Kingdom results from a large gap in those mountains, allowing moisture through. Other rain forests along the Sea of Fire result from the sea's moisture.

CASE STUDY 3—
MOUNTAINS AND MURDER

In this case study, we look at the impact of mountain ranges on terrain and sovereign powers. If following along with the maps online, expand the following sovereign powers sections: Erizon, Marula, Pell, and Siara.

The Winds and Rain Shadows

In the map below, the equator lies just to the south (off the edge). This means the prevailing winds are westerly. On the map's right side is a large, north-to-south running mountain range, the Marula Mountains, which acts as a rain shadow that causes the desert to its left. The Nemon Mountains (also on the map's right side) have a similar effect, causing another desert on their west, called Pell Pass. The War Peaks to the west would once again drain water from the atmosphere, leaving none to fall on the wider Anamaer Plain, which is wetter due to some moisture from the Sea of Fire to the south, resulting in grasslands instead of desert.

Figure 9 The Impact of Mountains

Some of this is open to interpretation. For example, Anamaer Plain could be another desert but two already existed in this region and more variety is good. No one from this planet is going to show up on Earth and announce that, in fact, no moisture from the Sea of Fire is coming north to result in more rain. However, it's unlikely that a full forest would stand there. If you don't understand why, this book will change that.

Forests stand to the north of these mountain ranges, as there's no rain shadow; the Marula Mountains don't go that far north and therefore don't block moisture.

THE POWERS

On the left third of this map (and extending out of view) is Erizon, a seafaring nation like the federal republic of Siara, on the northern coast. They are philosophically opposed and have competing navies with unrestricted access to the northern sea and a continent to the north. With the border between them short, most clashes are on water.

The remaining sovereign power in the image is the southern Pell Republic, which I decided has recently become a federal republic (in contrast with most other neighbors) like Siara. They became allies partly because Erizon threatens both from the west, launching wars on Anamaer Plain, a region filled with nomadic horse tribes. Caught in the middle, some of those tribes are allied to different powers, depending on who can benefit them. The landscape suggested these relationships, which is one reason to draw maps.

Pell Pass is how those of Pell and Siara meet and trade, but in the mountains to either side are unpleasant species and animals that attack any caravan or sign of life. Before Pell and Siara became allies, they contested Pell Pass and guarded it with castles at either end, seen on the map. These are now where caravans prepare for the dangerous trip through. The War Peaks are named for the battles that have often raged on either side of them.

The Pell Republic doesn't have the kinds of wood best for building ships and gets these materials from Siara, which has ships at Pell to access the Sea of Fire and lands beyond. This includes the Empire of Kysh, with whom Pell is on mostly good relations, partly because Kysh is also enemies with Erizon. Pell also has ships in Siara because it bought them from Siara.

The Kingdom of Marula to the southeast wants Pell's territory, including Pell Pass, partly to stop Pell and Siara from conspiring against it. Marula is at the heart of the slave trade and prefers those of Pell and Siara for slaves, increasing animosities.

CHAPTER TWO

CREATING A PLANET

T here are global issues to consider in creating a planet, such as moons, climates, the sun, and the rest of the solar system. Unless we're planning to do something truly unique with any of these, like two suns or moons, we'll probably want to go with an Earth-like situation, which is the focus of this chapter.

However constant celestial bodies appear to us in our limited lifetimes, their relationships are always in flux. We can invent a scenario that isn't likely in a four-billion-year-old solar system, but which is possible in a two-billion-year-old one. The reason is that gravity slowly stabilizes relative positions. For example, gravity causes satellites to *eventually* orbit in the same plane. If we have them in two different planes, we're implying the solar system's youth. Either that, or one of those moons was recently captured by the planet and hasn't stabilized with it yet. By "recently," we're talking in billions of years, meaning this happened well before our species crawled out of the ocean.

This may give us some leeway to invent a situation lasting long enough to tell our story, at the risk of eye-rolling by physicists. One goal of this chapter is to reduce such reactions and make reasonably informed decisions. Fortunately, physicists make up a relatively small percentage of Earth's inhabitants. Unfortunately, they make a far higher percentage of science fiction readers!

Some ideas and terms apply to more than one section. The alignment of three or more celestial bodies into a straight line is a called a syzygy. An eclipse is one type. Another type, called a conjunction, is when celestial bodies appear to be lined up from a low point in the sky to a higher one, as seen from another location (like Earth's surface). The term conjunction might be familiar to fantasy fans, as this has been used in stories, such as the films *The Dark Crystal* and *Pitch Black*, to indicate a rare aligning in the heavens, one that portends a great event. This is usually when some poor schlep is sacrificed, for example.

Appendix 1 is a template for creating a system and its planets, moons, and satellites. It includes more comments and advice, and an editable Microsoft Word file can be downloaded for free by signing up for the newsletter http://www.artofworldbuilding.com/newsletter.

ROTATION

Our planet is either rotating clockwise or counterclockwise. The Earth does the latter, which is why the sun rises in the east and sets in the west. We can reverse this for a quick way to thrust our audience into a different perspective. Of course, the stars, planets, and constellations will also travel across the sky in the opposite direction. Be aware that this affects ocean currents, covered later in this chapter. For world builders, this affect is largely that of which coast of a continent has warmer or colder waters. Prevailing winds will also be reversed in each hemisphere.

THE SUN'S IMPACT

Our lone sun is technically a yellow dwarf star of medium age. Most world builders, particularly in fantasy, will just want to go with the same and call their work done. More extreme situations might be better suited for worlds we'll only use for one story. In SF, with characters traveling across the cosmos to various planets, the viability of life in other suns' solar systems is debatable.

For example, a planet in the habitable zone of a red dwarf star would experience tidal locking (the planet's same side always faces the sun, just as one side of the Moon always faces Earth). This causes perpetual night on one side and perpetual day on the other. This sounds cool until we consider the huge temperature variations that would make Earth-like life difficult or impossible to form.

A moon orbiting such a red dwarf's planet could sustain life if it was also tidally locked to its planet, because that would cause the moon to not always have the same side face the sun. Even so, the lack of ultraviolet light also makes life unlikely, as does the variable energy output from the red dwarf (our sun is relatively stable). Maybe life can't originate there, but there's no reason we can't put a mining or research colony there. We can use such worlds but maybe not have much life originate there unless that life is extremely different from Earth's.

THE MOON(S) IMPACT

Earth has a stable moon with no atmosphere, but other moons in our solar system and beyond are volcanic, icy, or have toxic atmospheres. While our moon is relatively large in relation to the planet it orbits, and has a steady, close orbit, satellites orbiting other planets are often smaller, farther away, and have eccentric orbits. Most solar system objects orbit in the same direction, but some are backwards. This retrograde motion usually means a moon (or a planet) formed elsewhere and was captured by the planet (or sun). By contrast, a moon that formed when the planet did will orbit in the same direction. Large moons tend to match the direction while smaller ones can go either way.

TIDAL LOCKING

The term "tidal locking" will make many of us think of tides, but these are unrelated phenomenon. Our moon is tidally locked to the Earth. The same side is always facing us because the moon rotates on its axis in the same number of days it takes to orbit us. This might seem coincidental and unique, but most significant moons in our solar system are tidally locked to their planet; those nearest experience this first. Tidal locking is an eventual result caused by gravity. Early in a moon's orbiting, it might not be tidally locked, but ours may have become locked in as few as a hundred days (it's proximity and size having much to do with this). A moon that is not tidally locked may have recently formed or been captured by the planet. Either way, the stabilization process hasn't completed.

As world builders, we have some leeway to claim a satellite is locked or not. Most people are unfamiliar with the concept and we should only mention it if locking has occurred, as readers will assume the opposite without being told. Note that a close, large moon like ours will almost certainly be locked; during the brief period when ours was not, it and the Earth were molten and devoid of life.

Normally, only the satellite is locked to the planet, but they can become mutually tidally locked, as happened with Pluto and its moon, Charon. This means that each of them only sees one side of the other. If we stood on our moon, we'd see all sides of Earth as it rotates, but from Earth, we see only one side of the moon because they are not mutually tidally locked. If they were, the moon would stay in the exact same spot in the sky. About half the planet would see it, while the other half wouldn't even know it existed unless traveling to the far side of the world. This would eliminate most tides (see next section) except those caused by the sun.

We can create a planet that orbits the sun in the opposite direction from other planets, a fact which would likely be noticed. In a less technological setting, supernatural significance might be attributed to this. In SF, perhaps inhabitants of that planet realize it originated from another solar system and wonder what it's doing here. Where did they come from? We can also create a captured moon that orbits in a different direction than the planet or its other moons; these are typically farther away because gravity will eventually change that for nearer moons.

TIDES

Tides are variable. They are affected by coastline, currents, and other factors we can usually ignore as world builders and writers. But the moon is the greatest cause of tides, followed by the sun. If we want moons different from ours in number, proximity, or orbit, we should understand the moon's effect on tides. On Earth, tides can be so extreme that boats moored at high tide are sitting on the beach at low tide, which is one reason large vessels remain farther out and small boats are used to come ashore; such situations could be exaggerated with additional moons. Tidal forces are also causing our moon to get farther away, which would happen on any world we build (it if has oceans), but the rate is infinitesimal; still, a moon is unlikely to be getting nearer unless it's already very close. Gravity will pull it in and rip it apart. This can be a very real doomsday scenario for a world because the moon's debris will rain down on the planet's surface and cause destruction; the planet's tilt will also destabilize, affecting seasons and possibly causing dramatic and rapid-onset ice ages, for example (more on this in the next section).

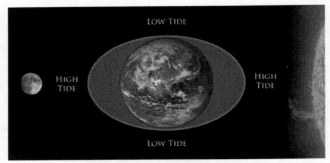

Figure 10 Figures

Our moon causes high tide on the side of the Earth it faces because it is pulling the ocean away from the planet. The moon is also pulling the Earth that direction and away from the ocean on the opposite side, causing another high tide on the planet's far side. The Earth's other two sides experience low tide (see Figure 10).

This causes two high tides and two low tides per day. Those two high tides aren't the same height, nor are the low. One reason is that the moon's orbit is not perfectly circular. If we invent a moon with a more elliptical orbit, the tide will be less pronounced when the moon is farther away. Imagine your characters being aware that such a moon is coming close in a week and they must get to higher ground or be flooded where they are, and that settlements have taken this monthly flooding into consideration.

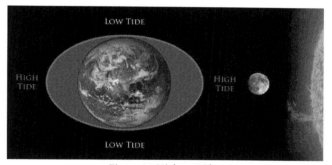

Figure 11 Highest Tides

Among high tides, the highest tides are when the moon, sun, and Earth form a straight line, such as Moon-Earth-Sun. But the very highest tides are when moon and sun are on the same side, such as Earth-Moon-Sun (See Figure 11), because the gravity of moon and sun are most strongly affecting the same side of the Earth. This is called a "spring tide" but has nothing to do with the season—it occurs twice a month, as does the corresponding lowest tides, called "neap tides." On a world of our invention, we might want to rename "spring tides" to avoid confusion.

A moon's diameter (apparent size) isn't particularly relevant for tides. Rather, mass and distance from the planet are the primary factors in tidal forces. Change either and we increase or decrease those forces and the resulting impact. More mass means more impact. More distance means less impact. Fortunately, our audience isn't expecting us to tell them the mass of a moon or how far away it is, especially as compared to Earth's, so we can usually ignore this, but we can at least know what we're ignoring.

We'll take a detailed look at how adding a second moon affects tides, as the observations can be expanded to additional moons and their impact. Using a clock face for orientation, with Earth at the center, what might the tides be like if the moons are:

- the same mass
- equidistant from the planet
- at 12 and 3 (to start) and never get materially closer or farther from each other while orbiting?

Picture Moon One's gravity pulling at the 12 and 6 positions (causing high tides there) while Moon Two's equal gravity does the same to 3 and 9 (causing high tides there, too). Would they balance each other's effect on the oceans, causing a constant water level (i.e., lack of tides)?

Unless we're physicists, we can get ourselves into trouble with this kind of thinking, creating impossible situations. Is that's why it's called "science fiction?" Not really. SF is fiction which combines science that does not exist while hopefully getting right science that *does* exist. We have leeway to invent but should aim for believability.

Lack of tides isn't particularly useful, interesting, or likely (without mutual tidal locking). The theoretical scenario above is a starting point for making observations that can help us make informed decisions. Altering that example, if two moons are at 12 and 6 and stay that way (always on a planet's opposite sides), we'd have more extreme tides. But if one moon had lower mass, it might have less impact on tides. This would also be true if one moon was farther away. Or had a more elliptical orbit.

Only distance, not mass, affects orbital speed. More distant satellites orbit slower, so two moons at different distances can't stay on the planet's opposite sides. Having two (or more) moons that are always in the night sky at fixed points to each other is unlikely. The nearer moon, moving faster, would appear to regularly catch and pass the farther moon. This will sometimes cause them to align in the sky. If they're orbiting in the same plane (and most moons of a planet do), this will cause at least a partial eclipse of the farther moon by the nearer. The degree of eclipse is determined by the relative size, not mass, of the moons. For a total eclipse, the nearer one must be large enough (as seen from the planet) to completely block the farther one as seen from the planet.

An elliptical orbit would also mean that a moon's effect on the world would ebb and flow depending on how far away it was; imagine it coming close once a month and causing a much stronger tide, and if this coincided with being on the same side as the other moon (and sun) every year, maybe we'd get a far stronger tide once a year.

If two moons are orbiting at different speeds (they do not stay at 12 and 6 in relation to each other), they can only do so at different distances from the planet. Otherwise they'd have crashed into each other, resulting in one merged moon and possibly a ring around the world from the impact's debris. The falling remnants would wreak havoc on life. If the moons are at different planes (but the same distance), they could theoretically survive, but gravity would eventually draw them into a collision because orbits stabilize to the same plane in time. This is a potential doomsday event for inhabitants.

When the two orbiting moons form a straight line with the planet, the tide would be more extreme. Otherwise, tides would be weaker.

In the most likely case of two moons orbiting in the same direction but at different speeds, at different distances, we could decide how long it takes for each of them to orbit the planet. We can just pick a number. Keep in mind that a number less than Earth's moon (which orbits in 27 days) means our invented moon is that much closer. A moon orbiting in 14 days is about half as close, when our moon is already very close. Anything that close will have a big effect on the planet, so unless we really want to emphasize the moon in some way, have the moon equidistant to or farther away than ours.

If our world has thirty days in a month, maybe we choose thirty days for one moon's orbit. Then decide how fast the other moon orbits. With this decided, we can then figure out how often they're on the same/opposite side of the planet. The formula is:

$$(P1 * P2) / (P2—P1) = C$$

P1 is the period that the closer moon takes to orbit the planet. P2 is the farther moon's orbital period. C is the conjunction (when they're together), though this could be any two relative positions. Assigning P1 to 15 days and P2 to 30 days, we get this:

$$(15 * 30) / (30—15) = 30$$

Breaking it down, 15 times 30 is 450. This is divided by the result of 30 minus 15, which is 15. So 450 divided by 15 is 30. Every 30 days, the moons will be in conjunction (or any other configuration).

If you'd rather not do these calculations manually, the "Moon Orbit Calculator" Excel spreadsheet included with the free templates allows you to type in the number of days for two moons and get the answer. If we're after a certain result, we can keep changing the numbers until it produces an answer we like.

For example, on my world of Llurien, there are 28 days in every month (because there are 28 gods and each gets a day). I want the nearest moon to orbit in 28 days, heralding the start/end of each month. Three months is a season of 84 days. Each season, an arrangement of gods changes. I wanted a conjunction of moons to occur each time, adding increased significance to this seasonal event. That means a conjunction at 84-day intervals. So how long does it take for the second moon to orbit? I probably could've used math, but I just kept typing numbers into the spreadsheet until 42 for moon two's orbital period caused the conjunction field to say 84, my goal.

Knowing when two moons coincide can help us determine how often eclipses happen. It also tells us when the highest tides are. Sailors and port townsfolk will be aware of this. A water-dwelling humanoid species might be, as would animals, both on land and sea, possibly taking advantage of this during birthing, hatching, or forays ashore.

This exercise can be imagined with more than two moons, though you'll have figure out the formula for that. Effects on the planet start getting complicated unless we keep most of the moons farther away, give them less mass, and keep them in a mostly circular orbit. All of this reduces their impact so that we can include them, but concentrate on the influence of the one or two most influential moons have on tides.

What happens if there's no moon? Probably very little tide; the sun would cause some tides.

THE SEASONS

Our moon also causes the stability of the Earth's tilt. As the Earth orbits the sun, one pole tilts toward it and causes summer in that hemisphere, while the other faces away and experiences winter. Without a moon, Earth would wobble chaotically. Seasons would end, as would most life, especially plants that evolved in a specific climate and wouldn't survive rapidly changing ones that could last unpredictable lengths, from days to possibly centuries. Worse, this would destabilize the Earth's orbit around the sun and cause us to acquire an increasingly elliptical orbit, meaning Earth will alternatively roast and freeze in a year.

Earth tilts at 23.5 degrees and is a kind of Goldilocks tilt, just the right angle to allow life to flourish. More extreme tilts up to 90 degrees, or down to 0, would cause heat extremes at poles and the equator, making an Earth-like planet impossible. On a world that never had a stabilizing moon, life might still evolve but would be adapted to sudden, extreme, and potentially long-lasting changes.

HOURS IN THE DAY

Our moon also affects the rate at which both it and the Earth spin. Both are slowing due to tidal forces they exert on each other. They will eventually stop spinning altogether, except that the sun will become a red giant and vaporize both before then. The moon is also getting farther away. If the Earth spun faster, as it did billions of years ago, we'd have much shorter days. Therefore, if we want a plausible reason that our invented world has very short days, no moons is one solution. Either that, or any moons are too distant to influence the planet in this way. Both scenarios inhibit life, however, so it might be best to decide that the planet is relatively young and still has a stabilizing moon. We don't need to ever tell our audience this, but if we wanted a character to remark that the planet was

4 billion years old and only has 12-hour days, this doesn't make sense unless the moon was captured (not formed) recently, as in a few million years ago.

MOONLIGHT

Since our moon is barren, it reflects the sun's light down on the planet as moonlight. If we create a habitable moon covered in water, earth (much of it forested), and the moon's atmosphere, it would absorb rather than reflect sunlight. The result would be far less moonlight. We should consider this when deciding that our nearest moon is habitable or covered in thick, dark atmosphere or a non-reflective surface. A secondary, farther moon might cast some light, but the effect will be reduced.

OTHER PLANETS IN THE SOLAR SYSTEM

Our invented planet is unlikely to be the only one orbiting its sun. This section discusses others within a solar system.

In SF, interstellar travel is virtually a given, whether that's within a solar system or between systems and galaxies. In fantasy, other planets are seldom mentioned unless there's an event of some significance like a conjunction of moons, stars, the sun, and planets. This might be an oversight, for magic or other supernatural means could allow characters to move between worlds (and moons). If a magic portal can get people from one place to another, the difference between traversing two sides of a planet and between two planets might be negligible. It could take tremendous power from a wizard or we can decide the ability has become commonplace. Perhaps magical doorways have been created, the magic imbued within them so that ordinary people can use them, just like a technology. We could similarly have magic-powered spacecraft.

When inventing other planets in a system, we should have rocky planets like Mercury, Venus, Earth, and Mars closer to the sun, and gas giants farther away; temperatures are too high for gas planets to form close to the sun. Saturn isn't the only planet in our system that has rings; they are just more pronounced, so don't be afraid to do this.

There's a habitable zone that's not too far from or too close to the sun, where Earth-like life can develop. Only so many planets can fit within this zone, limiting the number of habitable planets. With a yellow star like ours, this is two to three planets. With a red dwarf sun, scientists concluded that a maximum of five could occur, and closer to the sun, because a red star is cooler. With trillions, not billions, of years for life to develop, life might flourish on more than one world. Life would likely be quite different from Earth, however. Decide if you need more than one habitable world.

Determine how many planets are in your solar system, their names, order, type (rock, gas, ice), and impact, if any, on your world. Some will be visible to the naked eye, though this depends partly on luminosity, a measure of reflectivity of the sun's light. These planets can be mentioned for added realism, making our main world seem less like an island. Planets are rarely visible; significance is often added to their appearance, particularly in less advanced worlds.

STARS ABOVE

While many stars are visible in the night sky, only the brightest are likely to receive enough attention to be named. Names could be given by sailors or anyone else who watches the heavens. These stars are given significance, often heralding an important event, mostly because they were in the sky when something happened. Stars and constellations are not visible all year, for as the planet orbits, the stars overhead change. The same stars will appear each spring, for example. This is true with constellations.

CONSTELLATIONS

Constellations are an area of world building that can be avoided until we need it. A constellation is a group of stars that suggest an outline of a person or object. They are often attributed mythological significance. In a fantasy setting, people may still believe in such things. In a SF setting, the beliefs may no longer be held but the constellations may still be recognized. The visible constellations change with the season due to a planet's orbit around its sun.

Creating constellations that matter to our characters can be done quickly. If we've invented gods or other world figures, like those discussed in *Creating Life (The Art of World Building, #1)*, we can use them here. Deities, or objects they possess, such as Thor's hammer, might be associated with a constellation. Mundane items might also be constellations, like our Big Dipper. People see familiarity and therefore comfort in the stars, and we have great freedom to do as we like.

Figure 12 The Big Dipper Constellation

We should decide which constellations are near each other. This can be done without explanation, as apparent groups of stars have no actual relationship. More important is whether each constellation is near the equator or not. If so, then people in either hemisphere can see it, though it will appear upside down to half the world. Any constellation closer to a pole is only visible to people in that hemisphere. For example, on Earth, most people in the northern hemisphere can't see the "southern cross" due to its location in the southern sky. This would be a poor location for a constellation we want everyone to see.

If we want each of our gods to have a constellation, we might choose to place all the constellations at the equator so that the whole world can see them. Those living near the poles won't see all of each constellation, but they're a minority and we can resolve that concern for most inhabitants. We might choose to have a god's constellation only visible in the far north, however, if we want a stronghold of worshippers there and not in the south. What if all evil gods were north and all the good ones south?

If we have a winter god and their constellation is just north of the equator in winter, that makes sense for those inhabitants in the northern hemisphere, but those in the south will see that "winter" god's constellation in their summer. There is no solution for this unless we decide the god has no constellation or two, one near each pole, where each constellation would never be visible to those in the other hemisphere. The same formation of stars is unlikely, so one symbol might a trident while the other is a fish.

DARK CONSTELLATIONS

There are also dark constellations (such as the "Emu in the Sky"), which are mostly in the southern hemisphere on Earth and may be unfamiliar to some readers. Clouds of interstellar gas cause these apparent shapes, reminiscent of seeing familiar shapes in rain clouds. They appear dark because they're so dense as to block light from reaching us. This could be an interesting alternative for the constellations of evil gods. Good gods are light constellations. Evil gods are dark ones.

PASSING ASTEROIDS AND COMETS

Since the primary difference between asteroids and comets is composition, we can treat them similarly, with the caveat that the ice in comets causes their familiar tail. Our interest here is in those that come near our invented world and whether to invent ones that fly by at regular intervals. Our world's inhabitants can see significance in them, inventing myths or imagining doomsday scenarios (which might be accurate). Combining a comet with a conjunction might foretell a particularly influential event.

Figure 13 A Dark Constellation

UNDERSTANDING CLIMATES

While many factors affect life on our planet on the global level, climate is among the most important and has several world-wide aspects to it.

THE EQUATOR'S ROLE

The equator is an imaginary line equidistant from both poles. Days and nights there do not vary in length; this changes the farther from the equator we go. It's perpetually hot except at high altitudes. The four seasons of spring, summer, autumn, and winter hardly exist. Instead, residents think of a dry season and a wet one, which averages two hundred days a year on Earth; some places are uniformly wet all year.

If we're writing SF, the equator is a good place for space ports because the planet is spinning faster there and less fuel is needed to escape the atmosphere, though if we have imaginary propulsion systems, maybe fuel isn't an issue. On Earth, spacecraft must launch easterly to take advantage of this spin. Imagine a scenario where one nation has limited fuel and wants to launch easterly, but the spacecraft must then go over an enemy nation capable of shooting it down. This illustrates how world building research affects a story.

When drawing a continent, decide where it lies in relation to the equator. Position impacts climate and the direction of prevailing winds, which carry moisture that is either blocked by mountain ranges or not; see the section on "rain shadows." The location of deserts and forests (and what kind) are a direct result of this. The significance of position will be demonstrated by the rest of this chapter.

THE OCEAN'S ROLE

Ocean currents play a major role in climate. Oceans absorb more of the sun's radiation than the atmosphere, retaining and then distributing heat as the water flows around the planet. This effect is assisted by Earth's rotation, salinity, and tides (which are in turn affected by the moon). If we have a world without significant oceans, this occurs less and the heat will be concentrated at the equator, leaving the poles more frigid. We can use this to create greater extremes between regions. For Earth-like worlds, we could ignore the ocean's role unless we'd like to leverage it, but the effect on our work will be subtle and might not be worth the effort to some world builders.

For example, we could invent animals, plants, or species that are found on one coast but not another. Why? Because it happens on Earth. The Gulf Stream that runs along the eastern United States pulls warm water up the coast. The opposite happens on the western coast, where polar water comes south, resulting in much colder waters there. Most seal types prefer colder water and are found west but not east. This is turn means predators like great white sharks are also concentrated where the food is.

If we do this on our invented world, we could have someone from the west coast express disbelief that those around him are about to enter the water on the east coast. Aren't they afraid to get eaten by a sea creature we've invented? They'd likely wonder what he's talking about, as they don't exist there. This depends on technological level, as the population of a more modern world like ours is more likely to be aware of differences even if not understanding the reason. In other words, this is arguably more likely in fantasy than in SF.

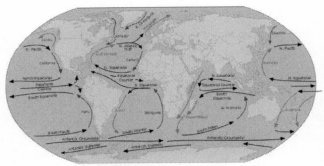

Figure 14 Ocean Currents on Earth

How do we determine where this happens? According to NOAA (National Oceanic and Atmospheric Administration), "Major current systems typically flow clockwise in the northern hemisphere and counterclockwise in the southern hemisphere, in circular patterns that often trace the coastlines." This means that a current is either carrying cold water from the pole toward the equator, or warm water from the equator toward the pole. On Earth, the western coasts are typically colder than the eastern ones. The online, color version of the above picture makes the difference in coastal temperatures easier to see, as the blue arrows are for cold water and are red for warm.

The details of this will depend on how many continents we have and their shape, but we needn't go overboard and can just decide eastern coastal waters are warmer. A caveat here is that this all depends on the planet rotating in the same direction as Earth. If not, just reverse this.

How does this affect climate? Warm coastal waters can moderate temperatures in one northern region relative to others, or conversely colder currents cause harsher winters. For example, parts of Norway have mild winters due to the Gulf Stream. We can note this in our files, but avoid explaining it, as explaining research we've done is among the worst, and most obvious, exposition errors.

UNDERSTANDING ZONES

The zones on a planet impact climate and will be discussed below. They are summarized in the next chart.

The exact latitude where a climate changes is not constant, as it can vary from continent to continent, so these numbers are generalizations and world builders can avoid worrying about getting it right. Besides, we're inventing a planet. Who can argue with us?

Climate Zone	Latitude
Tropics	The equator (0)—23.5°
Subtropics	23.5°—40°
Temperate	40°—66°
Polar	66°—the poles

Figure 15 Earth's Climate Zones

THE TROPICS

Extending north and south from the equator to roughly 23.5° latitude is a region called the tropics. This area is not defined by latitude but by the point at which the sun appears to be directly overhead at its highest point in the day, which is affected by the planet's axial tilt. Since our imaginary planet can have a different axis than Earth's, and therefore a different tropical zone, we can invent the area that is our tropical zone. Most of us will want to assume 23.5°, never mention this, and be done.

On Earth, the northern tropic is called the Tropic of Cancer while the southern is the Tropic of Capricorn. We'll want different names for ours. To make life easier on readers, it might be best to name a tropic after a prominent city located at 23.5°, though doing so requires having drawn latitude lines on a map. Or we can wing it. Stating that a map is not drawn to scale gives us some leeway to be inaccurate. Even on Earth, most people have no idea which tropic is which, where they end, or why they should care. Our readers won't remember either unless we name the tropics by something they're more likely to remember, like

a prominent city or a kingdom in that tropical zone. The
latter frees us from an exact location.

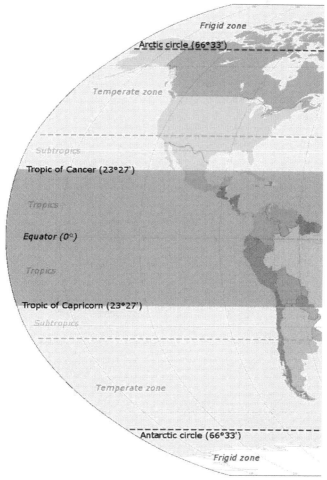

Figure 16 The Americans: Climate Zones

The tropics move heat from the equator toward the poles and are the primary influencer of climates on every continent. Ocean temperatures and mountain ranges further modify climate. A high-altitude area in a tropic zone might have a climate more like a temperate zone.

SUBTROPICS

The subtropics are the next farthest region from the equator, from 23.5° to 40°. On Earth, many deserts are in this zone, which seldom sees a hard frost or snow, but tropical storms and hurricanes can deliver as much as half of a country's rainfall.

TEMPERATE ZONES

In between the polar and subtropical zones, from 40° to 66° is the temperate zone, where most life on Earth exists. Coastal regions experience milder winters and summers than areas far inland, which experience a greater range in temperatures. Similarly, high altitude areas in this zone might have a climate more like a polar zone. The areas closest to the poles can be considered sub-temperate.

POLAR ZONES

The polar zones cover the north and south poles to 66° latitude and are largely covered in polar ice caps. There isn't much we need to worry about that isn't obvious. It's only mentioned to contrast it with the other zones.

PREVAILING WINDS

Wind direction varies at different latitudes (distances from the equator). These winds, along with geography like mountains, will determine where rain falls. This affects both climate and where vegetation and deserts are. Understanding this helps us create sensible topography.

Figure 17 Prevailing Winds

If our planet is tidally locked to the sun, it won't rotate, one side burning and the other freezing. This extreme is not covered by this book, so we will assume our planet is rotating. On Earth, this rotation causes winds near the equator to travel east in the tropics, while winds in the temperate zones travel west. In the polar zones, winds are again eastward but are light. Technically, the westerly winds are not entirely westerly, as they move from near the equator toward the poles. Similarly, the easterly trade winds move toward the equator, not just easterly. Our invented planet can be rotating in the other direction, reversing these winds.

A continent situated in the northern hemisphere like the United States or Europe will have westerly prevailing winds, which are called the westerlies for that reason. The easterly winds are called trade winds; sailors used them to cross the world's oceans, expanding trade. Ships benefit from sailing in the direction of the wind (prior to the invention of engines). We can call these winds what we want in our world, but it may only come up in the context of ship-oriented stories.

In areas with light winds, factors such as mountains, valley breezes, or the difference in air pressure between sea and land breezes affect wind patterns. These are local phenomenon and not something to consider when creating land features.

RAIN SHADOWS

Mountains cause moisture-carrying winds to rise. The clouds dump all the rain on one side of the mountain range, causing lush vegetation. On the mountain range's other side, there's no water left to fall. This causes a "rain shadow," an area that receives little to no rainfall. Deserts are the usual result. This process plays out across the Earth. A large list of examples can be found here: http://www.artofworldbuilding.com/rainshadow.

Rain shadows often occur near a coast and can cover half a continent, such as in the United States. Desert-like conditions occur closest to the mountains, though this is less severe farther from the mountains that are causing the rain shadow, partly because moisture doesn't come exclusively from the oceans and will be picked up in the atmosphere to fall as rain (albeit less of it). As we progress farther from the mountains, desert may give way to grasslands and finally forests.

THE CLIMATES

Climate impacts all life and is important for understanding how much rainfall occurs in various areas and the resulting vegetation, or lack thereof. It's an easy way to distinguish one location from another in stories. A humid region will impact the style of clothes and even customs of inhabitants. Maybe it's so hot and humid in midday that people work in the morning and late afternoon but take a long noon break. Those in northern climates might make the most of noon heat.

Climate is a long-term weather pattern, rather than day to day changes. Many factors influence climate and can be daunting to consider. Terrain, altitude, nearby bodies of water and their current, and latitude (distance from the equator) all impact climate. The ratio of land to water, how distant that water is, and the location of mountain ranges also have an impact. Another factor is the density and type of vegetation, which increase heat retention and rainfall. How far inland we are also changes things.

These variables cause the changes in rainfall amounts, temperature, and humidity. This might seem trivial, but areas can be well known for their climate. Examples include India's monsoon season, the humidity of the southeastern United States, and the dryness of the southwestern United States. As the latter two demonstrate, we can't rely on latitude to explain climate, as both areas are equidistant from the equator but one is hot and dry and the other is hot and wet. The prevailing winds and rain shadows from mountain ranges will be partly responsible for where forests and deserts lie.

Africa map of Köppen climate classification

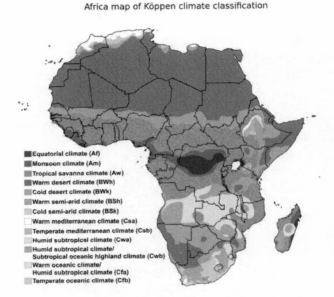

Figure 18 Köppen Classification Map, Africa

There are different climate rating systems, but the Köppen climate classification is the one we're familiar with (even if we've never heard of it) because it has terms like subtropical and rainforest, so we'll use that one. In this system, climates are divided into five main groups, each with subtypes or subgroups. Much of the information in this section comes from Wikipedia's Köppen Classification Summary at http://www.artofworldbuilding.com/Koppen.

Some excellent color images online can give a quick peek into just how variable climate is on even one continent. One is below, but the rest of Earth can be viewed online at this link:

http://www.artofworldbuilding.com/KoppenMap

TROPICAL

Located in the tropics (nearest the equator), tropical climates have year-round high temperatures at low elevations, and average temperatures of 18° C (64° F) or higher. Of the three below, we'll most often use the tropical rainforest climate, as the differences between the others are too subtle to matter to most of us; they amount to less uniform rainfall throughout the year.

TROPICAL RAINFOREST

In this climate, each month has average rainfall of 60 mm (2.4 in), and this climate is usually found within 5-10° of the equator but can sometimes extend up to 25° away. There is little seasonal change here, because the temperatures stay the same year-round, as do the number of daylight hours (changes are small). Many places are uniformly wet unless a rain shadow causes less rain there. Land at a higher altitude will have a milder climate and, due to a rain shadow, might even be relatively dry. Assign this climate to most areas near the equator, such as Brazil and Peru.

TROPICAL MONSOON

This climate is rare enough that we may want to ignore it during world building. Monsoon winds are those that change direction with the season and last several months. These winds cause this climate, which has a driest month just after the winter solstice. The wet season is months long. Some areas alternate between being arid, like a desert, to lush with green vegetation in the wet season, the stark contrast happening within weeks. The trade winds can bring enough moisture to cause rain in the winter months, preventing an area from having our next climate. Miami has this climate.

TROPICAL WET/DRY OR SAVANNAH

This climate has a more pronounced dry season of very little rain and is usually in the outer edges of the tropical region, farther from the equator. Some of the wettest places on Earth have this climate, with incredible rainfalls during the wet season, sometimes in a single day. Examples include areas of Africa, Brazil, and India.

DRY

Dry climates produce less than ten inches of rain a year. Some areas may receive more but lose it all due to evaporation. These desert climates can be hot, cold, or mild and are generally low in humidity.

The hot deserts have perpetually sunny, clear skies year-round and extremely high temperatures, though these can drop to freezing at night due to the same clear skies that permit heat dissipation. They are almost always in the tropics. Assign this climate to tropical deserts.

The cold deserts have similar hot summers, but the winter can be far below freezing. They occur at higher altitudes, are drier, and are in temperate zones (north of the tropics in the northern hemisphere, south of them in the southern). They are also usually in the rain shadow of a mountain range.

The mild desert climates are mild throughout the year and are usually found along the western edges of continents or at high altitudes (plateaus or steppe deserts). They are caused by cold ocean currents offshore. Deserts by the coast often have fog and low clouds.

TEMPERATE

Temperate climates are where most of Earth's population lives, though that's partly because much of our land is there. These climates have an average monthly temperature above 10° C (50° F) in their warmest months and an average monthly temperature above −3° C (27° F) in their coldest months. Some have dry winters, dry summers, or significant precipitation throughout the year.

There are several versions of temperate climates, discussed next.

DRY SUMMER

Dry summer climates, also known as a Mediterranean climate on Earth, usually occur on the western sides of continents between the latitudes of 30° and 50°. Summers are hot and dry except in coastal areas, where summers are milder due to nearby cold ocean currents that may bring fog but prevent rain. Winters are mild with rainy weather. Most rain is during winter, hence the name "dry summer." This climate is found around the Mediterranean and much of California.

WARM TEMPERATE

Warm temperate climates occur on the eastern sides of continents, from 25° to 45° latitude, such as the southeastern United States. Moisture from the tropics causes air to be warm and wet. More rainfall occurs in summer than in winter. The air flow out of the tropics brings warm, moist air to the southeast of continents. This flow is often what brings the frequent but short-lived summer thundershowers typical of subtropical east-coast climates.

MARITIME TEMPERATE/OCEANIC

These climates usually occur on the western sides of continents between the latitudes of 45° and 60° and immediately poleward of dry summer climates (such as north of them in the northern hemisphere). This includes the Pacific Northwest and New Zealand. They have changeable, often overcast weather. Summers are cool due to cool ocean currents, but winters are milder than other climates in similar latitudes, and very cloudy. This climate can be found at higher elevations in latitudes that would otherwise be subtropical or temperate. These high-altitude climates are called oceanic even if they're not near an ocean.

TEMPERATE HIGHLAND TROPICAL WITH DRY WINTERS

This is characteristic of the highlands in the tropics. Winters are dry, unlike other tropical areas. Summers can be very rainy.

MARITIME SUBARCTIC OR SUBPOLAR OCEANIC

These climates occur poleward of the maritime temperate climates, such as Iceland. They happen on narrow coastal strips of land on the western poleward margins of the continents or to islands off such coasts. There is very little precipitation and temperature variations are extreme between winter, at -40° C (-40° F), and summer, up to 30° C (86° F). The ground is frozen in winter to depths of several feet.

DRY SUMMER MARITIME SUBALPINE

This climate is very rare and only exists at very high elevations where the ocean influence keeps the temperature from going below -3 C° (26° F). As a world builder, we can largely ignore this unless we need it.

HUMID CONTINENTAL

These climates have an average temperature above 10° C (50° F) in their warmest months, and a coldest month average below −3° C (−26° F). These usually occur in the interiors of continents and on their east coasts, normally poleward of 40°. Precipitation (with thunderstorms) is evenly distributed throughout the year, snow cover often being deep. Summers are warm to hot, and often humid. Winters are cold, sometimes severely. Forests thrive in this climate, including evergreen and conifers, as do grasslands. Oak, fir, spruce, and pine do well in wetter areas and the fall foliage is noteworthy.

From a world building standpoint, the subtypes below offer little in the way of things we need to consider. That a summer is hot in one latitude vs warm in another is of little importance, but they are mentioned for reference.

HOT SUMMER CONTINENTAL

This usually occurs in the high 40° and low 50° latitudes, with an average temperature in the warmest month of greater than 22° C/72° F. This includes southeast Canada, some parts of the western United States (such as Utah, Montana, and Wyoming), and Serbia.

WARM SUMMER CONTINENTAL

This climate is just north of hot summer continental climates, generally between 45° and 58° latitude in North America and Asia, and in central and eastern Europe and Russia, between the maritime temperate and continental subarctic climates, where it extends up to 65° latitude.

CONTINENTAL SUBARCTIC

Climates occur poleward of the other continental climates, mostly in the 50° and low 60° latitude, although it might occur as far as 70°.

CONTINENTAL SUBARCTIC CLIMATES WITH EXTREMELY SEVERE WINTERS

Places with this climate have the temperature in their coldest month lower than −38° C (−36° F). These climates occur only in eastern Siberia. The names of some of the places with this climate have become veritable synonyms for extreme, severe winter.

POLAR

Polar and alpine climates are characterized by average temperatures below 10° C (50° F) in all months. The tundra climate has a warmest month of between 0 and 10° C. It occurs on the northern edges of Earth's land masses, in the north hemisphere. The ice cap climate is perpetually below 0° C and occurs at the poles and on extremely high mountains.

CLIMATE CHART

Highlights from the previous sections have been summarized in the chart below and are ordered the same, from the equator toward the poles:

Climate		Summary
Tropical	Rainforest	5-10° from equator, no seasons, steady temperatures, hours constant, uniformly wet
	Monsoon	Wet season of several

Climate		Summary
		months, otherwise dry, rare climate
	Wet/Dry or Savannah	Very little rain, outer edge of tropical region far from equator
Dry	Dry	**Hot deserts:** year-round sunny, clear, very hot (frigid nights), found in tropical region **Cold deserts:** similar summers but drier, brutal cold in winter, found in rain shadows/high altitudes and temperate zones **Mild deserts:** year-round mild, found in high plateaus and western edges of continents, prone to fog/low clouds if coastal
Temperate	Dry Summer	30-50°, western side of continents, hot/dry summer but milder on the coasts due to fog, mild winter with rain
	Warm	25-45°, eastern side of continents, warm/wet air, more rain in summer, frequent short summer thunderstorms
	Maritime/ Oceanic	45-60°, western side of continents, cool summers, mild cloudy winters
	Highland/	Found in tropics at high alti-

Climate		Summary
	Dry Winter	tude, dry winters, very rainy summers
	Maritime Subarctic	Found poleward of maritime/oceanic on narrow coastal strips/islands on western side of continents. Very little rain, ground frozen several feet in winter, temps from -40° F to 86° F
	Dry Summer Maritime	Rare, very high elevations
Humid Continental	All	40° latitude and above, found in continent interiors and east coasts, rain all year, warm to hot summers (often humid), cold winter (sometimes very). The four variants are all similar.
Polar	Polar	Average -10° C all year

Figure 19 Climate Chart

WHERE TO START

If we're using a sun unlike Earth's yellow star, we'll need to start there because this impacts much about our world, but otherwise little is dependent on another subject from a world building standpoint. Our biggest decision beside sun type is whether our world has a moon and how many. It's recommended to have at least one unless we're certain of what we're doing without one, because the absence of a moon will cause more changes than we might be aware of. The world's going to have an equator, prevailing winds, climates, constellations visible, and possibly other planets in the system, but none of these affect us until we start creating continents. Enjoy the rare privilege to embark on a world building subject in whichever order pleases you.

CHAPTER THREE

CREATING A CONTINENT

Despite the term "world building," we usually build far less than that in detail. Fantasy tends to utilize one continent. SF will typically use multiple planets, but on each, a single location (like a city) is used. Chapter Six, "Creating a Settlement," covers the invention of single cities, so this chapter discusses inventing a continent, even if we'll only use portions of it in detail. Multiples continents can be created following the advice herein. It's also possible to create a single, large supercontinent, like Pangaea or Gondwana.

We don't need to invent every region of our continent, but some basic thought should still be given to areas we won't utilize as much. It adds depth to our work to say that a product, like wine or furniture, came from a certain region. We can invent that on the fly instead of planning it, but there's more to life than products. Different sovereign powers will exist and have histories with each other. Allies and enemies flourish. Grievances are to be nurtured. Stereotypes, racism, and ethnic hatreds blossom. We can do all this and more by laying out a continent so we know where these people in conflict live. It's crucial for any story involving travel, like a quest, which typically involves a journey through hostile places; otherwise, any schlep could go get the quest token.

MULTIPLE CONTINENTS

We don't need to invent more than one continent, but to make our main one seem less like an island, we can name other continents and decide what they're famous for. We might never use them. But maybe people on our main continent know of another where people are free, and those in an oppressed kingdom dream of going there. Travelers from faraway lands will eventually reach our shores. Why not have some ideas on where they originated?

Creating multiple continents doesn't necessarily mean laying out each in detail. Here's a simple process we can follow to get started for one:

1) Draw a rough shape on paper
2) Decide where the land mass lies in relation to the equator and where it is in relation to the others
3) Give the continent a name
4) Carve it up into sovereign powers
5) Add names to those powers
6) Decide what each power is like, using Chapter 5, "Creating a Sovereign Power."

That can be it for now, or maybe we'll go one step further and decide on some reputations for the entire continent or various regions in it. Think about the Earth and what intrigues us about a place, then create such a one somewhere. We might want to save the best ideas for our main continent, but some things will be true of multiple places, like naval powers. There's usually at least one per continent. We can ask ourselves some questions for inspiration:

• Is there a kingdom known as a naval superpower, whose ships and raiders will reach our main continent's shores?
• Is there a slave trade somewhere?
• Huge rainforests?
• Impenetrable mountains?
• Vast deserts?
• Exotic animals?
• A spice trade? Or trade in something of our invention, like supernatural or technological elements?

WHICH HEMISPHERE?

The differences between a planet's northern and southern hemispheres is largely trivial but has various consequences. What matters most is where our continent lies in relation to the equator. The reasons this is important are laid out in Chapter 2, "Creating a Planet," but amount to determining climate. We can draw mountain ranges without having decided this, but no desert, grassland, or forest should be placed without this decision. The combination of prevailing winds, which are solely determined by latitude, and mountains will influence the location of vegetation, as discussed Chapter 2 under "Rain Shadows."

Those who travel between hemispheres will note that moons look upside down. So will constellations. Moon phases are also reversed, which can matter if we're planning to do spells that depend upon the moon's phase. An old game called *Ultima IV* had moon powered portals that only operated at certain moon phases, but the continent spanned only one hemisphere, presumably.

SEASONAL ISSUES

Those world builders who are used to living in one hemisphere might need to remind themselves, when creating a continent in the other hemisphere, that cold regions are not north/south but poleward. The seasons are also reversed; when it's winter in the north, it's summer in the south. This matters more during storytelling, but it also impacts constellations, as noted in the previous chapter. It can impact our calendar if we're not careful; this is discussed in Chapter 10, "Creating Time and History."

UNDERSTANDING PLATE TECTONICS

Understanding plate tectonics will help us add mountain ranges that make sense. A planet surface is composed of an outermost shell of slowly moving plates, which either converge on each other, diverge, or transform. The first two are the motions that create mountains ranges and volcanoes. Most volcanoes occur where two plate boundaries intersect, but some volcanoes exist in the middle of plates due to flaws in the plates; this means we can have a volcano anywhere on our map and no one can tell us otherwise.

There's a reason the western United States has major earthquakes and volcanoes and the eastern doesn't. The continental shelf is the area of land that's underwater just offshore. It is shallow compared to the deeper ocean. On the east coast, the shelf is wide, which means the plate boundary is also far away. By contrast, the west coast's shelf is narrow, ending just offshore. This means the deep ocean isn't far away. More importantly, the plate boundary is near the west coast, causing dramatic boundary activity that results in mountains and volcanoes.

Such a situation is true on other continents and is something to consider. If we say that deep water lies just off the coast of a continent, there are probably nearby mountains, some volcanic. We can also approach that in reverse: a coastal mountain range likely has deep water not far from shore. Ship wrecks there will be far under the waves. If we have a water-dwelling, humanoid species, or even sea monsters, they might be found here. Using the U.S. as an example, a giant sea monster is more likely to be encountered near the west coast than the east.

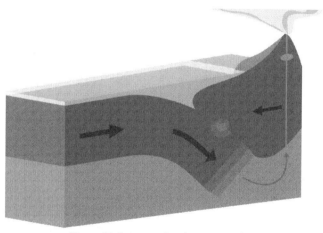

Figure 20 Ocean to Continent Boundary

Convergent Boundaries

When two plates converge, one destroying the other's edge, the results can be varied.

If subduction, in which one plate is forced under another, happens at an ocean-to-continent boundary, the ocean plate plunges under the continent, causing a continental mountain range. This range will be parallel to the coast (plates), with volcanoes that are the most explosive.

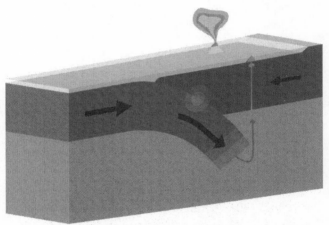

Figure 21 Ocean to Ocean Boundary

If subduction happens with two ocean plates, one goes under and causes a chain of volcanoes, which will eventually breach the ocean surface and become land. These volcanic islands will form a subtle arc shape in relation to each other because a planet is a sphere. A deep ocean trench will also form. This can be over two miles below the rest of the ocean floor there. It can also be a hundred miles away. If we have a sea monster we'd like to give a home to, here is where it lives. In a world with sea monsters, a place like

Hawaii would be prone to at least one creature; it almost doesn't make sense for one not to be there.

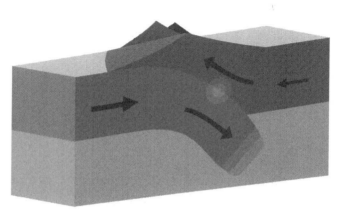

Figure 22 Continent to Continent Boundary

At a continent-to-continent boundary, the plates can converge, fold, and lift, forming very tall mountain ranges with no volcanoes. These will be the tallest ranges on our world, located in the interior of continents.

DIVERGENT BOUNDARIES

When two plates move away from each other underwater, small volcanoes form, which can result in volcanic islands. When this happens on land, a low area of land can form and then fill with ocean water to create a sea.

The Earth continents were once a super continent that broke apart. Divergent plates caused this. Evidence is apparent just from looking at the globe, as South America and Africa look like adjacent puzzle pieces. We can use the same idea for our continents, a small detail that may impress an audience if they notice.

TRANSFORM BOUNDARIES

Transform boundaries means two plates grind past each other without destroying either. These plates sometimes slip suddenly, causing strong earthquakes. Aside from this, evidence of their existence is less obvious. There are no mountains or volcanoes. If a paved road is broken, one stretch having moved ten feet away, this means the roads spanned the fault, an earthquake happened, and now the road will never connect unless repaved. We needn't consider this when drawing continents.

SEAS VS. OCEANS

Though there's no real difference between Earth's oceans, there are five that comprise the "world ocean:" the Pacific, Atlantic, Indian, Arctic, and Southern Oceans. The latter two are sometimes considered parts of the others. Some oceans cover both hemispheres and are therefore said to have a North Pacific vs. South Pacific, for example. When creating our continent, we might want to give different areas different names, too. These names refer to huge areas of sea separating the continents but which are one continuous body of water.

If you've ever wondered what the difference between an ocean and a sea is, that's because there isn't one. They're the same thing. "Sea" is typically used to denote a smaller area than an ocean, an area that is surrounded by land on several sides.

By contrast, a lake is a body of water that is surrounded by land. Sometimes a very large lake is called a sea. This may happen because the lake is so large that it seems like a sea to those living on its shores. Or "Sea of So-and-So" might've had a better ring to it. Or someone unfamiliar with the differences named it and the name stuck. "Sea" can also suggest a wild expanse of water with nothing (or at least, no civilization) on the far side; this can represent a judgment by inhabitants that only barbarians, for example, are found on that far shore. World builders can do this, too, though some snarky know-it-all may tell us it's really a lake and we don't know what we're doing.

An ocean region may have a reputation not based on fact, such as our Bermuda Triangle, where ships are thought to mysteriously disappear with regularity. We can invent such places, making them real or not. We can do this with aircraft, dragons, or anything that flies. Maybe dragons refuse to fly somewhere due to this.

Some ocean areas are prone to hurricanes and tropical storms, which are affected by water surface temperature, air temperature, and prevailing winds. This sort of thing plays into culture and a region's viewpoints on the ocean and its consequences. There can be mythology about gods being angry with them and sending these powerful storms. By contrast, the Pacific Ocean is so named for its calmness, possibly owing to its enormous size (nearly a third of the Earth's surface).

BAYS AND MORE

The information here is mostly about naming water bodies.

• Like a sea, a **bay** is a body of water surrounded on several sides by land. It can be part of the ocean or a lake

• A **gulf** is a very large bay

• A **cove** is a smaller bay and is usually circular, with a narrow passage into or out of it.

• A **fjord** is a narrow bay with steep terrain around it

• An **inlet** is a narrow, long indentation of a shoreline and which often connects a bay to another body of water. A group of many inlets can be called a "sound."

• A **sound** is large enough to draw on our continent-sized maps; they can be as big, if not bigger, than bays. A sound can give ships many places to hide.

• If two large water bodies are separated by a narrower area of water, that's called a strait, channel, pass, or passage.

Since bays lessen the effects of wind and waves, they are safer spots for fishing. Our world will have settlements along a bay. Some of our oldest cities will be there. It won't make sense to have a bay with no settlements on its shores, unless something is keeping everyone away, like a sea monster; in that case, the bay is likely named for that creature or its effect ("the Bay of Death"). Sometimes a monster is named for the water body instead, like the Loch Ness Monster.

ISLANDS

The difference between an island and continent is interesting reading but has no real bearing on world building. For most of us, it comes down to size. Use your judgement.

A continent often has large islands nearby, with those islands part of the same continental plate. This means relatively shallow seas lie between the island and continent. This won't be the home of a sea monster that likes depths.

These continental islands are distinguished from oceanic islands, where are almost exclusively volcanic in nature (whether that volcano is still active or not). Some oceanic islands result from plate tectonics, meaning we'll have a mountain range on it, possibly with the resulting rain shadow and desert.

Our world will have tens of thousands of islands, whether our species have discovered them or not. We needn't draw any but the largest near a continent. Most island nations consider their territory to extend far offshore in every direction. In addition to naming individual islands (or chains like Hawaii), we can name large regions that contains many islands. An Earth example would be Polynesia, which is a big swath of the Pacific Ocean and islands, all within an imaginary triangle. We also name land regions this way.

WHERE TO START

Though adding land features is part of the next chapter, making a list of the ones we'd like to include can help us determine how large a continent we need. Our story requirements can also help this. An early decision is hemisphere, as this determines whether hot or cold is north or south. We might also want to know other continents' direction and distance, as this influences population and more; try not to think of the continent as an island. We should also determine where bays and other water ways are when drawing our map, as this can influence the sovereign powers we place there. I recommend following the steps in the bonus chapter, "Drawing Maps." We can also start by imagining what powers we'd like in various areas of the land mass and rough ideas on their world view and impact, which can be fleshed out more by following Chapter 6, "Creating a Sovereign Power." There's no right or wrong way to start creating a continent because it's somewhat vague until we start filling it in, so use whatever inspires you to get going.

CHAPTER FOUR

CREATING
LAND FEATURES

While laying out land features can be fun, it's even better when we've first reminded ourselves of the possibilities and what they can mean for our world's inhabitants, our audience, and ourselves. This chapter is a roundup of the salient details world builders should consider. We can start placing items without having outlined a continent or even a coastline, but it's often better to know where the sea is, to determine plate tectonics, covered in Chapter 3, "Creating a Continent."

MOUNTAIN RANGES

MOUNTAINS

Mountains are covered first because their effect on precipitation determines the locations of forests, deserts, and rivers. We all know what a mountain is, but scholars have not agreed on a definition. What this means is that our characters can refer to something as a mountain when it isn't that tall (less than a thousand feet), so remember this option. The land just needs to stand out from the surrounding area.

Roughly 24% of Earth's surface is mountainous. Glaciers can create various shapes, including cirques (an amphitheater-like circle) where lakes form. If two parallel glaciers recede and carve parallel valleys, they can leave a row of peaks between them. If three glaciers recede from the same central point, a pyramid-like, sharply pointed peak or glacial horn is formed, like the Matterhorn. While these are interesting, they seldom matter on the large scale for world builders and are instead ideas for characterizing individual peaks our characters have noticed.

The highest mountain discovered in the solar system is Olympus Mons on Mars. Its extreme height (69,459 feet vs. Mount Everest's 29,035) is due to the absence of tectonic plates on Mars. Land stays over a hot spot indefinitely, causing eruptions and lava flows in the same place, which increases local elevation. By contrast, on Earth, tectonic plates shift land (or ocean) across the hot spots, causing things like a chain of volcanic islands like Hawaii. If we want a truly enormous, standalone mountain on our world, we can decide tectonic plates don't exist, but this would cause various changes like a potential lack of earthquakes or mountain ranges (and a resulting lack of rain shadows). Such a world might have many very tall, volcanic mountains but few if any ranges.

Such enormous mountains may not be as interesting as they sound. Olympus Mons is so wide, as big as France, that our characters wouldn't even realize they're on a mountain if walking on it. If we want something dramatic, than a single, solitary peak is better. Images of Mt. Shasta in California can give you inspiration. While it's only 14,000 feet, it's so large compared to its surroundings as to be majestic, and majesty is arguably what we're after. We don't need a giant Olympus Mons and its accompanying problems for our world.

Mountain ranges can have peaks formed by different forces, meaning some are volcanic while others aren't. Several ranges can be back to back; this means one is north-to-south, and where it ends, another north-to-south range begins. To the layman, we sometimes don't realize this; neither will our audience, but we can give two different names to a range if they're separated by a pass or a little offset from each other. For example, the Appalachian Mountains include the Blue Ridge Mountains and White Mountains. These are regional names for the same range and are technically the smaller ranges that make up the larger one. If we have a truly long range, a thousand miles or more, it might not be realistic to say it's a single mountain range. It's probably several ranges.

VOLCANOES

We often speak of volcanoes as being active (they erupt regularly), dormant (it hasn't erupted in centuries), or extinct (it hasn't erupted in written history). These distinctions aren't scientific and a supposedly extinct volcano can erupt again many years after the last time. By human life spans, they're extinct, but active compared to the planet's life span. For our purposes, these classifications work, but we can surprise our species by having a supposedly extinct volcano erupt; maybe it's part of a prophecy.

Some volcanoes on Earth have been erupting continuously for hundreds of years, but these aren't the explosive ones. We can have our characters believe an evil is ongoing in the world as long as Mount So-And-So is erupting.

Or the reverse—a volcano's been erupting for as long as anyone remembers and then suddenly it stops as foretold, with consequences everyone's heard of.

A large eruption of ash can cause a volcanic winter (when the sun is blocked out for months). This has caused some of the worst famines and even mass extinctions.

CHARACTERIZING MOUNTAINS

HEIGHT

Some mountain ranges are only 3-4000 (914 meters) feet tall while others tower above 10,000 (3000 meters). This is a critical difference. Lower mountains are less likely to cause a rain shadow, while taller ones absolutely will; the surrounding terrain is affected for as much as a thousand miles. Travel across a range differs according to how high one must climb to traverse them. Survival conditions deteriorate, too, as some mountains are so high that oxygen deprivation occurs (above 2400 meters or 8000 feet). The increased cold is another factor; it is possible to freeze to death. An underground species like dwarves may tunnel through, as could monsters, to solve this problem.

The ability of flying species, giant birds or dragons, to cross these peaks might also be impacted, particularly if they're carrying a load, such as our characters. We can narrate that our giant birds can take them as far as those peaks but no farther. The air becomes thinner at higher elevations and even birds struggle to fly over. The additional lift required by something the size of a dragon may preclude it from flying over the highest peaks, except that we like the idea that they're all powerful, but the point is worth making.

The higher the peaks, the less likely they are traveled, meaning a settlement there might be safer than one at lower altitudes. This will determine how many visitors the place is likely to get and even how receptive the residents are to that. This can work in different ways.

For example, a settlement in high mountains might be rarely visited and therefore suspicious and hostile toward outsiders. Then again, maybe it has no reason to be so hostile because no one poses a threat to it. Perhaps a settlement in smaller mountains is the one that's very protective and suspicious, refusing admittance to others. We can create different scenarios for each range, making the settlements therein different. Higher altitudes also pose problems with oxygen deprivation and higher mother and infant mortality rates.

RESIDENTS

Which species live in each mountain range? It's likely that the same ones live in every one, but that may depend upon attitude. I have a species that likes to prey upon other species but which is simultaneously at risk of being preyed upon by others. The result is that, if their prey isn't present, they tend to not be there either. Some of our species might have massive numbers in the peaks, which they use as a base to amass armies or from which to launch raids.

Another issue is whether we have a species, or more than one, known for tunneling into mountains, like dwarves. They can have underground civilizations that mine for gems and minerals like gold. This can make their lairs desirable for conquest. They may also unearth monstrosities buried deep in the earth and better left undisturbed. Maybe their place has been destroyed as a result, with all manner of ghosts haunting the ruin. Or perhaps they've controlled whatever they've unleashed and can send it after those who try to conquer them.

Dangerous animals and monsters can also be present and impact travel. Their presence can be known or not. Do our characters prepare for an encounter or try to evade them? Do they assume a certain number of them will be killed before they get through? If the mountains are low enough and our characters can afford aerial flight, maybe it becomes a moot point, unless these creatures can also fly or knock out of the sky anything that does. Then our people must escape alive.

EXAMPLE DESCRIPTIONS

Below are two example descriptions similar to those you'll write for your files.

FORBIDDEN PEAKS

These intimidating mountains are shorter than most, being less than 5,000 feet tall, but the stories of evil wizard towers and monsters have kept most people from entering. Those who do often don't return or return insane, babbling nonsense about hundred-foot-tall cave trolls, talking trees, and rocks that come alive and chase people. The wizards of Nivera have investigated these rumors and found enough evidence to prove the claims, though they have admitted that only to the royal court in Nivera.

SOARING PEAKS

Volcanic in nature, these peaks still rumble with activity so that those nearby have long thought the gods must visit here. The tallest peaks are over 10,000 feet while the average is a couple of thousand less. Heavily forested, they are home to all manner of dragons and other flying creatures, many of them preyed upon by the dragons. The southern pass is inhabited by ogres and goblins, making travel hazardous and the city of Nivera hard to reach or escape. By contrast, the northern pass is well protected, courtesy of castles at either end and a legion of knights.

WATER

RIVERS

Rivers flow downhill to other rivers, lakes, or the ocean, but sometimes they dry up first. Other times they fall into a hole in the ground to become underground rivers. They seldom take the shortest route to their destination but simply go downhill, cutting through the softest material. Wide rivers can have a floodplain, which is where all the water goes when a river floods its banks. A floodplain can be many miles wide and have multiple settlements in it.

The age of a river can determine some of its characteristics because the erosion deepens over time. Young rivers like the Brazos River, Trinity River, and Ebro River tend to be steep and fast, with few tributaries but deep rather than broad erosion. Mature rivers like the Mississippi River, Ohio River, and Thames River are less steep, flow more slowly, and have more tributaries, with wider channels. Old rivers are slow, don't erode much, and have flood-plains; examples include the Tigris River, Euphrates River, and Indus River. When adding rivers, we should note their age in our files and consider how to draw them: a nearly straight line suggests a young river while a winding river suggests an old one.

The impact of rivers is mostly felt on settlements, but wide and long rivers have often been the boundary between nations. Keep this in mind when laying them out, for it's an easy way to decide where one kingdom ends and another begins. There will be many more rivers than the ones we put on the map, so when it comes to drawing, we're talking about the big ones, like the Mississippi River. Waterways can also impact travel, as we'll discuss later in the "Travel by Water" chapter.

LAKES

Lakes are found in natural depressions and along the courses of mature rivers, which are moving more slowly than young rivers. Most of them are also in higher latitudes. When deciding a lake exists somewhere, we need no explanation other than that a river flows into it. Sometimes two lakes that are near each other are connected by a strait. Most lakes on Earth are freshwater, but some are not, such as the Dead Sea and Great Salt Lake.

Lakes have natural outflows in the form of rivers or streams, which serve to keep the lake level consistent (excess water drains off). But some lakes don't and maintain their level via evaporation or underground drainage; we can have a river end in a lake and not continue out the other side. Lakes sometimes vanish quickly, even in a few minutes, if something like an earthquake opens up a hole through which the lake drains into ground water. This is another scenario we can use in our writing if our inhabitants attribute this to something supernatural. Incidentally, Baikal Lake in Russia is the deepest lake on Earth and is over 5,300 feet (1615 meters)—deep enough for a monster, certainly.

There's no real difference between lakes and ponds and in fact there's argument about what the difference is, the usual determining factor being size. That said, ponds far outnumber lakes. Geologically speaking, all lakes are temporary because they'll eventually fill with sediment, a fact which only becomes relevant if we have time-traveling characters who go far into the future and wonder why a lake is gone.

FORESTS

There are more than eight hundred definitions of "forest," and we're going to cover them all. I'm kidding, but if you're like many, you simply write "forest" in your stories and leave it at that. Here's a chance to be a little more specific and populate a world with different types of forests.

The tree types are covered in more detail in *Creating Life (The Art of World Building, #1)*, but it helps to know the basic types: evergreen (literally green all year), coniferous (needle-like leaves), and deciduous (seasonal loss of leaves, flowers, and fruit ripening). All trees actually lose their leaves but deciduous ones do so all at once in dry or winter seasons. The others lose and replace their leaves continually. Coniferous trees are the tallest in the world, including the redwood, so if we have elves that are living in enormous trees, they are conifers, which also means a single straight trunk.

FOREST

Most of the time, we will indeed want to say a forest is just a forest. Only when choosing something more specific, as defined next, will we need to deviate.

Figure 23 Forest

A forest typically has a tree canopy covering 60-100% of the land within it. This allows for some underbrush but not something impenetrable. Half of the Earth's trees are in the northern temperate zone, though this is partly because there's so little land in the southern temperate zone. Temperate zones have both evergreen and deciduous forests; evergreens are the most common trees unless it's very cold temperate, where conifers dominate.

The latitudes between 53-67° (Polar Regions) have boreal forest, which are predominantly coniferous, with some deciduous trees.

Tropical rainforests are found within 10° of the equator and are *almost* the only kind of forest found there; the trees there are considered evergreens. Jungles are found there as well (see below). Smaller winged creatures can fly beneath the tall tree-canopy of rainforests but might find it difficult to reach the open sky unless a clearing is available. There is very little underbrush due to the canopy preventing sunlight from reaching the ground.

WOODLAND

Figure 24 Woodland

A woodland has less tree density and therefore less canopy than a forest and is relatively sunny, with only a little shade. Otherwise the tree types are similar to forests. Most people probably think they're the same as forests and might call them "light forests." When naming forested areas, "Forest X" vs. "Woods X" can be used interchangeably, regardless of the tree density. In our notes about the area, we might want to specify it's a woodland.

A woodland will be easier to ride horses or other animals through than a forest or jungle. The sparser underbrush limits ambush opportunities, so an animal or humanoid species we've invented and which relies on ambushing prey is less likely to be found here. While animal trails will still exist, the sparse underbrush means life doesn't need an existing path (created by other animals) quite as much.

SAVANNAH

Figure 25 Savannah

A savannah has virtually no tree canopy despite the trees, which is one reason grass covers the land. This results in more grazing opportunities for animals than in forests. Some people wrongly believe that widely spaced trees indicate a savannah, but some savannahs have more trees per square mile than forests do. Savannahs cover a fifth of the world's land surface and typically lie in an area between forest and grasslands.

There have been times in human history where we've set fire to a savannah on purpose. The goal is to prevent a forest from forming by killing the smaller trees and shrubs, maintaining the open canopy.

Animals that hide in tall grass will use a savannah to their advantage. Some of their prey will be skilled at climbing trees to escape. The lack of underbrush means riding animals or driving a caravan of wagons is easy.

JUNGLE

Figure 26 Jungle

The term "jungle" is poorly defined in its vernacular usage. It's basically a very dense forest with enough underbrush to be difficult, if not impossible, to traverse unless we hack our way through. It's often implied to be in the tropics but needn't be. This contrasts with rainforests, which have very little underbrush due to the tree canopy that prevents light from reaching the ground. Jungles often border rain forests due to the light at the edge allowing underbrush to grow; we might have to cut our way through a jungle to reach the rain forest. The wildlife in jungles is dependent on where the jungle lies.

If you're confused as to the difference between jungle and rainforest, that's partly because the latter term replaced the former. To quote Wikipedia, "Because European explorers initially travelled through tropical rainforests largely by river, the dense, tangled vegetation lining the stream banks gave a misleading impression that such jungle conditions existed throughout the entire forest. As a result, it was wrongly assumed that the entire forest was impenetrable jungle."

Due to underbrush, a jungle is largely impassable so that even people on foot will have trouble. Horses or other steeds cannot be ridden and might even be abandoned. Creatures who ambush will abound in such conditions.

CHARACTERIZING FORESTS

By now it should be clear how to characterize the forests we invent. The thickness of canopies and underbrush and the types of trees will determine what life is like for those who live here or pass through.

RESIDENTS

Which species and animals live in each forest? Benevolent species can make a forest safer to travel if they've been thinning out any nefarious species. Or obnoxious species, intolerant of others, may prevent travel. Or perhaps they've been driven into certain areas that are not safe to travel.

If we've invented any plant, especially ones that prey on species, are those plants here? Do people know that? What do they do to protect themselves? Avoid the place? Carry measures for protection, like an antidote to poison? Maybe those plants are only predatory at night so people feel safe in daylight but must stand guard at night.

If there are settlements near, people will use the forest for wood, hunting (for food and sport), and other activities that possibly put them in harm's way. To that end, their armed forces might have outposts or castles there and have cleared nearby areas to be safer. Or they might guard anyone going into the forest.

EXAMPLE DESCRIPTIONS

Below are some sample descriptions like those I use in my files. These might give you a sense of what we're after.

HORN WOOD

Named for adjacent Horn Bay, the Horn Forest lies near the southern coast, twenty degrees north of the equator, where the climate is temperate and often humid. It is a sparse forest with a mix of deciduous, coniferous, and evergreens and is known for its general lack of underbrush, sunlight streaming between the trees. Ogres and other obnoxious species are seen primarily near the eastern side close to the nearby Lima Mountains they call home. The woods are therefore considered safe and are used for casu-

94 | RANDY ELLEFSON

al riding by the residents of several cities nearby. However, in the event of a flying menace, there's nowhere to hide. A lookout tower stands toward the eastern edge as much for ogres as dragons that also call the mountains home.

DARK WOOD

Dark Wood is so named for being seemingly impenetrable. Hacking through the underbrush is time-consuming, but using the few trails is dangerous due to the ogres and the like that wander those trails, but several monsters are believed to have made them. The trees are so thick it becomes difficult to see any threat coming. Poisonous plants abound here, as do criminals seeking to escape the law. For all these reasons, people generally avoid Dark Wood, skirting its perimeter by a wide margin. It is often not flown over either, for if a crash landing occurs, you'll never make it out alive.

THE ADELIA FOREST

The beauty of the deciduous and evergreen Adelia Forest, which stands upon gently rolling hills on the eastern coast, has attracted visitors for years. Unfortunately, while the eyes draw people here, something foreboding makes them regret traveling far into the woods. Rumors swirl as to the cause—it may be haunted or protected by a wizard; both stories have attracted adventurers who have sometimes never been seen again—or haven't been right in the head since emerging.

PRAIRIES/GRASSLANDS

These lands are characterized by grass, whether tall, short, or mixed. The taller grass occurs where there's more rain, resulting in abundant grain crops. The short grass can be less than a few inches tall. In tropical grasslands, sometimes all of the year's rain occurs within just weeks.

Figure 27 Grasslands

In North America, when the Rocky Mountains rose, they caused a rain shadow that killed the forests for hundreds of miles east of them in the Midwest, resulting in the prairies of the Midwest. For tens of thousands of years, Native Americans periodically burned these grasslands, preventing trees from growing there. This was done to extend the land for their livestock to graze.

Trees will steadily encroach on prairies without the interference of humans or grazing animals, so keep this in mind when placing them. They will exist due to rain shadows. Our species may cause them to remain intact; otherwise, the land will first turn into a savannah and then a forest. We'll want some nomadic peoples to dwell there, with herds of grazing animals, like the American Indians.

WETLANDS

A wetland develops its own water-oriented ecosystem from being saturated with water either seasonally or all year. The aquatic plant life is what distinguishes it. The water can be fresh, salt, or brackish (somewhere between). They are good places for monsters to hide, if they're fine with being wet all the time, because humanoid species are often uncomfortable with entering wetlands; we tend to like solid ground.

There are four basic types of wetlands, and most are found in temperate climate zones or the tropics, but they can be in polar areas. Many fish species, including ones we create, use wetlands for nursery grounds, and many animals are typically found in them. This means food and products come from wetlands, including rice, honey, sugar, natural medicines, dyes and textiles.

There are far more lakes than we're going to draw during world building. Usually we depict the largest ones, which can have mires (discussed next) at various places along their shores. Take a moment to state in your files that there are wetlands in various places on these lakes and how far these are from various settlements. While this is good, it won't result in nearly as many wetlands as there would be, but the goal is not accuracy per se; it is including these potentially useful land features. I suggest that after building settlements, world builders take a moment to determine which settlements have a wetland nearby, what kind it is, and where it's located in relation to the community. This will necessitate deciding there's a smaller lake nearby, the kind not drawn on a continent-sized map.

MIRES

Bogs and fens are similar types of mires. Both get water from rainfall, but fens also have surface water (water that collects on the ground, contrasted with rain or a spring). The water quality is therefore different, but your readers will not care. Both form at the edges of a lake and can eventually cover the entire surface.

BOGS

A bog forms in land depressions or old lakes, typically in the mountains in colder temperate climates. They collect deposits of dead plant material (like mosses) and form peat. The water is acidic and sometimes comes entirely from rain partly because the bog is domed-shaped land that is higher than its surroundings. A bog can be many meters deep over a wide area. Evergreen plants can grow there, including trees in drier locations, in which case the bog can appear to blend in with an evergreen forest adjacent to it

Sometimes carnivorous plants exist in bogs. They survive by eating invertebrates. Or we can have them eat bigger animals and our species. Some large animals like moose and caribou are found in bogs, as are otters and smaller animals. Peat is itself a product that can be used for fuel (heating and cooking).

In *Creating Life*, the possibility of undead plants was discussed. What if a bog contained undead plant material and the remains of either animal or humanoid undead? This could be where the undead emerge from and return to in between terrorizing the living.

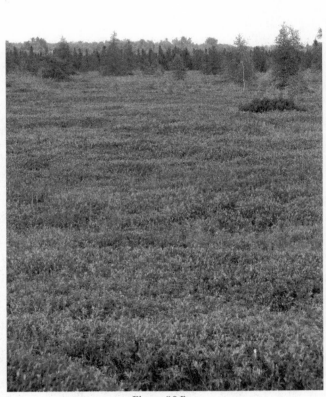

Figure 28 Bog

FENS

Fens are similar to bogs but are covered in grasses and shrubs instead of peat, looking like meadows. They occur along lakes and rivers where seasonal changes in water level occur and are often in the mountains. Fens are located on slopes, depressions, or flat land. Water is supplied from the ground more than rain. A fen may eventually become a bog.

Figure 29 Fen

World builders can use fens for inventing plant life that is only found in one. Since fens are typically in the mountains, fetching an herb for a magic spell could place someone in danger from all those nasty ogres and the like that one must bypass to reach the fen. Some of the plants can be more dangerous if carnivorous and willing to consume humanoids. Since a fen looks like grassland, they can be deceptive so that characters enter them before realizing the potential dangers.

MARSHES

Marshes form along slow-moving rivers, at lake edges, or in depressions of land. They are often a transition between dry and wet ecosystems. Grasses and reeds dominate (not trees) and they can be home to fish, birds, amphibians, aquatic mammals, and dangerous water-dwelling predators we design. The water level is shallower than other wetlands. Saltwater marshes are found farther from the equator along coastlines where the tide floods them. They must be protected by lagoons or estuaries.

Figure 30 Marsh

SWAMPS

A wetland with a forest is called a swamp. They occur near large rivers and lakes. A hammock is a dry land area within one, albeit with aquatic vegetation that can survive occasional flooding. The difference between a swamp forest and a brush swamp is the amount of tree cover, as the shrub version has far fewer, and shorter, trees and is instead largely bushes. The shrub version is also drier and the shrubs are mostly on the hammocks.

Figure 31 Swamp

While elves are known for their love of forests, they don't appear interested in swamps, but maybe world builders can change this, creating a new variant on elves. How might these elves utilize the water and animals within it?

DESERTS

Deserts take up a third of Earth's land surface but can be larger or smaller on the world we've created. They play a role in regulating Earth's temperature, so deviating from this could render our world less habitable, but our audience isn't likely to know that.

Figure 32 Hard Desert

While lack of rain causes some deserts, others do receive rain, just not enough to compensate for high levels of evaporation. Our characters might express surprise about being rained on and not realize why the water doesn't remain. Ten inches or less of rain causes a desert, while semi-deserts receive ten to twenty inches. If there's grass, it's called a steppe. A given desert may be one of these, but have portions of another type, especially if the desert is large. Since rainfall causes the differences, we should use our understanding of prevailing winds and rain shadows to determine what type of desert exists where. Land near a mountain range might be a desert while the area of that desert that is farthest from the mountain might turn into a steppe (because it's getting more rainfall).

When it does rain in deserts, it's often a violent downpour. This can cause flash floods to occur miles away from where the storm is.

A desert normally can't form near the equator due to heavy rains in the tropics (from 0° to 30° latitude). However, high elevations (above 5,000 feet) cause a temperate climate to exist where we'd normally expect a tropical one. This can combine with a mountain range to form a rain shadow, resulting in a desert, such as those in Somalia.

Only 20% of deserts worldwide are sand, and in some areas, like North America, sand only covers 2%. The rest is a virtual pavement of tightly packed small stones (like pebbles) left after the dust has blown away. Once this happens, the ground is stable. Therefore, it's not accurate to always state that humanoids or hooved animals are trudging slowly through sand.

Drifting sand accumulates as a series of sand dunes, or more rarely, a single dune. Extreme temperature changes from night to day cause rocks to break apart before further eroding occurs via wind, creating sand. Some deserts feature outcropping of rocks that help form an oasis when ground water remains. Established trade routes are often used to make crossing a desert less perilous. This is where we can add a settlement; most of these are likely to be small, not a megalopolis.

Hot deserts like the Sahara and Mojave have strong winds and low humidity. Cold deserts like the Gobi occur at higher latitudes and/or altitudes. Some deserts are farther inland because moist, warm air rises over the land closer to the sea and dumps rain there, leaving none for areas farther inland, causing a desert; this means we can have a forest between our desert and the sea. Some deserts are far from oceans or other large bodies of water, but others form to leeward of a mountain range, in its rain shadow, resulting in a long narrow desert near the coast. In other words, a north-to-south coast might have a north-to-south mountain range and then a north-to-south desert on the other side.

Sandstorms and dust storms aren't the same. The dramatic images of towering storms are dust storms. Sand is too heavy to be lifted that high and doesn't get much higher than a person when blown by the wind. It's inaccurate to state the sand is falling on people from such a storm; dust is falling. Sand will pelt people in the body and face sideways, not from above. People can die from repeated exposure to dust storms when dust causes an incurable respiratory illness that ultimately causes them to suffocate.

SETTLEMENTS

Chapter 6 includes details on creating individual settlements, but when creating our continent, it's wise to also decide where cities and towns are, drawing them on the map. Villages won't appear on a continent-sized drawing (there would be too many) but can be on maps of smaller regions. Laying out settlements helps start the process of imagining different sovereign powers and where those on our world live, travel, and what they must contend with to survive and get what they want from life.

Historically, people build near water to have a steady drinking supply, to dispose of waste in, and for transporting goods. The biggest cities tend to grow from a particularly useful spot on a river, lake, or by the ocean. We can't drink salt water, so such port settlements often have a river emptying into the ocean there, too. Always draw your settlements by water unless you've decided ground water, like a spring, is the settlement's supply.

CULTIVATION

Consider how much impact our sentient species has had on the landscape. On Earth, we've done all of the following:

• Bulldozed entire forests out of existence, whether for wood, farmland, or to create living space
   • Diverted rivers so that they've dried up
   • Created dams that have caused new lakes to form
   • Turned uninhabitable deserts into cities
   • Tunneled through mountains and under lakes
   • Altered our atmosphere with carbon monoxide and other emissions
   • Caused global warming and sea levels to rise, altering coastlines
   • Dumped toxic waste and garbage into landfills and the oceans
   • Surrounded our planet with satellites and space junk
   • Paved over seemingly everything
   • Heavily fished the oceans
   • Driven animals into extinction with many of the above

On our invented world, the current civilizations might be the most advanced ones. This can suggest they're the ones altering the environment in these ways, in which case the perpetrators might have protesters and supporters like Earth has. If an apocalypse has occurred (possibly resulting from these acts), then a previous generation might have been responsible; authors have done these cautionary tales before. Decide when the most advanced societies existed and what marks they might've left on the world and the psyche of those alive now. In the "Creating Places of Interest" chapter, we'll look at ruins they might've left behind.

WHERE TO START

Mountains are the first item to place on a continent due to their impact on precipitation, which affects where forests, rain shadows, and deserts form, and which direction water is flowing. Mountains indicate where rivers start, while a coastline will determine the end, but we will be suggesting the altitude of the topography as we draw our rivers, so keep this in mind. Once we have determined winds and rain shadows, we can get a sense of vegetation as impacted by mountains. Use the knowledge gained in this chapter to determine which sort of forest, desert, and wetland is likely in each area; try not to bog down in doing this "right" because we have creative license. What we really want is to be plausible. If you have ideas on settlements and sovereign powers, indicate them and worry about the details later. Cultivation will also impact land features; we can determine how species have impacted this, though a decision might need to wait on placing settlements.

CHAPTER FIVE

CREATING A SOVEREIGN POWER

This chapter delves into the differences between kingdoms, nations, countries, empires, and more. In addition to allowing us to name sovereign powers appropriately, it helps us create different types with varied rights, outlook, and overall feel. Different governments are often ideologically opposed, and inventing such places, whether adjacent to each other or not, helps create friends and foes. The subject is an enormous one to which entire books have been written, so while this is not exhaustive, it's enough information for world builders to understand powers at a high level. Details on creating one are later in this chapter, but I highly recommend that world builders understand this material first; it may suggest possibilities that hadn't occurred to you.

Appendix 2 is a template for creating a sovereign power. It includes more comments and advice, and an editable Microsoft Word file can be downloaded for free by signing up for the newsletter.

http://www.artofworldbuilding.com/newsletter.

SOVEREIGNTY

A concept impacting all powers is sovereignty, which means the right to govern oneself without outside interference. It's a matter of recognition, both from other sovereign entities and from within. Generally, the power structure of sovereign powers is hierarchical, with the typical king or emperor at the apex and a dizzying array of nobles and aristocrats beneath. This book doesn't delve into this because the subject warrants a book by itself, and because this book series is aimed at contrasting overall differences between power types—and what life is like for inhabitants. Those world builders who intend to write a *Game of Thrones* style narrative, one dealing with those nobles and aristocrats and their struggle for power within their hierarchy, can find details in any number of available resources to become informed.

The issue of whether sovereignty is recognized by others is crucial. Recognition broadly falls into two categories: external or internal. In other words, do other powers acknowledge the country's sovereignty? Do the residents recognize it? This impacts the attitude of others and can result in events like war, peace, or revolution.

EXTERNAL SOVEREIGNTY

A sovereign power may or may not be recognized as having sovereignty by other sovereign powers. When Napoleon declared himself emperor of France, most European nations refused to recognize his sovereignty and repeatedly attacked France (together) to prevent a French Empire. We can leverage such real-world events for our invented one. It's recommended but optional for world builders to read about the rise and fall of various sovereign powers through history to get a sense of how this works.

One factor influencing sovereignty is exclusivity. Is a sovereign power the only one claiming control over somewhere? This place can be the land itself or something on that land, like a weapon or source of power or wealth. If someone else is also claiming it, then one of them must be destroyed, engulfed by the other, or otherwise proven illegitimate, or neither of them is truly sovereign; they cannot both claim it and have this mutual claim last and be respected by the other. Sometimes a sovereign entity has a legal right to exercise control but doesn't have actual control due to lack of might, an uncooperative population, or other impediments.

It's possible to achieve sovereignty but not be independent due to needing help from other powers. This assistance can be military, technological, magical, or humanitarian, to name a few. To build ships, one might need access to materials located in someone else's territory. The territory could be landlocked and need an ally on the sea. Perhaps our power has no territory near the equator from which to launch spaceships, and must find an ally who does. Note that a desire for something doesn't necessarily cause dependence; it's only when a power cannot continue existing without support from another that it becomes dependent (but still sovereign). These situations can cause tension, assisting storytelling. Our monarch might need military aid for which he must bargain, possibly offering crops or natural resources. A power can be independent but not sovereign because sovereignty is claimed by more than one political group within it.

During a military occupation, a sovereign nation can retain its sovereignty because the occupying force does not contest it. Storytellers might be loath to waste such an opportunity for conflict, but this respect of a nation's sovereignty can show the benevolence of another power. The United States and its allies are a good example, such as after the Second Gulf War, when Iraq retained its sovereignty despite defeat. A republic may do this, but a dictator likely won't.

Sometimes one country can take over another's territory. The conquered sovereign entities (royalty) can continue to exist in exile and still be recognized by the international community, who see the occupying force as an invader and not someone with a true claim to that territory. This can lead to our deposed king claiming his rightful place has been stolen; perhaps he promises rewards to those nations who help him get it back. This is reminiscent of *Game of Thrones*.

INTERNAL SOVEREIGNTY

The relationship between a sovereign power and his subjects might also be strained. In extreme cases, the people overthrow him, and murder, imprison, or exile him. The latter two offer further chances for mischief by our deposed monarch, should he choose it or have those loyal to him who are willing to assist. Leaders are overthrown when they are weak. Weakness includes inability to:

1. Restore or create peace
2. Squash rebellion
3. Enforce laws when those laws are broken in particularly costly ways

Promises made to one's own police and military forces must be kept. Failure to do so can result in internal war and a coup, possibly resulting in a military junta or dictatorship. A strong leadership can bargain with opposition to keep peace.

Centuries ago, many believed a single person should rule because this provided a single voice of decisions. In time, this fell out of favor so that an elected body, such as a parliament, assumed authority.

GAINING SOVEREIGNTY

So how does a power acquire sovereignty? Conquest is the most entertaining for us. Other times, one power cedes land to another via a treaty, or grants the other the right to control a territory. If no state exists in that territory, a power can just take the territory, which explains the attitude of Europe on discovering North America. With the Native Americans not having a state recognized by the Europeans, British, French, and Spanish conquerors just took the land. Each declared sovereignty over different regions; overlaps between these areas led to wars. Then the soon-to-be United States declared its own sovereignty and threw everyone out. Other powers eventually recognized this sovereignty.

THE DIVINE RIGHT OF KINGS

You may have heard of the "divine right of kings," which on Earth means that someone is sovereign by the will of God and answers to no one but God. Tyrants tend to like this idea, which suggests any attempt to thwart them is treason. If our invented world is polytheistic (many gods), we can still do this by having someone claim a single god they worship has given this right. Someone from a different religion could make the same claim. Conflict is good. This also gives our protagonists someone to destroy.

This divine right can be expressed differently, both here on Earth and in ways we invent. For example, in some parts of Asia, such a sovereign is only considered legitimate if he is just; unjust behavior will have him stripped of sovereignty, which is then given to someone else—or taken by someone else claiming they've got it due to the tyrant's abuses. It's easy to imagine the tyrant seeking retribution on his replacement. This concept of the divine right justified rebellion against a tyrant.

Opposition to the divine right helped lead to modern ideas of democracy. Those questioning it can be philosophers or those who can write influential papers. We can have similar people in our invented world. We can have a monarch execute someone who has suggested that this divine right:

1) Is unjust,
2) Doesn't really exist, or
3) Should be abolished

Sometimes such rulers instigate mass executions like burning people at the stake as heretics. Such actions inevitably lead to more rebellion. Other monarchs are more benevolent toward individual freedom or have limits placed on their divine rights.

LOSING SOVEREIGNTY

The section on gaining sovereignty also implies various ways to lose it. This includes being conquered, but a sovereign power can be overthrown from within, as evidenced by the French and American Revolutions. The concept of freedom and equality for all people led to rebellion that violently ended the rule of sovereign powers. A new government must take its place. If a weak one does or if the transfer of power doesn't happen fast enough, sometimes the military leaders seize control, resulting in a military junta or dictatorship.

OTHER FACTORS

It is possible for multiple powers to form a collective sovereignty, such as the European Union. This means they've reached an agreement that they will jointly make decisions on matters impacting a region or even the world. Those writing SF might find this particularly useful because technologically advanced worlds are often depicted as being so urban that there's hardly a blade of grass left. With nations competing for resources like water, cooperation must happen on some level to ensure survival. While mutual need can bring powers together for this, animosities can strain the relationship and eventually destroy it.

When space-traveling powers have an armada, they likely must leave some ships behind to protect their land and ventures. Other defenses might exist, but only something extreme is likely to cause all ships to depart for space. This will be true even if an alliance exists, regardless of how well allies get along. Importantly, if an alliance exists, isn't it possible, even likely, that ships will have crews drawn from more than one sovereign power?

Sovereignty affects a federal republic, which is a collection of individual states (like the United States). Each state has some sovereignty (to rule itself) but also falls under the federation's sovereignty. Members of a federal republic (the states) do not have the right to leave the federation. By contrast, in a confederation, they do. This is partly responsible for the American Civil War, when several states in the federation seceded to form a confederacy, but Congress declared the action unconstitutional. We can use similar scenarios.

CONCLUSION

Some sovereigns (kings and emperors) are absolute, meaning they can do whatever they want, being above the law. But others have restrictions by custom, laws (whether created by predecessors or not), a constitution, or even outside forces like other nations, with whom they have agreements. Due to the likelihood of the latter, absolute monarchs are rare. They also tend to abuse their power and get overthrown by their own people, which is one reason they're fun for fantasy and SF stories.

Not having enough military might to prevent this is one reason a monarch might not be absolute; they might be unable to enforce their own policies. An all-powerful wizard monarch, or one possessing a superior technology, might be more successful if he doesn't need to rely on troops.

If all of this sounds like too much to consider, think of it this way—does our monarch have the control to do what he wants or is something or someone in his way? Can he do something about it or not? Is his power recognized or disputed, and by whom: his own people or outside forces? Things change over time, too. Through history, no sovereignty remains the same. The British Monarchy of today isn't the same as 200 years ago.

ROLES

In any government, there are roles and titles. A few are most important for us as world builders.

HEAD OF STATE

The "head of state" is the visible representative of a sovereign power. He often has no actual power or authority, being ceremonial, such as the Queen of England. This leader sometimes appears to have power in making appointments to the government, but this is often a formality, as the real power to accept—or reject—these appointments lies in the legislature. Other functions are also ceremonial, including the signing of bills into law. The head of state is also the highest military leader, or commander-in-chief, but as with other matters, the responsibility can be ceded to others who have control (in this case of the military).

Examples of heads of state would be kings, emperors, and presidents. Presidents are sworn in. Monarchs are coroneted. In a hereditary monarchy, the head of state provides continuity with the past. Sometimes the image of the head of state (actual portraits, statues, or images on coins) replaces national symbols like the flag, resulting in a cult of personality. Ceremonial heads of state often attend events to add excitement to them.

One power they do have is to grant knighthood, nobility, and other honors. They can also declare martial law. As world builders, we can grant them whatever powers we wish. On Earth, governments and previous heads of state have granted the position a wide variety of rights, many of them reflecting the nation's culture. As a general rule, however, heads of state have few powers unless they're also the head of government, which is where their real powers originate.

Monarchs generally inherit their position as head of state. On Earth, the role is typically reserved for males unless none are available. If we'd like to be more modern, we can include females. These bloodlines and the order of succession are sometimes not clear, leading to wars when two people think they're the next king.

HEAD OF GOVERNMENT

The "head of government" is the person leading it. He has a title like prime minister or chancellor. This person might also be head of state, in which case they'll have a title like king, emperor, or president. Be aware that the duties of a role, such as president, change from country to country. This means world builders have some leeway to give or take away rights from someone should our situation require it.

Writers tend to state someone's title without providing much idea on the person's powers. Some of this is natural to avoid some potentially boring exposition, but it might also be a lack of thought given to this subject. There are many potential acts various heads of government can do and it's worth researching them to gain some idea. For example:

- Can they veto laws or sign laws into existence by themselves?
- Can they be booted from office? By who? The congress or a popular vote?
- Are they protected from prosecution?

- Can they be executed?
- Can they raise and lower taxes?
- Do they need permission or cooperation from others in government to get things done?
- Can they get away with conflicts of interest?
- Can they declare war?
- Can they oppress/suppress media, communications, and the people?
- Are there exceptions to any of this?

Regardless of our decisions, I recommend a scene giving some idea of the person's limits. They could be in a bad mood because they're thinking about laws that constrain them from doing something. They can think about what consequences they might face. Rather than coming across as exposition, it sheds light on their turmoil, obligations, conflicts, and character, hopefully all of it relating to the present storyline and whatever is bothering them right now.

For example, "As the steward departed, leaving him alone, King Davos hurled his full goblet at the wall, red wine splattering like the blood he wanted to spill. It dripped down the painting of his grandfather, which seemed appropriate. What good was all this power if he couldn't quash a rebellion? He snorted in derision, powerless to crush anything more than the golden cup rolling around the polished floor. He was a useless head of state who knighted star fighters and blessed new warships. Prime Minister Kier had all the power, making his puppets in the parliament dance to his merry tune.

"The Davos line deserved better. That damn grandfather had signed away all their rights to parliament, the last act of the last absolute monarch. Maybe the time had come to wrest power back once more. He smiled coldly, knowing just the right people to stage a massacre. That new neutron bomb he'd secretly had developed would end this government once and for all. He could frame the rebels, too. And in the power vacuum to follow, who but dear old King Davos would the people turn to? He suddenly lamented the spilled wine. Revenge was thirsty work."

Such a passage not only gives us insight into a character, but their situation and how their role is impacted by history and their form of government. It's arguably better than just calling the guy King Davos and never commenting on any of it. Providing vividness to our readers requires having clarity ourselves. This chapter aims to provide this.

It can be assumed that if a sovereign power has a prime minister as head of government, there's also a ceremonial head of state who has less power. If you've ever wondered why the U.S. President (head of state and head of government) regularly meets with Britain's Prime Minister instead of the Queen of England, it's because those meetings are between heads of government. If the President and Queen meet, it is ceremonial, as heads of state.

Prime ministers can have other titles and are sometimes temporarily a minister of something else (see next section), particularly in times of war (Minister of Defense). Some heads of government serve a set period of years while others can remain in power indefinitely; it depends on what the power (or the author) has decided on and passed into law. The head of government has an official residence like a head of state, though not nearly as grand. This home is well known, having a recognized name, similar to the White House in the United States. That's also the head of state residence, but you get the idea.

MINISTERS

There are sometimes multiple, other "ministers," each overseeing a different area like finance, defense, or foreign affairs. Or wizardry. Or interstellar travel. They usually have simple titles like Minister of Space. *The Harry Potter* series is full of ministers, like the Minister of Magic.

BRANCHES OF GOVERNMENT

It is important to understand the difference between executive, judicial, and legislative branches. The differences in how they interact with each other and heads of state/government are part of what distinguish one type of government from another. An executive branch administers the state and enforces laws passed by the legislative branch, whereas the judicial branch interprets those laws.

This separation of powers exists to prevent tyranny and is an advancement over earlier forms of government like an absolute monarchy. To some extent, we are implying a level of government, political, and philosophical sophistication when we assign a form of government to our sovereign powers. The reason is that these improvements to governance arise out of dissatisfaction with earlier forms. That dissatisfaction stems largely from abuses of power that subsequent ideas on government are designed to prevent (with varying degrees of success). Sometimes a good improvement is made but still has flaws.

Far more than two paragraphs can be written on branches of government, but when world builders are deciding what sovereign power type to create and where, we don't need much more than this. Such details are more useful when creating stories or doing a deep dive into political intrigue.

PARLIAMENTARY SYSTEMS

In a parliamentary system, the legislative branch, often called congress or parliament, has a prime minister as head of government. He answers to them and can be removed *by* them with a vote of no confidence. This means that the executive branch gets its power and legitimacy from the legislature, who can take it away. In some cases, the head of state (such as a king) can appoint and dismiss the prime minister. We can invent how this works for our sovereign power because variations exist on Earth.

In the example I wrote above, King Davos removing Prime Minister Kier from office isn't possible because I implied it isn't—that would've ruined my example. For this reason, it's suggested that world builders don't worry about such details in a sovereign power until setting a story there, because we might have to later change how that government works to make our story work.

As for how a prime minister is chosen, there are several versions:

1) Being selected by the head of state and then voted on by the legislative branch
2) Being outright appointed by the head of state
3) Election by popular vote (people) or parliament

Despite the relative lack of power for the head of state, a king could usually still declare war. Similarly, a king could sometimes surrender without consent of parliament, which is an interesting scenario for causing the ire of the people, who then take action.

One advantage to a parliamentary system is faster passing of laws and avoidance of stalemates, which can happen when the executive and legislative branches are led by different political parties, as happens in the United States. If the parties can't cooperate, little progress is made.

Power is also more divided, which can benefit minorities, who might be better represented by factions within government. Only members of legislature can become prime minister, as opposed to anybody with the monetary and political backing to run for office, as in the United States, for example.

GOVERNMENT TYPES

Most of us don't find a discussion of government entertaining. We don't want to research it and explain what's going on to our audience any more than they want us to explain it to them. But stories can be improved when told by someone with a high understanding of different power structures and their sources. These can cause conflict that affect our characters, whether our story heavily features government characters or just causes life to be hard.

The usefulness of Earth analogues abounds. Somalia's destabilized government has caused pirates to seek a better life through plunder, which can affect us if we sail near. The United States is admired for personal liberties, causing millions to desire fleeing to it; it is also despised by dictatorships. Some countries are known for their corrupt governments, police, and drug cartels, and the resulting problems citizens face. Our world's inhabitants should be aware of how desirable various kingdoms are or whether they should be avoided, and why.

This section provides details on the various sovereign power types. Entire books have been written on each, but we're not going that deep here. If you need more detail, this section can help you decide which government type you want to create before making such a deep dive via another resource.

Each name for a government type has implications, but sometimes a sovereign power has the wrong name. The Empire of Kysh might be a federation if one "looked under the hood" at how its government functions. A dictatorship is unlikely to call itself one. World builders should strive to get it right most of the time, but we might like "Empire of Kysh" better than "Federation of Kysh"—or our inhabitants might have some reason for the deception/inaccuracy. We have some leeway here.

Another issue is that a government type doesn't last forever in a given sovereign power. They rise and fall, replacing each other. For this reason, when writing in our world building files about our new sovereign power, include a note about what government type it has *right now*. We can also include other types from which it arose. Each will have left an impact on the present in some way, whether that's structures, statues, or military. The cultural impacts will be felt, too, including languages spoken and general feelings among the population, such as relief or dread about the most recent change. Working these out is optional but adds color and depth.

Government types can be organized, such as by power structure or power source. The latter is used here.

AUTHORITATIVE STATES

AUTOCRACY

A government where one person can do what they please without any inhibition, or fear of consequences from government or society, is an autocracy. These are great for fantasy and SF villains running a country. These are the sort of people our hero can destroy. However, when this individual is destroyed, the power vacuum can be devastating and lead to even worse. Absolute monarchies, like Brunei and Saudi Arabia, and dictatorships are the main forms of autocracy and will be discussed below.

TOTALITARIAN

In a totalitarian government, the state has total control of everything, including military, communications, and infrastructure. There's only one political party, which uses propaganda to remain in power and control minds. Citizens have no power at all and no laws to protect them or advance their wishes. Dissent can bring brutally harsh punishment, including death (and mass killings), long prison sentences, or hard labor. The military is used to enforce the will of a leader, who can often be part of a cult of personality designed to worship him. Many of Earth's most evil figures were leaders (usually dictators) of such regimes. They are typically very charismatic.

The ownership of weapons is highly restricted, as is free speech, assembly, art, science (magic?), morality, even thoughts. Even architecture symbolizes the hulking, brutish dominance. The state terrorizes its subjects into submission and has secret police.

This state will have an all-encompassing effect on any story we'd like to set there, as there's no such thing as living in this regime and not having it impact you deeply. Such states make for excellent enemies of our characters or threats to their way of life, particularly when the regime seeks to expand and conquer the place where our hero lives. Think Nazi Germany and the resulting world war.

This form of government can arise from the destruction of war, when a power vacuum is created and a political party seizes control, particularly when it controls mass weapons and then communications. Imagine a Kingdom of Illiandor defeating the Republic of Kysh, but Illiandor leaves because it lacks the resources to control Kysh, or its army is needed on another front, or some other reason. Now Kysh is on its own again but its government is destroyed. A military leader in Kysh takes power and it becomes a totalitarian government.

This government also forms after anarchy—a lack of government.

AUTHORITARIAN

An authoritarian government is a less extreme version of totalitarian ones. It has a single political power, whether an individual or group, and the leader is not particularly charismatic and may even be disliked. Separation between society and the state still exists, but the state constrains political and other groups, and the legislature, while also having so much red tape to regulate everything that it can stall out progress it disagrees with. Corruption is high and personal connections and favors are important to maintaining power. Elections, if held, are rigged. Unlike a totalitarian government, the state is only concerned with aspects of political life, not everything else. This allows the people to have at least some illusion of control. As long as society is not challenging it, the regime allows some liberty, such as a private business.

Examples include the United Arab Emirates, Laos, Egypt, and China, Sudan, Vietnam, and North Korea.

DICTATORSHIP

When one person or party rules a country, it's a dictatorship. It can also be seen more as a role in government than a type of one. This is partly because it's not possible for one person to truly do it alone; he must have others supporting him, such as with an oligarchy. Sometimes the apparent dictator is a figurehead, chosen by an inner circle that holds the power. The government is typically authoritarian or totalitarian. There are no elections and the people have no power, which rests exclusively with the dictator (and his inner circle) and is achieved by force.

Dictators sometimes arise after the collapse of a government, when they lead a military group that exerts force to take control. If the existing government is weak in any way, these soon-to-be dictators can seize power. Sometimes these military leaders appoint themselves political stature (like declaring yourself emperor). Elected presidents and prime ministers can seize power by crushing opposition and creating one-party rule, which is possible when the government is weak. These leaders typically live in opulence by stealing the nation's wealth.

Some dictatorships are temporary, to resolve a problem, with the dictator intending to return power to government after a crisis is over. Other dictators never intended doing so despite what they may have said. This gives us a few scenarios for creating such a character, though we'll need a motivation for their decision.

A stable dictatorship can last a long time. A dictator may avoid too much provocation. Why would the dictator risk their extravagant lifestyle by stirring things up? It helps if an established dictator refrains from aggressive tactics such as war against neighbors, because losing a war tends to undermine their stature. New dictators, however, may need war to establish their power, earn respect, and enrich themselves (from foreign wealth they promise to their people but keep for themselves). They have less to lose. If a dictator dies and is replaced by a son, for example, this individual might need to establish himself, destabilizing the dictatorship. When creating a dictatorship, decide how old and stable it is.

Examples of dictatorships include the Soviet Union under Joseph Stalin and Nazi Germany.

DEMOCRACIES

A democracy allows people to participate in government by having influence over what policies are made into laws. Direct democracy means that the public votes directly on initiatives that can become law as a result of that vote, but this becomes unwieldy as the population increases. In an indirect democracy, people use free elections to elect officials who vote on those initiatives on their behalf; the indirect approach is far more common on Earth, one example being the United States. Indirect is the one we'll typically want to use. Having representatives running government frees the rest of the population for other things.

The ability to elect and remove government officials also eliminates the need for revolution to cause change.

While democracies have existed in some form for thousands of years, it wasn't until the last two hundred years that greater equality for citizens became the norm. Before that, there was often an elite class in control. Even in modern democracies, there are sometimes oligarchies or monarchs affecting affairs. This causes some ambiguity about the power structure, which is one reason world builders might want to avoid that.

Examples include the United States.

RIGHTS

In a democracy, laws are supposed to apply to all people, but this isn't always true. A democracy is a rule by the majority, which means minorities are sometimes overlooked, abused, and not offered equal protection. This is arguably truer in a newer democracy. In time, progress is typically made amid occasional setbacks so that an older democracy might offer more equal rights. Generally, greater freedom allows people to travel, learn skills and information, and have opportunities not available in something like a totalitarian regime.

Our characters can run into problems anyway. Someone with talent for magic might be prevented from training due to race, gender, or another issue. One character can be forbidden to carry a weapon while others can. If we don't want to focus on such things in a story, it's still a good way to give characters a sense of entitlement or bitterness about their life and opportunities. This can be the reason they've left home, to escape a lack of freedom. It can work in reverse, such as a female wizard allowed to be one in her home country only to arrive in another where it's not allowed and she is jailed.

Human rights abuses tend to be smaller or non-existent, compared with authoritarian powers. Citizens have laws on their side and courts through which to seek resolution of disputes. Freedom is central, including freedom of speech, political and religious views, and the press.

In theory, anyone can become a representative in congress, though money and influence often restrict this. In this way, a democracy can resemble an oligarchy, where a small group (the wealthy) are running government.

THE RISE AND FALL OF DEMOCRACY

A democracy can arise from revolution and wars that overthrow or otherwise destroy previous governments. Religion and economics can also cause a sudden change. The Great Depression in the United States caused hardship around the globe. It also sullied the idea of democracy, leading many to believe it was a failure. The result was a rise, in other countries, of dictatorships. A decade later, when those countries lost World War II, another swing back toward democracy took place; this was partly a rejection of such regimes.

Epic fantasy fiction often includes stories where someone must save the world, usually from an evil dictator or kingdom. Should our heroes be victorious, we can choose to have a similar rise in democracy in the aftermath, if we continue using the world.

A democracy can fail when it's not structured to prevent the balance of power from tipping too heavily. When a branch of government gains too much strength, it effectively stops being a democracy even if it doesn't rebrand itself. Some groups may be prevented from having power, which can also lead to trouble and an overthrow.

There's a tendency to take our current government for granted. In the United States, this complacency reveals itself in low voter turnout that sometimes surprises those in foreign countries who wish they had that right to vote. In countries with less stable government and fewer rights, the average person is more likely to care quite a bit about the current government because life under it isn't fair, kind, or likely to change. They may dream of escape. Give them somewhere to dream of.

TYPES

There are many different types of democracy, but we'll only cover a few basics.

Direct democracy was discussed previously. So was indirect, which is commonly called "representative democracy," and when the head of state is also elected, indirect is called a democratic republic. A republic may or may not have the word itself in its name, like "Republic of Nivera." As with other government forms, the idea of a republic has changed over time, giving us some leeway to tweak details. Republics eventually replaced absolute monarchies as the most common form of government on Earth.

Since a government representative is free to exercise his own judgment on how to "represent" the constituents who elected him, there's room for abuse and resulting dissatisfaction that may lead to being ousted from office in favor of a new representative.

In parliamentary democracy, the people elect members to parliament (the legislature), who in turn elect a prime minister as head of government from among their ranks.

This prime minister is chosen from the majority ruling party. The people cannot remove a prime minister, but parliament can remove him via a vote of no confidence. The people can vote members of parliament out of office at the next election.

By contrast, in a presidential democracy, people elect the president, who is head of state *and* government and appoints his own cabinet. The election date is set, but the term of office (how many years they can be president) may or may not be. The president cannot be easily removed, nor can he easily remove legislative members. If the president is in a different party than the legislature, they can block each other, causing stagnation.

Even in a representative democracy, there can be aspects of direct democracy when the public votes directly on referendums or initiatives. This is how individual measures are voted on by the public, causing a kind of hybrid democracy. The United States allows this, particularly at the state and local level, as each has some sovereignty over its own affairs.

FEDERATIONS

FEDERATION

A federation is a union of self-governing states or regions that give up some of their freedom for a national government and the advantages it offers. A constitution outlines the status and division of power and cannot be altered by political powers, the federal government, or the regions in the union. One goal is greater stability, especially economic, but if the economy of one state experiences severe troubles, it can threaten the stability of all. Territorial disputes are also resolved with the agreement, which also creates greater uniformity between disparate states.

The states have some sovereignty over themselves but nothing at the federal level or with other foreign powers. They have some rights to control local laws and administer their own affairs. Some states may have more autonomy than others, possibly because they joined a federation sooner, before the constitution changed. Federations can also provide a common military front to shared enemies. A federation is helpful in managing a very large area due to the ability of the small states (sometimes called provinces) to manage their more local affairs. Membership in the federation is not voluntary.

A challenge for all federations is that individual states sometimes have opposing ideas about what they can do and the central government must find a way to resolve this. Failure to do so can lead to civil war, states seceding, or even states being expelled. In extreme cases, the federation can collapse. One example is the United States Civil War, where southern states believed the constitution provided the right for slavery. Other states and the federal government disagreed. This caused the southern states to attempt seceding (to create a confederation, explained below). Seceding is not allowed in a federation and led to civil war as the federal government attempted to bring the southern states back in line. No foreign country recognized the south's Confederation of the United States as being sovereign.

Federations, like Canada, sometimes do not include "federation" in their name, but others will. Titles include federation, federal republic, confederation, dominion, kingdom, and union. In other words, we can't always tell what form of government a power has by its title.

132 | RANDY ELLEFSON

UNITARY STATE

A unitary state is similar to a federation except that the federal government can eliminate the autonomy of the states. Their formation is also different, as a federation comes together from independent states joining forces. A unitary state originates from a pre-existing central government granting more autonomy to previously dependent states. What the government giveth, it can taketh away. These subdivisions can be created and abolished by the central government at will. Laws can also be forced on the states or taken away. Sometimes the states cannot create any of their own laws.

These details may be the sort of thing we and our audience don't care about, so we could ignore unitary states as an option for our sovereign powers and just have them be a federation instead, partly because we've all heard "federation." Fewer have heard of "unitary state," requiring explanation that is likely dry. If we use a unitary state, we may not want to call it one to avoid that reaction. This gives us the best of both worlds: a unitary state without reader confusion. If our story ever involves the government giving or removing rights to a state, then we can admit its form of government.

The United Kingdom is a unitary state.

CONFEDERATION

A confederation is a group of sovereign powers who form a permanent union so as to act together against other states. Membership is voluntary, unlike a federation. Any agreements made by the confederation are not binding until the member states enact laws in accordance with those agreements. The actual confederation has no real power and any changes to its constitution require a unanimous vote. The formation is usually by treaty, but a constitution will be created shortly thereafter. One confederation might be quite different from another, meaning we have some freedom to create the rules of one; some will be stricter, like a federation.

Switzerland, Canada, Belgium, and the European Union are confederations.

EMPIRE

In an empire, multiple sovereign powers are ruled by a single power via coercion. The individual powers are still self-governing because the central government allows it, similar to a federation. An empire can include territories across the sea and other territories not adjacent to it, like the British Empire. Sometimes a ruler, such as a king, names himself emperor, making his territory automatically an empire, even when it doesn't fit the details outlined here (it's still a single sovereign power).

In addition to controlling by conquest, an empire can gain control by exerting pressure due to having an advantage of some kind. This can include superior economics that make another sovereign power subservient to it. Using force requires keeping soldiers in each country. This limits options for further conquest, so other forms of coercion are attractive.

A weak state may also seek to be annexed by an empire for protection and other advantages such as trade. Imagine being the ruler of a kingdom sandwiched between an empire and a wasteland of nomads known for violent conquest; we might want the empire's protection from the barbarian horde. This protection comes at the expense of current autonomy but is better than the alternative of being destroyed. In SF, a planet could be blockaded by space ships and prevented from interplanetary trade unless it joins the empire blockading it.

Due to this absorption of other countries, an empire includes multi-ethnic peoples and will typically force its culture on all its territories to consolidate its hold. When an empire fails, it often breaks into pieces based on these cultural and ethnic divisions, and the previously independent states (prior to the empire) don't necessarily return to what government they were before the empire. An empire's collapse is often catastrophic for its former territories, leading to enormous upheaval and uncertainty. If we want traveling characters to experience unexpected challenges wherever they go, an empire's recent collapse provides believable chaos across many areas.

An empire can become a federal republic or a more loosely bound commonwealth of nations all governed by the previously dominant nation. For example, Britain still governs states that were part of its empire. The impact of having been part of an empire is long lasting even when full independence is achieved. Economic and cultural changes take root more deeply the longer a state was part of an empire.

Examples include the Roman and British Empires.

MONARCHIES

A kingdom is technically a monarchy, which was the most common form of government on Earth until the republic took that honor. In fantasy, it's the most common, whereas federations seem dominant in SF. In a monarchy, one person (the monarch) is the sovereign until death or abdication, though there have been cases of a monarch serving for only a few years, with this planned in advance. This is done to achieve a goal, like quelling an insurrection. When the crisis is over, the monarch steps down.

Someone can simply announce they are a monarch after seizing power, as Napoleon did in France to create the First French Empire. Doing so resulted in other European countries repeatedly attacking France as a unified coalition because none of them wanted a French Empire. He rebuffed them but eventually succumbed.

Monarch titles are familiar: emperor, king, duke, prince, and so on.

SUCCESSION

Monarchies are typically hereditary, where only members of the family (usually male) can become monarch. Heirs are raised in a royal family and taught what is expected of them, and if the same family rules for generations, it's called a dynasty. The heir is most often known in advance to ensure smooth, uncontested transition. George R. R. Martin's *A Song of Fire and Ice* (aka *Game of Thrones*) is largely based on the failure of smooth succession. Competing ideas on who is the rightful heir can cause strain and outright war.

An heir can be chosen according to the proximity of their bloodline to the king. A son is in close proximity while a cousin is farther removed. Primogeniture is different and stipulates that the first born male is to inherit everything, followed by younger sons, then daughters, and finally siblings. We don't need to know too much about this for world building unless getting further into the details of a kingdom to tell a story there.

The rules for succession vary so that we can invent our own if desired. We could decide that the king's eldest son is next in line but only if he's been a knight or star fighter in the past. This becomes justification for forcing military service on a prince, but maybe such a prince fails and the next oldest male heir is now first in line to the throne. The quality of one's bloodline can be a determining factor, as can religion, age, and even mental capacity. The most famous disqualification is gender; our modern audiences might prefer the abolition of that one. Sexual orientation could also be used, one justification being that a homosexual is less likely to produce an heir.

Another option is for those within a group to elect the next monarch from those who are eligible. Maybe the next king must be a wizard, and this requirement trumps everything else so that even someone who is otherwise unqualified to rule becomes king. In SF, it could be a scientist chosen by other scientists. We can decide there's a reason for this, such as this specialized skill set enables the fulfillment of the king's duties. Or we can just decide it is part of the kingdom's constitution and never remark on why that is until we think of a rationale.

ABSOLUTE MONARCHY VS. CONSTITUTIONAL MONARCHY

In an absolute monarchy, the monarch has unrestricted power over the people, who have little or no say in government. He can enact laws by decree and impose punishments. He has full control over the military. In practice, he may be limited by a priesthood, the aristocracy, or middle and lower classes. The monarch also needs help from an inner circle that often acts like an oligarchy, since many are relatives. An absolute monarchy often gives way to a constitutional one.

If a constitution exists to place limits on the monarch, that's called a constitutional monarchy. The monarch is often the head of state but not head of government, making him largely ceremonial. Some constitutional monarchs are also head of government and have considerable power. Otherwise, power lies with the legislature and a prime minister who is head of government. Other powers can exist due to laws, precedent, or tradition. The monarch has an official residence and sovereign immunity (he cannot be sued and technically can do no wrong because the government is considered responsible). Succession is usually determined by law of the constitution.

OTHER LIMITS

A monarchy might not be absolute due to other limitations, such as military groups who retain authority over themselves and dominate the monarchy. In ancient times, there were several instances of the military electing a monarch or even killing one before replacing him; the Praetorian Guard of Rome exemplified this.

OLIGARCHIES

An oligarchy is any form of government where power is controlled by a small group of people. This can be beneficial in smaller populations, particularly if a group like village elders is in power, because wiser people tend to be less selfish. But in larger populations, oligarchies tend toward being tyrannical and make a good idea for evil sovereign powers on our world. Anything can be the basis for an oligarchy but is usually something like wealth, military power, status, family, higher education, or ability (like wizards). Owners of large corporations could qualify, especially in SF. There is sometimes a figurehead who appears to be the leader while the real power structure is unknown to the public. The military is used to maintain control and order.

Several types of oligarchies are discussed below.

ARISTOCRACIES

An aristocracy is a form of government where a privileged class, supposedly the most qualified, rule. They might be the most famous and will usually be wealthy or otherwise influential. Belonging to the aristocracy requires inheriting the right or having it conferred upon one by the monarch. The people have few if any rights while the aristocrats have many and might even be above the law.

Historical examples include medieval nobility in Europe and ruling classes in India, Athens Greece, and Rome.

PLUTOCRACIES

In a plutocracy, a small group of rich people are in control. The leaders may enrich themselves at the expense of the poor. And they do not make life better for everyone, just themselves, so we typically won't see them creating social programs to aid the general population. In such a sovereign power, opulence will dominate areas where the rulers dwell while poverty might spread everywhere else.

Historical examples include merchant republics in Venice, Florence, and Genoa, and the Holy Roman Empire.

MILITARY JUNTAS

A military junta results from a military conquest of a country, the power now being held by multiple military leaders as a political group. The state is fundamentally authoritative, as you'd guess, and there are no elections. There's also no constitution or laws adding legitimacy. Those in power typically emerge as leaders after combat, whether personal or military.

Past examples include Thailand, Burma/Myanmar, and Argentina.

STRATOCRACIES

Like a junta, a stratocracy is a military government, but this one has a constitution, laws and formal government, where every position is held by officers. If people can join the military, voluntarily or not, they become eligible to be part of this government. They therefore acquire the right to vote, for example, provided they are in good standing, such as having been honorably discharged. The rights of people are often limited, much the same way any military places limits on the conduct of its population. Since officers can be promoted on merit, this can be a meritocracy where only the most worthy advance.

Examples include Burma/Myanmar and the fictional Cardassian Union of *Star Trek*.

TIMOCRACIES

In a timocracy, only property owners can participate in government. No one else can hold office or vote, for example, and their rights are limited. Acquiring property might be difficult. It's easy to imagine red tape and other barriers, or plots to rob an heir of property that would be inherited. Perhaps the government has recently eliminated the inheritance of property by individuals, which goes to itself instead of the heir.

MAGOCRACIES

We could also have a magocracy, where only people who have magical power can be in government, hold office, or vote, and no one else has much in the way of rights. There could other versions of this, replacing wizards with one thing or another—vampireocracy, undeadocracy, or elfinocracy. The latter could be more simply a "raceocracy," a term used regardless of the race in power, although it doesn't sound as good, but you get the idea.

OTHER IDEAS

Other ideas, which are sometimes theoretical or just rarely seen, have been suggested, going all the way back to Plato. Each of them amounts to rule by a select group, whether it's the strong, wise, technologically advanced, or whatever other criteria we invent. This is an opportunity to make things up. Another variant is rule by thieves, such as might be found in a corrupt city or pirate den. Rule by corporations or banks might be useful in futuristic SF. For more ideas, visit http://www.artofworldbuilding.com/government.

OTHER GOVERNMENT TYPES

THEOCRACIES

In a theocracy, a religious person or group rules and all laws are based on the religion's beliefs, which are based on the concepts of a god (real or imagined). The god is considered the ultimate authority, thus legitimizing the state; the god is head of state, which implies that someone (a mortal priest or "living god") is head of government. The latter is appointed by a group of high-ranking priests from their ranks, though in a fantasy or SF world, an actual god could make this selection personally.

Any laws stated by the leader are considered to have divine origin. These religious laws will be interpreted by religious courts. The leader may be responsible for appointing people to government positions, such as the military leader. Some theocracies allow people to elect officials while others don't. The level of control by the people can be negligent to substantial. This gives world builders leeway to invent what we desire.

Examples include Vatican City (Rome), Pakistan, and Saudi Arabia.

NATION

We've all heard "nation," but that isn't a form of government. The word refers to a people that have common characteristics (cultural, language, and especially ethnicity). The physical borders of a nation might not coincide with the physical territory of the state. For example, Russia recently invaded Crimea, on the grounds that Russians were living there and therefore the Russian state included that territory, which lay outside Russia's borders. Some Russians in Crimea likely agreed and welcomed this while others might not have.

We can leverage this scenario. Maybe some elves have left their forest kingdom Lorelai and taken up residence in another forest, which is inside a human-dominated Kingdom of Illiandor. The Lorelai elves could decide their nation extends into Illiandor and attack to acquire that other forest and the territory in between. This sort of thing can embroil our characters. We can include such incidents in the present or past of a region, causing lingering animosities and distrust.

The word "nation" is political. If we choose to call one of our sovereign powers either a nation or country, we'll still need a more definitive term (even if we never tell our audience what it is) for its form of government. Nonetheless, informally, nation can be considered the same as a state (which is a government) or country (an area).

Due to ambiguity about what constitutes a nation (there is no agreed upon definition), we may want to avoid calling our sovereign powers one. From *Creating Life (The Art of World Building, #1)*, you may remember that the concept of race (instead of species) is just a concept, one that may have no biological basis. Similarly, a nation is a concept more than a well-defined entity like a monarchy, which implies an actual border and a specific form of government. "Nation" implies neither, its vagueness making it less valuable to us. The concept of nations is relatively new on Earth; prior to (and even after) this, people sometimes felt allegiance to a ruler, religion, or their city.

COUNTRY

Like "nation," "country" is a vague term that is often used as a synonym for a state, or former state. It is similarly not useful to us as world builders because it doesn't define a type of government. Why call Nivera a country and then point out that it's really a monarchy, when we could just call it a kingdom to begin with? The word "country" can be used informally to refer to a geographical region, one that has been associated with a sovereign state, and this is where this synonymous usage likely originates. Individual states of a sovereign power can be called countries, as in the case of the United Kingdom (the sovereign power), Wales, Northern Ireland and Scotland (countries).

Like nation, country is a word to use in storytelling but maybe not in our world building. There's no problem with having characters call a sovereign power a country, and if we've never determined its type of government and don't want to be specific, the vague "country" or "nation" nomenclature is a good way to dodge the issue. This is weaker than being specific, which should be much easier now that you've finished this section.

Next we learn to create sovereign powers.

CHOOSING A GOVERNMENT

The type of government is the first choice we should make because it affects so much of life in a sovereign power. A dictatorship, constitutional monarchy, and federal republic offer wildly different experiences for everything from personal freedom to opportunities for employment. Most of us take for granted the form of government in our own land because it likely hasn't changed in our lifetime

144 | RANDY ELLEFSON

unless we're in a war-torn country. But those who are suffering due to government failures for infrastructure, human rights, and other issues are keenly aware of their government and foster a desire for change or escape.

With the government type decided, we should decide who the head of state and head of government are; these may be the same person. Names are not important, just the roles. In a constitutional monarchy, just state the monarch is head of state and the prime minister is head of government. See the previous section for roles.

Decide the head of state's role. Does he have actual power, and how much? What can he make happen? If his role is ceremonial, what does he do, bestow knighthood and appear at big sporting events, like a joust? Does he bless new ships, space stations, or weapons?

No ruler rules alone. Decide who else has power (it may be a group) and whether they're helping or thwarting him. Is it the legislature in a constitutional monarchy? Is it an inner circle of trusted sycophants in a dictatorship? It might be the people in a federal republic, voting legislators out of office. Special interest groups can lobby for power and control events.

When deciding to use a parliamentary system, for example, we can write in our files something like this: "This sovereign power is a parliamentary system with a prime minister (head of government) chosen by the head of state (king) but who can be removed (by the legislative branch) with a vote of no confidence. The king's role as head of state is largely ceremonial."

To recap, follow these steps to get started:

1) Decide on government type
2) Decide on head of state and head of government
3) Decide head of state's role
4) Decide who else has power

HISTORY

The history of our sovereign power doesn't need to be created, but doing so often enriches our writing. A previous section provides ideas on how each type of power rises and falls, lending ideas for a changing political landscape and fortunes for our inhabitants. It's unlikely that our sovereign power has had the same government type through history. Changing it can provide opportunities for stories, such as abandoned places that might now be harboring something deadly.

In all likelihood, our characters won't know that a current aspect of their life originated in a previous form of government. But in certain cases they will. This includes shared coinage that a long-gone empire might've caused to spread. Grand buildings could be ancient and in disrepair like those of Egypt, the government that created them long gone. Common languages and customs arise from such things, too.

We don't need a complete history. Just decide that some previous versions existed, choose a point in the past and work your way forward (dates can be added later). For example, an absolute monarchy can give way to a constitutional one, which then collapsed during a war that left a power vacuum that a dictator filled. Maybe that guy was destroyed by a hero, who became an absolute monarch, then conquered other nations, becoming emperor.

States sometimes fail because they no longer provide something a state must provide. This could be economic stability, enough military might to control its territory, or basic services to the people.

Try to think of a legacy that each government left in its wake. Maybe it increased learning, language, and literacy (more likely in a democracy), voting rights, laws (which may not be honored later or can be), coinage, slogans, and improved the general disposition of a population. Maybe knights are far more widespread now, or plants and animals were imported from other regions. Perhaps a species was banned or allowed in after a ban and introduced cultural ideas. Maybe ships of a particular type weren't allowed but are now, or vice versa.

When creating history we can write something like this in our files: "Up until a hundred years ago, this was an absolute monarchy. This changed as a result of the king burning heretics, a rebellion, war, or some other events. This led to the current system of government and a curtailing of the king's powers" (i.e., removal as head of government while keeping the role of head of state).

How Many Powers to Invent

Now that we have a high-level understanding of different sovereign power types, we can create one with better clarity. The process of inventing each is similar unless we go into details on roles and responsibility of individual government officials, which is not the focus here. We're taking a higher aim at overall subjects because those apply to the broadest issues in decision making and affect the most number of world builders. If you want the nitty gritty on any government type and its operations, numerous books by experts can provide the insight you need. I've created scores of sovereign powers over the years and have seldom needed more than what's discussed herein.

While this chapter focuses on inventing one sovereign power, we likely need more, particularly if we're going to reuse the world. The variety of government types outlined in a previous section should provide ideas for options. Strive to have differing governments.

Authoritative states and oligarchies will have abusive leaders and a suffering public. They are great for being overthrown by our hero, as the source of some evil that is threatening the world, or as a dangerous place that has valuable things our characters want to plunder at their peril. Monarchies can differ in severity. They can be benevolent but with few options for lowborn people to advance. Federations and democracies are more likely to be decent places to live, minimizing abuse from the state itself, but evil can lurk anywhere. Our characters from such a place might be better informed about the world and have far more opportunities to make their own way.

INVENT FOR TODAY

The invention of time and history is covered in more detail in Chapter 10, "Creating Time and History," but when creating a sovereign power (or settlement), we're usually deciding what it is like right now. "Now" is when we're planning to use it. We can just write in our files, "present day Nivera Kingdom is..." without deciding what year that is. Or we can omit the "present day" comment and assume that, unless we say otherwise in our files, we're always describing present day conditions. Eventually, we might decide present day means 5403 AE, but it isn't necessary now. Just make a note in your files or in your head about what you're doing.

POPULATION COUNT AND TYPE

When considering population, we should include land features in our thoughts. Dwarves are unlikely to be present in high numbers when there are no hills or mountains. The same is true of elves and forests. The form of government can also inhibit an entire species (or cultures within the species) from living somewhere if too much ideological separation exists between species and government. A territory may include land features that house undesirable species (and monsters), which in turn might cause repeated efforts to keep them at bay. The result will be armed forces who specialize in dealing with them, and possibly a famous hero for our world.

INCLUSION

Our sovereign power's population determines much of what life is like, partly because they'll decide the form of government. Or at least, the population around at the time will. We can look to the U.S. as an example, for with white men in power at the time of the country's creation, life has favored them ever since. The increasing introduction of other races has led to racial tension. While many believe other residents should be afforded the same rights, and these were intended by the founding fathers, this wasn't the case. New laws had to be enacted and other races and women are still trying to catch up hundreds of years later.

We can leverage such a situation. Decide who founded our invented power. This will be whoever we want to dominate it. Keep in mind that a power has a capital somewhere, and within the power's territory will be other settlements. As discussed in "Creating a Species: Habitat" from *Creating Life (The Art of World Building, #1)*, more than one species likely created our places. There's a tendency to decide humans built everything and all other species are bit players on that human stage. These locations can be dominated by another species instead.

We should decide what percentage of each species filled our sovereign power when it was formed, and what that proportion is today. And we should consider whether the percentage of any species rivaled or surpassed that of humanity. If the territory is half elven, that suggests they are present in many settlements (as at least a strong minority). In turn, they are prominent enough to insist on a form of government that takes into account their world view. By contrast, if they are only rarely seen outside their forests, they won't have a voice. Minorities are always excluded in some way, even in the most benevolent society.

Since government forms change in time, this means that a power could collapse and rebuild more than once. Earliest forms of government might not have considered the elves, for example, but a thousand years and several government types later, maybe now the elves are so numerous that they impact the current government type. There could be prejudice against this or not, but it gives us a realistic viewpoint into how a sovereign power can be more equal about who's in power.

EXCLUSION

Are there species that aren't allowed in our sovereign power or are suppressed, openly or not? We'll need a good reason, such as hostility, distrust, or other problems they might cause, like spreading disease. If a nefarious species is frowned upon, they might still be present. Sovereign pow-

ers cover much territory that cannot be completely po-
liced, even with technology or magic designed to do so
(nothing is perfect). Decide where in our land this unwel-
come species tends to be, and how they reach that point.
Do they land there (whether via ships or wings)? Maybe
they can burrow to reach it. A spell or portal can put them
there.

Why does an excluded species want to be here? They
might be hunting animals or species for sport or food,
whether there's a famine where they live or not. They may
covet a resource. They could be spying for later conquest.
A benevolent species might come to spread its ideology or
help people.

We might have sympathizers to the excluded species in
our sovereign power. These can be people who want to
overthrow the government. Perhaps they want to use
these excluded species to help despite the risk. This
might've happened in the past, too, and can be one way to
create history and a fallen government long gone. The result of this can be an influx of the species and whatever
good or ill they bring with them. It isn't just evil species
that might be excluded, but the good ones during a benevolent power.

We might consider the price these species pay for being caught. Imprisonment, torture, forced servitude, and
death are the more extreme options.

NUMBERS

Most of us have little idea how many people are within
a geographic area. Rather than citing hard numbers, percentages can be more useful while also freeing us from
unrealistic statements. Numbers might be needed when

stating how large an army is, for example, but this can be bypassed with descriptions of how a sea of troops spread farther into the horizon than could be seen. This is more useful than a number, for it describes the impact or impression a force creates; a number tells the audience little.

WORLD VIEW

There is considerable overlap between a sovereign power's world view and government, but some ideas are bigger than the resulting government, which they can sometimes outlast. An idea can guide the formation of laws and the separation of power (or lack thereof).

We should decide what ideas drive our sovereign power. We can do this by deciding who the ruling class was/is at the time the current government formed. The group will promote its own self interests. This is true even in a democracy, where ideals of freedom for all are still seen as being in the best interests of not only all people, but those putting forth the idea.

If businesses are in power, they might craft laws that only they can own business, expand, or do advertising. Wizards in power might believe in the rule of might by magic and create laws and government supporting this. Those who fear wizards could undermine their power and might ban magic. This can be true of technological advances . Some people are selfish and want all the power and riches, being willing to force millions into poverty to gain it. A dynastic ruling class will try to preserve its way of life. Generally, any oppressive regime will undercut the people while also trying to prevent an uprising. By contrast, a more democratic one will empower the people.

The world view of those in charge can diverge from those they rule, regardless of the population's freedom. Those in a dictatorship might despise their government (quietly, to avoid being murdered by it) while democracies can have opposing parties that are starkly at odds with each other, despite sharing broader views that unite them. Inventing more than one political party can make our invented sovereign power more believable but isn't necessary unless we intend to write stories using them.

What we're looking for are a few broad ideas to characterize this place. They will be generalizations, as not everyone will hold the viewpoint. Take some ideas from here as a starting point:

- Wizards are evil and therefore magic is banned
- Aliens will only destroy us and therefore we must be prepared
- The ocean offers a chance to visit and conquer or explore other lands
- The world/cosmos is wonderful and must be explored for continued advancement
- Space must be explored because the planet is in jeopardy and another one is needed
- Territory or natural resources must be protected from aliens, immigrants, or barbarian hordes and therefore military might is cherished
- Freedom is a central right of all people and therefore democracy must be spread, prompting support of other countries and being "world police"
- The race/species in power is superior and deserves to rule the world
- Other races/species are inferior and deserve extermination or exclusion/expulsion from lands
- Gods have given a divine right to dominance that must be pursued

LANGUAGE

Decide if this power has its own language, which will often be named after it; sometimes the power's name changes, but the language's name doesn't, a minor detail that adds depth if we have occasion to mention it. Even if many cannot read and write it, a written language will almost certainly exist. Higher forms of governments arguably require it.

Secondary languages can also be widespread. These may originate from other species. The language of neighboring powers will be spoken by some people but isn't something we need to consider unless these languages are widely spoken. The presence of other languages could bother those in power to the point of suppressing them, as an authoritative state might. Writings in other languages might also be banned. In extreme regimes, reading and writing might be withheld from the population to keep them ignorant. We should decide whether areas bordering other lands have secondary languages or not.

Humanoid species are often widespread enough that territory isn't the deciding factor in whether others know the language. Rather, personal experience with that species will cause people to pick up words. In such a case, understanding will be limited instead of deep and broad; this is known as a working knowledge of language—enough to get by on the streets but not hold deep conversations. In more educated worlds, a language could be taught in school much as it is on Earth. This might be truer in SF, where education is generally assumed to be far greater than in fantasy settings, but we can challenge that assumption.

Fantasy often includes the concept of a common tongue, one that most humanoid species can speak well. This concept is useful on film, reducing the need for subtitles at the least, but it also frees authors from inventing languages. Despite the nomenclature "common tongue," not everyone will truly be fluent, as barbaric species are often depicted as being barely coherent. Anatomy sometimes causes this. So can the common tongue diverging too strongly from their natural language so that they sound guttural in speaking it. This common tongue will be the language of somewhere. When choosing a name for it, we might first want to consider what empire of the past conquered so much of the world that its language became the common tongue.

In SF, language is rendered moot by universal translators. Characters are unlikely to learn other languages unless for curiosity's sake or because the equivalent of Starfleet Academy from Star Trek (italics) demanded it of officers. In the event of a universal translator failure, our characters may be unable to communicate with alien species at all without said training. It seems reasonable that on a large ship, at least one person would be fluent without the devices, not by chance, but due to protocol. A ship's A.I. would serve the purpose, but that can be comprised. The machine translators are typically not present onscreen but are portrayed as largely infallible when that's unlikely to be the case. Subtle nuances are lost on even people, let alone machines. Relying on just the words and not the tone or body language of the speaker is also problematic.

CUSTOMS

Customs will be affected by culture, a subject in volume three, *Cultures and Beyond*. In the context of sovereign powers, the kind of custom we care about is the kind that will cause misunderstanding between different powers. For example, a culture clash often results when a society has expectations that a visitor, ignorant of the custom, runs afoul of it. This can cause unintended offense, though that will depend on our characters; some people might recognize that the offense is accidental and attempt to educate the visitor. Others are more foolish and are eager to be offended, ignoring attempts to diffuse the situation. Maybe they behead someone for it, and depending on who that is, risk war.

Especially when deciding on greetings, we might wish to focus on these expectations. Do people in one power expect gifts of a certain value upon meeting? Or is that considered an insult? Is an amount of flattery expected? Do people expect a visitor to have researched the one being met, with well wishes given to the entire family by name? We can take cues from Earth societies. All we need is a set of expectations that might be unknown, or conversely, expertly followed by the more knowledgeable characters.

LOCATION

The adage that "location is everything" applies to an entire sovereign power. This determines climate, neighbors, and what natural resources are available (and which are not). The form of government will have little to do with location, however, as anything can exist anywhere.

Despite the latter, creators sometimes allow landscape to influence or characterize a power. If we desire this, then mountainous areas are good for an authoritative state and an impregnable fortress or city. An island nation lends itself to being a seafaring power that raids other lands, but it can be democratic or authoritarian. A desert's foreboding landscape can be good for authoritarian states, but then so can an area heavily forested enough that travelers must struggle through the vegetation.

If none of this seems definitive, that's because we can make a case for anything if we characterize it right. When we desire a desert dictatorship, just claim the harsh landscape inspired it. Imagination gets us whatever we want and helps avoid oversimplified clichés. If we've already decided on our government type, we can consider this, or not, when choosing a region to place it in.

Having a map while inventing a sovereign power is advantageous (mapmaking is covered in Chapter 12). This allows us to place the capital somewhere and know where borders, other settlements, and land features are. If we don't have a map yet, then use a piece of paper to sketch regions as ovals marked with the land feature type, like "forest." We can also draw an arrow off the page and indicate an ocean or a dictatorship lies that way. Colored pencils can help; drawing a jagged coastline isn't much help if we can't remember which side the water is on. Use blue for water, green for forests, yellow for desert, and brown for mountains.

Having a sense of the sovereign power's overall disposition (benevolent vs. domineering) can lend ideas for the land features we might like there. This includes how those land features are characterized. A foreboding forest or mountain range might suit one need while a pleasant, coastal savannah with numerous islands offshore might suggest another use. If you have a map, look at it for possible areas to include within the borders and what features might be contested by neighbors. If you don't have a map, you can sketch it using the same mindset.

Decide on the overall territory and where current borders are. Leave room on a map for other sovereign powers, being aware that the more land this one takes, the less there is for everyone else. This is a greater issue if our map already exists and we don't want to alter it. Country boundaries on Earth make little sense to most of us, suggesting we can do as we please, although major rivers often form boundaries, as is the case in the United States with the Mississippi River.

CLIMATE

In "Creating a Planet," we discussed prevailing winds and rain shadows. With this knowledge, we should have a good idea of our sovereign power's climate. There could be more than one if the territory spans hundreds of miles north to south (changing its distance from the equator), or if it's east-to-west with a coastal mountain range on the windward side, or if the altitude changes significantly. The climates will determine the type of vegetation, or lack thereof. This will, in turn, impact what life is like.

For example, high mountains will inhibit travel, be a place for dragons or an underground species like dwarves to live, hide bandits, and be a source of wealth (precious gems and minerals mined from the earth). A forest provides wood for paper, furniture, and wooden ship building, but it can make travel difficult if nefarious creatures are within it. A rain forest provides unique plants and wildlife, some of them useable for medicines or spells.

Review the available climates from chapter two and make a decision, which can be as simple as, "the west is hot, arid and dry while the east is very humid."

Climate will impact the inhabitants in other ways. People in a humid, wet, and warm area near the equator might be used to wearing little clothing and find nudity more acceptable. If not willing to go that far, they might still be more tolerant of showing skin, resulting in bared midriffs or legs for females. Tight fitting, long gowns might be unusual. The climate can inspire people to avoid working outdoors during midday in summer. Colder climates can have the opposite effect. *Cultures and Beyond*, will have more details on deciding cultural impacts.

RELATIONSHIPS

Whether a sovereign power is physically isolated (like an island) or borders other nations, it will have allies and enemies who shape the past and present. In the early stages of building a world, it's best to focus on the high-level aspects of these relationships, such as who is friend or foe. If we don't have a reason for our decisions now, we can add it later. There are some basic reasons we'll cover, however.

CAUSES OF TENSION

ETHNICITY

Ethnic hatred and other forms of racism are an unfortunate reality. We can pretend they don't exist in our world, but if so, that's best done by never commenting on it, not explicitly stating it doesn't happen, as this strains credibility. If we choose to invent this sort of tension, understanding the source helps. Generally, unfavorable attributes are assigned to a group of people who often share physical traits that make them more easily identified on sight; this is part of where the superficial aspect of this enters. Don't use only skin color for this, as facial features like eyes and noses can be used, too, such as how Asian and Jewish features have been on Earth.

The source of that unfavorable trait can be cultural, ideological, or based on government. For example, people living in an authoritative state might despise people in a relatively free democracy. This can be jealousy but is more likely to be propaganda put forth by that authoritative state condemning democracy and vilifying various aspects of it. Those in the democratic power might have similar negative views in return. Even if these governments change in time, the character assassination will linger (on both sides). These ideas are attached to the people.

In practice, borders change and people move, resulting in a mix of ethnicity that leads to conflict. This can cause one kingdom to attempt exterminating or expelling those of a different ethnicity. While we see this with humans, it can be done with other species, like elves against elves, or between species, like elves expelling humans from conquered territory.

This sort of expulsion can lead to perpetual war, particularly if cherished ground lies in contention. Jerusalem comes to mind. Retaliation can linger so long that each is convinced the other struck first or that they can never let an action go unanswered. The original reason for conflict can be lost to antiquity, which gives us some leeway to invent a conflict and a current claim by each side that justifies its stance, without worrying about having it "right."

We might feel that some of our species and powers are more enlightened than this, and they may well be, but racism can still run deep and be hard to eradicate.

RESOURCES

Natural resources can cause tension when sovereign powers can't share them peacefully. This can happen when one power has the resource entirely within its territory or if the resource spans both powers. Newly discovered resources might cause a struggle to possess it. Weaker powers might also control a resource only to be threatened by a stronger one. While Earth-like resources are fine, materials of our invention can include items needed to power space ships and weapons, cast spells, heal people, or anything we imagine. Rarer resources are more valuable and we can decide what's common on our invented world, but try to avoid making gold, for example, largely worthless, and something that's cheap on Earth be prized on your world; this tends to confuse and it might be better to just create a new resource than to do this.

TERRITORY

There are many reasons territory can cause tension. This includes resources, ethnicity (discussed above), religious significance, and the access the territory provides to other destinations. In the latter case, a landlocked power might wish to conquer another to gain access to the ocean. Territory sought is typically held upon acquisition unless something prevents this, such as the conquering army losing so many of its troops in victory that it cannot hold what it has gained. It might also become vulnerable to threats from elsewhere. Such fears can keep an invasion at bay unless something tips the balance. It might also succumb to local disease to which it doesn't have immunity.

WORLD VIEW

Ideological differences can cause one power to want another's destruction or to become allies against such threatening powers. These differences may be not only political, but cultural, religious, and moral. Some populations, or at least their government, want to impose their own way of life on others, and see differing ideologies as a threat. This is one reason the United States supports struggling countries and why Russia supports different ones. The resulting conflicts are proxy wars where two superpowers are fighting each other via smaller countries they seek to influence. This can make for strange allies.

INTERNAL CONFLICT

In extreme cases, internal conflicts can lead to rebellion, civil war, or government collapse. These dramatic events are useful in creating not only history, but a current situation that embroils our characters. A story taking place during such events is often about those events, however, so if doing this, we will need to work out the details of the conflict. If we don't want to focus on such extremes, then lesser tensions might be needed. These less dramatic issues can eventually reach the extremes we avoid until later, if at all. Don't be afraid to set these stories in motion out of a desire not to deal with the result now.

The conflict often involves freedom, abuses by government, or basic needs not being met, such as infrastructure or economic failures. It can be ideological in that people have lost faith in a leader or what he stands for. These reasons often merge, such as when slavery led to the American Civil War. This was both ideological and economic, as the south's economy depended on slave labor that the north wanted to abolish for ideological reasons.

WAYS TO IDENTIFY THE POWER

A sovereign power is keenly interested in symbols, flags, and even slogans that are associated with it; this is also true in a feudal society. Although outsiders can stigmatize a place by associating it with something undesirable, this section focuses on inventing identifiers a power has chosen for itself. The goal of an identifier is to embody and portray a fundamental trait of a sovereign power. As such, the identifiers acquire power. They can inspire love, loathing, and indifference. They can be a rallying cry for resistance in war. They should not be overlooked. With travel such an elementary part of SF and fantasy, our characters will be looking for them when approaching space stations, ports, and fortifications. Failure to mention one is an oversight.

Despite this, world builders may need to invent them later in the process of creating a sovereign power when our idea of a place is more firmly established in our minds.

SYMBOLS

A sovereign power often has a symbol, which its reputation may influence. Symbols may change when the government does to signify the change to outsiders and a country's own people. Inventing a symbol allows us to emblazon it on flags, ships, buildings and more.

To invent a symbol, we should decide how our sovereign power wants to be viewed by its citizens and by outsiders. An authoritative government will have a more intimidating and bold symbol (and colors) to imply oppression and dominance. A show of strength might be desired, either to intimidate potential attackers, or to bolster itself against a sense of weakness. A democracy might want to appear more inclusive and benevolent. Some symbols are negative like the skull and crossbones of pirates, while others show unity, like the United States flag and its stars representing each state. A symbol might not accurately reflect the power.

If we choose an animal to represent the power, this animal doesn't need to be specific to the landscape there, or even be found there, particularly if it's considered a wide-ranging animal. This is also true of plants. However, a distinctive landscape feature like a mountain with a peculiar peak should be located within the territory; for inspiration, consider Crater Lake, the Matterhorn, or the Devil's Tower. Other symbols can be based on the sovereign power's reputation (see the section in this chapter), regardless of which came first.

When deciding on a symbol, we should remark upon the impression it creates. If we're an artist, we can draw a hawk that looks vicious or that appears noble and proud. Simply saying it's a hawk doesn't convey this important distinction. While implying an impression can be fine, the ambiguity leaves room for uncertainty—and a sovereign power typically wants to be quite clear with its symbolism.

COLORS

While black or white colors can be used for identifiers, other colors can be used to increase the impression an identifier creates. Domineering governments often choose bold primary colors. The black, white, and red of Nazi Germany springs to mind. Benevolent countries might choose softer and lighter shades of colors like yellow and green. While this approach can yield results, it is unrealistically simplistic. Usage is everything. Don't be afraid to use colors for no apparent reason. We needn't tell the audience what each color represents, assuming it represents anything. They'll care about the impression it creates. The meaning of colors will be lost upon us unless explained, and explanations are best avoided unless done quickly and artfully.

When choosing and creating sovereign powers, try to prevent too many of them from having the same color combination. Having a list of them will assist with this. Organize the list by continent, region, or alphabetically.

FLAGS

Flags often include the symbol in the power's colors, but not always. Many flags are quite simple, being strips of colored fabric. In a world with less technology, flags should be simpler to produce because they're likely being made by hand. This doesn't mean they need to be three strips of colored cloth sewn together, but simple geometric shapes are helpful. There are talented seamstresses who can embroider something extravagant, but this takes longer and there aren't as many of them to do the job. In SF, more elaborate flags (and symbols) might abound because machinery can crank them out.

On Earth, we often don't understand why a flag has its design unless it's from our own country. In SF, with so many things to distract us, we might tend to care less about such things, but even in fantasy, fewer people will know, or care, about a flag's design. This gives us some leeway to invent without much justification. To make life easier, it's recommended that world builders decide on a symbol and place this on a flag, killing two birds with one stone.

SLOGANS

Our power might have a slogan. These are short, memorable phrases that epitomize a fundamental aspect of the sovereign power's outlook. They can inspire greater passion, loyalty or fear, such as "Resistance is futile" by the Borg of *Star Trek*, though the Borg aren't really a sovereign power as we think of it. Games of *Thrones* used this to good effect ("Winter is coming") and so can we. Inventing this calls on our skills as writers to sum up a truth in a catchphrase. Like the other subjects in this section, it requires knowing what our power is all about.

REPUTATION

Our sovereign power is likely associated with certain traits. These can include basic quality of life and freedoms (or the lack thereof), but we might want something more specific, such as an item from this list:

• A mad king
• Slavery (this includes being the source of exported slave s)
• A space craft design or type of man-o-war
• Raiders (like Vikings) or conquerors (maybe a specific individual like Genghis Khan)
• Wizards being banned

• Unique plants, animals, or products
• An unending war, either internal or with another country
• The first place something happened (a launch into space, a discovery, an invention)
• A horror, whether supernatural or technological
• Superior weapons, armor, technology, or devices
• Nomadic tribes with expert horsemen
• A seafaring or spacefaring superpower controlling territory
• Being near the elven homeland (or any other species, pleasant or not), and having good/bad relations with them

Make a list of options you'd like to cover and begin assigning them to the powers you create. Using Earth analogues makes this easier. Remember to change details and mix and match traits to obfuscate the source; see Chapter 1 from *Creating Life (The Art of World Building, #1)* for why. These issues don't have to dominate a nation, but they can be good starting points we expand on.

To get started, consider geography and government. For example, a naval or spacefaring superpower will need ship builders and may export ships. A seafaring one might be an island nation that excels at fishing and facing sea monsters, with legends, myths, and famous sailors. Animals or plants from the sea might be harvested. They probably also have a history of colonization attempts. Where am I getting some of this from? Great Britain.

WHERE TO START

We should first decide on a purpose for our power. Is it to be a force for good or evil? With that decided, choose a government that influences this disposition; more freedom for people is typically good in many ways while less is bad in many others. Next we should decide where on a continent it lies, as this will determine neighboring powers and what land features are near, which in turn affects who lives here; if our power covers a wide area, species' distribution will vary by location. With population so important, it's a good idea to decide on the general makeup of the residents. Are they 40% human, 20% elf, 15% dwarf, and the rest a mix of dragons, ogres, and whatever else? Now that we know who lives here, determine the power's relationships with its own people and other locations. This has a huge impact on our world building and could arguably come first when inventing a power. Remember that everything in this book is a recommendation but there's no right way to world build. Finally, we can attend to lesser issues like identifiers, language, and customs.

CHAPTER SIX

CREATING A SETTLEMENT

Without cities, towns, and villages, no world building project is complete. In this chapter, we cover how to create more vivid settlements for our characters. Appendix 3 is a template for creating one. It includes more comments and advice, and an editable Microsoft Word file can be downloaded for free by signing up for the newsletter at http://www.artofworldbuilding.com/newsletter/

DETERMINE LOCATION

A settlement's location affects everything about the way it develops, from the reason it exists in that spot, to what it has to defend against, climate, species, culture, and more. Location is the first decision to make.

CLIMATE

Weather is much more than how the air feels outside. Consistent weather patterns, known as climate, affect rainfall, temperature, and air quality. These all affect life in the area, from native plants to animals and the people living there, including their culture and customs. Some life (including crops) will develop there while other life must be transplanted, which is more likely in worlds with good transportation, such as in SF. Chapters two through four touched on what climates exist in which latitudes and elevations. If we've drawn a continent, it can be helpful to draw rough ovals to indicate climates in each area. This largely solves the problem of determining a settlement's climate for us; we've already done the work. Just place the settlement in that zone. A high-level idea on climate is all that's needed at first, such as whether it's humid or dry, rainy or arid, hot or cold. Being more specific about when each of these variations occurs can be fleshed out later.

TERRAIN

In addition to altering a settlement's climate if the land is very high or low in altitude, terrain impacts how challenging it is to reach, not to mention live in, a settlement.

TRAVEL, FARMING, AND PRODUCTS

Mountains inhibit travel to and from a settlement over land, whether those mountains stand between this place and another, or if the settlement is among the peaks. The steepness is relevant, as this can eliminate farmland, requiring pastures be located farther away from the actual settlement. With airborne travel, these issues are reduced, as food can be shipped in, though this does make a settlement vulnerable to shipment tampering. Stones from the mountains can be used for construction, while mines can produce gems, precious metals, and fuels like coal.

Deserts offer few farming opportunities unless modern irrigation or magic is at play. However, the settlement needn't be surrounded by desert. An adjacent desert allows us to utilize it for our work while not causing too much hardship for characters. While travel over sand is difficult, many deserts are rocky, though this hard-packed earth is unkind on the feet (or hooves).

A forest can also be adjacent to but not surround our settlement, but if it does encircle it, the trees can be cleared to make way for farmland. Woods provide rich biodiversity and therefore greater food and medicine choices. The trees can also be used for the construction of buildings, furniture, weapons and siege engines, tools, ships, and household products.

An adjacent river or lake not only provides drinking water and abundant food, but a trade route that can bring travelers to the settlement, in addition to providing fishing opportunities. Ocean water cannot be consumed, but the ocean provides wide-ranging exploration opportunities and more danger from enemy vessels. The livelihood gained from the sea outweighs its dangers, but a strong navy can be a significant aspect of the settlement's life. The sea provides for a multitude of products, from the fish themselves to items like the candle wax from whales. We can invent our own sea life and the resulting products gleaned from them.

IMPACT ON LAYOUT

Terrain can impact a settlement's layout, especially rocky areas that prevent anything from being built upon them. In stony terrain, consider placing the occasional boulder in random places. Some can be as high as a house and offer lookout opportunities, or even the chance for youths to climb it; such a rock might be named, and a town square might be arranged to include it because it's preventing anything from being built there. Rocky ground is harder to dig into for support beams for buildings, which may also result in open areas where only temporary, small structures are placed.

Higher areas are more easily defended, such as a castle location; they are also highly prized so that wealthier neighborhoods are typically there. A river or lake is also a highly sought area, but some industry will be located there, usually downriver from the settlement, due to pollution. Consider having the more luxurious homes farther upstream. Rivers, lakes, and ocean will cause progressively more room for docks, with the port dominating this region of town. This can bring out criminals, beggars, and other undesirable people, causing more touristy areas to be in a nicer section of port.

There are sometimes areas that offer natural protection, such as a rocky cliff or rock outcropping where a castle or other fortification can be built. A settlement will be planned around these and may be farther from a river precisely because a natural defense area is farther removed from it. A river can also serve as a one-sided moat.

Aside from these considerations, buildings need to be constructed on level ground or in such a way that uneven ground is taken into account. This can mean homes where the second floor is higher off the ground on one side, or leveling the ground prior to building.

Decide what terrain is impacting the layout and if it's resulting in anything typical, such as boulders, homes built into hills, or the town being divided up based on zones for commercial, residential, or industrial needs.

WATER SUPPLY TYPE AND LOCATION

There must be water for our residents, which is one reason to place our settlements by water sources on maps. Our basic options are a river, lake, spring, or well; the size or number of these water sources will place limits on the size of community they can support. Remember that sea-water doesn't count; it can't be consumed without making people sick. In an advanced society, desalinating large quantities of water (in treatment plants) is less of an issue than in medieval-like times; magic could change that.

The water supply is central to our settlement, whether it's physically in the middle like a well might be, or adjacent like a river; we always have the option of having a city with a river running through it, but this is more likely when the city expanded to both sides in time, not at the start. One justification for that expansion is to guard a bridge on both ends, first with a guard tower, then a garrison, then an inn and stables, and the next thing they know, the city straddles the water.

Decide where the water is early on because "Old Town," if it exists, will probably be closest to it.

OLD TOWN CONSIDERATIONS

Cities and larger towns often have an "old town," consisting of the settlement when it was just a town or village. This area often has a wall around it, one that's sometimes just a few feet tall. It might be badly in need of repairs, partly because its stones might have been raided for nearby buildings when the town expanded and the wall wasn't needed, thanks to a newer wall farther out. "Old towns" tend to be more crowded, with buildings in closer proximity to one another. This can become deadly in a fire that spreads between buildings.

Old town is the oldest and possibly most rundown area; in modern times, we've restored such places as tourist attractions, so this might not be the case in a more futuristic society. The streets will be narrow, the buildings in disrepair, and roads just spotty cobblestones or even mud. It might be poorer, with all manner of less desirable people, from the innocently down-on-their-luck to scoundrels. It likely smells and will be the place where a plague takes hold. It might be a warren for thieves and worse. It's the perfect place for someone to lead visitors into an ambush.

Not all of this may be true, however, as this could be a good market district and the center of life. If a religious site is at the center, for example, maybe this has always been well kept and preserved. We have leeway to create differing old towns and have a character from one place be surprised by how old town is in another community.

WHO ARE THE NEIGHBORS?

SOVEREIGN POWERS

Our settlement is either deep within a sovereign power, near the edge of its power (and therefore near another power's border, most likely), or in a land without a power ruling it. Each scenario will have impact on that settlement.

A settlement deep into a power won't be reached by an invading army as quickly and therefore might enjoy more peace of mind. This depends partly on the relative strengths of the powers and invaders. A power may weaken due to famine, wars sapping its inhabitants and straining resources, or poor leadership. All of these invite conquests of our settlement, or inspire our settlement to conquer a neighboring power having those problems. This settlement might not always have been far from the current border, so it could still have substantial fortifications that may not be well manned or maintained anymore.

When a settlement has long been near a border, it has likely been attacked and even conquered more than once. It will have substantial and well-maintained defenses with an active garrison and some of the more elite fighters, some of whom may be legends. The military group might be famous too; an individual member might have esteem conferred just by association. This idea makes it easier to invent an intimidating character who has this in their background. This settlement is a likely first line of defense against invaders and may also be the source of attacks on others, even if the command came from another city within the sovereign power. This place may feel safe or perilous depending on the current state of hostilities.

While some cities are quite powerful, an independent settlement is more vulnerable even if it has a few allies. If it doesn't belong to a power, a nearby power may decide to annex it. Such a place may have good defenses, but without a sovereign power to lend it aid, it may not have the best fortifications or soldiers. Decide how long this settlement has been in its current state. Who last conquered and ruled it, and for how long? How did this end? A rebellion? Or did someone manage to kill this ruler and oust his followers? What sort of abuses occurred? If he was benevolent, what sort of problems now abound?

If a settlement has been conquered, consider how long the occupation lasted. The longer this endured, the more a foreign culture will have imposed itself on life in the settlement or region to which it belongs. This is true even after occupation ends, though certain things will be eliminated while others last. Architecture typically remains, as do deeply ingrained cultural elements like widely accepted customs or even laws. It's the elements that people chafe against that disappear sooner. Some residents might be of mixed descent and will continue to live here, whether accepted by others or not; they might also be rejected by the ousted conquerors if they try to go there.

Weaponry will also determine how much a settlement has to fear. A country with long range missiles can strike deep into a territory. Magic portals that transport people— or bombs—can render location less relevant. So can aircraft or spacecraft that move at tremendous speeds or have cloaking devices. This is one reason we might want to decide the boundaries of sovereign powers before we start placing settlements there or deciding what life is like for the residents.

OTHER SETTLEMENTS

Virtually every settlement has friends and enemies.

Friends are easier to decide on if a sovereign power rules there, as cooperation between settlements under a sovereign power is part of the benefit of sovereignty. This sort of thing needs little explaining or working out for world builders partly because it's assumed and is also not entertaining for readers. Few are interested in how cooperation is working out for everyone or the details of it, such as favorable trade prices, crop exchanges, and shared military might or training of each other's soldiers. The latter is one of the few we could mention for a character, that they trained in so-and-so city known for its warriors. Decide which settlements have skilled warriors, healers, wizards, and more so you can leverage this when needed.

Despite all of this, some animosity can remain between settlements in one sovereign power even if that doesn't lead to open warfare. Think of different cities within your own country and how stereotypes persist and strain relations. Individual cities might have good or bad reputations. Decide how yours might be viewed and why, and if it's a fair criticism and observation or just inspired by jealousy, for example. What views have residents taken of other places, near or far? These will be generalizations, as not everyone will accept a stereotype, but one character being chastised for spouting slander helps characterize both the world and our cast.

Enemies offer richer conflict. Settlements of true enemies are unlikely to be part of the same nation. One exception is a settlement recently conquered by an enemy power, which is now expected to incorporate into its former enemy. This is a tough pill to swallow and can lead to openly acting like friends while secretly (or not so secretly) loathing their new sister cities. For more open hostility, the easiest way is to not have them be part of the same sovereign power. Isolated settlements could also mean many friends and enemies.

Few settlements stand alone. Realistically, a city has towns nearby, and towns have villages, but we won't typically draw all these on a map or even name them unless needed. Some may be considered almost part of the larger settlement's domain and enjoy protection in exchange for something, like their agriculture or dairy, for example.

REGIONS & LAND FEATURES

We looked at how terrain can impact travel between settlements or even how they're laid out, but we should also consider the impact nearby land features and regions will have. With a forest or mountain range, dangers lurking within will influence the number and type of fortifications our settlement has. This can trigger decisions on where the castle stands, if one exists, or where the strongest weapons and troops are located. This will affect the city layout, as well. The armed forces might also venture into those land features to reduce the threat. Maybe warriors from other places come here for practical experience and training in dealing with a local danger.

Aerial threats are another consideration. Does our settlement have a wire mesh or something similar strung above it from towers as protection? Are there armed forces who fly on giant birds or dragons as defense and offense, undertaking missions into the peaks to cut down on the population of threats or report on their movements? Think about the impact of these dangers on settlement life.

A desert is less likely to be home to enough dangerous creatures that our settlement needs fortifications against them, unless we invent our own animals. Unless a body of water contains life equally at home on land or in water, it will not pose a threat. A large sea creature is unlikely to threaten the settlement itself unless it has huge tentacles or something similar, but even then, the water is too shallow in most places for such a creature to do this without getting beached.

POPULATION CONSIDERATIONS

Along with setting, our residents are the most important aspect of a settlement. This includes the species and their collective dispositions, leaders and others in power or exerting influence, and whether everyone is segregated into their own neighborhoods, or intermingled.

WHICH SPECIES ARE HERE?

We should decide which species are present in our settlement and in what percentages. Someone is a majority. There's a tendency in fantasy for that to almost always be the humans, unless another species originated the town. In modern times, a melting pot is increasingly common, and with travel easy in SF, a mix seems more plausible. In less advanced times, as is often the case in fantasy, with less travel, each settlement or region will be more homogenous. That's believable but a little restrictive. Perhaps we should have a few well-visited settlements that run counter to this assumption. If you choose one, select a politically neutral city along a trade route, rather than an out-of-the-way settlement that's also a hotbed of war, where strangers might not be welcome. This place is also more likely to be a city due to these factors. A port that lies on a continent edge, so that visitors from this land mass and others arrive here, is a good candidate, with visitors not necessarily moving on to other settlements.

Consider the nearby land features. In fantasy, elves go with forests and dwarves with mountains or hills, for example. A settlement near either feature with a native population is significantly more likely to have that species living in the settlement. However, with their homeland so near, they may not. If there's no such land feature near, then why would they be here long term? They likely wouldn't be if truly attached to their native habitats. We can invent species that aren't so caught up in their origins. Why can't a dwarf be sick of living underground? He can be, but would enough of them feel that way as to live here? What is it about this place that draws them? A good reason is encouraged. Perhaps there's work to be done cutting stone. Maybe tunnels are needed. Can they create a home away from home?

In SF, travelers get around a lot and might find habitats on other worlds which differ only somewhat from their home. This gives them enough of what they grew up with while providing something new. Consider that in artificial environments like ships or vacuum settlements, the climate control can be set to accommodate the species residing there—or purposely not set for them by those who are indifferent or cruel, like our villains.

With multiple species in a democracy, we might have an elf be president with a human for vice president, for example. In a hereditary monarchy, we may not have such variation, but who's to say that an elven ruler doesn't have some human in their ancestry? When this sort of thing is included, contempt for 'half-bloods' may surface, where that person is considered bad by both sides, but some societies might even insist the ruler be such a half-blood (to represent everyone). Strive for variety among your settlements and sovereign powers.

The military might have people of different species at different ranks. Restaurants can certainly be elven, dwarven, or whatever. Shops can cater to a niche or everyone, whether this is clothing or weaponry. Why can't the humans fancy elven clothes and buy some or just have human clothes influenced by other species? Integration has its advantages for making our world more believable.

As an example, let's take Jai, a human character. Maybe she fancies elven styles for aesthetic reasons and is considered to have high ambitions by her peers, who misunderstand her style choices because they like the idea she has a big ego. Maybe Jai spends a lot of time with dwarves and swears like one, or uses their expressions. Maybe she's considered a dwarven sympathizer when the dwarves have political issues that are causing tension. Jai could love dragons and get herself an apprenticeship to one that can shape shift, so she's assumed to have access to all sorts of powerful items or information, which places her in danger.

To integrate species, we might have to rethink how they get along, and this can change from one locale to another, which also adds variety. We can have a traditionally segregated continent, and a more integrated one elsewhere. This can seem like a radical departure from expectations, but this is a good thing. It's also one reason to invent our own species—we're not beholden to anyone else's ideas. Despite this, there will probably still be settlements that are predominantly one species and which are preferred that way by the founders.

Decide how each of your world's species is welcomed and viewed in this settlement.

WHO ARE THE LEADERS?

The smallest settlements, like villages, may have no formal leader but will still defer to someone who makes good decisions or who has some power, such as a wealthy farmer. This may change if that leader makes a few poor choices, or even one disastrous one is made. A large village, and certainly towns and bigger, will have a definitive leader, who might rise to power in the same way as a village leader, or through actual elections in a free society, or by appointment from someone within a sovereign power. This is largely a function of government, which is discussed in chapter five, so what we really care about within the settlement is who this person currently is, what sort of influence they wield, and what curbs their power.

On one extreme is someone who can enact laws or simply declare something a crime and someone guilty of it, and what punishment would happen. Such tyranny tells us much about a place and the quality of life there. We may use this in authoritative states but not elsewhere. Conversely, a place with elections and laws that reflect the moral code of the population is likely to be fairer to all, though minorities can still suffer. Leaders of such settlements can be accountable for their actions, decisions, and even be the victim of poor situations, such as an economic downturn that isn't their fault but results in losing the next election. In between these extremes is a wide variety of possibilities that provides us leeway to create limits that impact our story.

DETERMINE POWER STRUCTURES

The larger the settlement, the more formal its structure, but unless our story features this, we can skip this stage and focus on our actual leader. If we need it, we can decide on a structure such as a city council made up of individuals who represent each ward, or neighborhood of town, each of whom are elected by their ward.

A mayor might be little more than another member of the city council, albeit one who presides over all meetings and has ceremonial duties, but little power to act independently. He might have final say over financial matters or anything else we assign to him, such as decisions on magic or technology. Other mayors have more power, including veto rights, the ability to hire and fire staff within administrative bodies, and some legal authority. They are more definitively in charge but still need cooperation from the council on certain initiatives, which are at our discretion to decide upon. Great variety exists on Earth and gives us leeway to determine what we need.

When inventing a settlement, only decide on the details of power structure when you need to use it. Otherwise you might just contradict yourself later, or find yourself needing to change it for another story. That a council and a mayor exist can be assumed in any place larger than a town, so all we might need to do is decide who the person is and the influencers on them, then worry about council and mayor interactions when, and if, needed.

Our characters might need to understand relationships if they want cooperation. This is when the mayor's power, or lack thereof, becomes an issue we can leverage. They might think they can appeal to him only to discover that he's powerless to help. An appeal must be made to the council, meaning several people must be swayed, not just one. This adds complexity and makes goals harder to achieve, even if an audience cares little for the details of government; the workaround is to make this about the council members' personalities, turning them into characters with agendas that interfere with our main characters.

WHO HAS INFLUENCE?

Before we decide on power and limits, we might also decide if there's someone other than the nominal leader who is in control. A clandestine group might have corrupted settlement officials and be getting their way. Lobbying groups can bribe and otherwise influence someone, or get their chosen people into government and then exert control behind the scenes. Some leaders become little more than figureheads. In these cases, the apparent authority they wield is sharply curbed. This creates a good conflict where the public might know the leader can do something but he refuses because someone is controlling him, and yet he can't admit this. Our characters might also run afoul of this influencer and find a more challenging situation than they had prepared for.

It doesn't have to be "evil" people who influence leaders. A benevolent wizard could insist things be a certain way. Those running a space port might need a degree of cooperation from town officials. A group of farmers may influence decisions that benefit the crops, which aid many in town. A resident hero might inspire not only the population, but the leaders into doing some things his way.

Decide what role this settlement plays in your story and whether some complication can help enliven it. If not, we can decide a leader is truly in charge and then change this later if needed. A new influencer can always arrive.

IMPORTANT PEOPLE

Aside from leaders, other significant figures could be associated with the settlement, whether they reside here, have been born here, or visit frequently. This includes world figures such as heroes. Monuments might exist for them, whether that person is alive or dead. Where do they reside in town? What made them a hero? Did those acts occur here so that they're adored for having saved citizens or the town, or did events happen elsewhere so as to make people proud they call this home? Decide if they were born here, or just moved in at some point, and whether that was before, during, or after the associated heroics. There might be some who resent him. This person might be one of our town's secrets or have powerful friends who come to visit openly. Is there any spectacle associated with the hero-in-residence?

Villains might also be here. They could be hiding after a horrible act or just use this as a clandestine base of operations. Is there something that tips off others to the villain's presence, such as a specific type of arrow? Clothing they're seen in, or even technological/digital trails could also lead some to realize their presence. Do they moor a distinctive vessel, whether a spaceship or a sailing ship, in the port? Do they have a feared stronghold nearby?

Our settlement might also be home to other similar people so that they fit right in; this could be the reason they're here. Just as heroes bring pride, villains bring shame unless they're expected, tolerated, or even welcomed. Remember that a villain to some people is a hero to others, so we might need to decide on their values and those of our settlement before we know how they're viewed. Their means might be despised while their end results are admired.

Wizards could have a tower or a more modest home that doesn't call attention to them. A priest likely lives in or near their temple, and makes their presence known for healing or guidance. We might have celebrities, depending on our world; actors, musicians, athletes, and other performers seem more likely in SF than in fantasy, where life is often too hard, and mass consumption is unlikely, for people to have elevated these people to celebrities.

We might also have monsters or creatures here, on the outskirts of town, in a tower, or beneath the ground in catacombs. We'll need a good reason why they haven't been destroyed, if known. Maybe someone has control of them. Perhaps there's a use for them, like the way Jabba the Hutt of *Star Wars* fed enemies to them. Decide on the creature's capabilities before figuring out how it can be used, where it is, and how it manages to survive if people know it's here.

POPULATION DISPOSITIONS

The quality of the population can be affected by settlement size. Small towns can be romanticized as wonderful places devoid of evil (no crimes are supposedly committed) but can also be prone to everyone knowing everyone else's business and gossiping. A large city offers the good and bad, from too many people and their problems and trash, to greater numbers of skilled laborers and higher quality of materials and goods. We might want a wholesome settlement in one place and an obnoxious one in another for variety, so don't be afraid to experiment with what's going on in a place. We should decide on the general feel, such as:

- Dangerous or safe
- Quirky
- Boring
- Sleepy or bustling
- Transient or stable
- Hard/easy to reach
- Welcoming (or not)
- Rich or poor
- Artful
- High-minded or down-to-earth
- Religious
- Militaristic
- Prevalence and use of either magic or technology.

Every settlement will have a reputation for one of these. How do we decide? We don't need a reason and can sometimes go with a feel we have, but if we want reasons, consider what surrounds it. A remote town will likely feel safe, sleepy, stable, poorer, down-to-earth, possibly religious, and have less technology, though magic may still abound if it's prevalent in the world; otherwise, skilled practitioners will be uncommon. A more urban settlement is likely more dangerous to live in, bustling, transient, welcoming (if more indifferent) to visitors and travelers, richer in some areas but poorer in others, high-minded, and has more technology and magic.

While these characterize an overall population, we'll need to consider which species are here and whether each has an attitude different from the overall feel than the dominant species. Is one species more high-minded, artistic, and welcoming than the norm? Is another one more dangerous, militaristic, and standoffish?

QUARTERS

You've probably heard of the French Quarter in New Orleans. The name originates from this being the original town, which we could call "old town," but it's called the French Quarter because the French founded it before Americans took over the city. We can do the same, having a settlement that was originally a town by elves, for example, before humans took over, causing an Elven Quarter.

Such a quarter might be full of trees like New York's Central Park. A city with dragons might have a similar huge park with plenty of livestock for them to devour. A water-dwelling species might have a quarter like Venice, Italy, with easy access to water, which can include under-

188 | RANDY ELLEFSON

ground rivers and lakes. A dwarven one would have buildings with smaller interior spaces, presumably, except for places catering to taller species, assuming they're welcome. A species' preferred architectural style will prevail, with customs being more honored here than elsewhere. If multiple species with differing environmental needs are traveling on the same space ship, they may have climate-controlled common areas in separate parts of the ship. This is especially true if that species' presence was expected, such as for crew members.

Consider where a quarter would exist based on each species and these questions:
- Why is it there?
- How easy is it to reach?
- Is it centrally located or off to one corner of town?
- Is the entrance guarded or open?
- Are visitors encouraged?
- Is the species' culture preserved within?
- What rules must other species follow while there?
- For what is the quarter known?

Decide which species have a quarter. There could be none or, in a very large city, one for each, but in many settlements, only those with a significant percentage of the population, and who are perpetually present, are likely to have one. A quarter doesn't necessarily have to be built for a species. They could just take over an area bit by bit, resulting in shops and other venues catering to their needs.

UNDERSTANDING ZONING

Young settlements will have no clear zoning, which is a designation of how the land can be used (residential, commercial, industrial, agriculture, mixed). The longer a place exists and the larger it becomes, the more zoning takes place to handle incompatible land use, such as dirty factories being beside homes. A place advanced enough to have sizeable industry is also advanced enough to have zoned that into separate areas. More mature towns may also have separate housing areas for the wealthy or upper class, but this is not always the case and we can have different classes mixed.

When laying out a settlement, consider whether these zones exist. Unless it's been rezoned, "old town" will have mixed use, possibly with buildings that are a store on the first floor and a home on the second; this might have been the original purpose, now changed. Upper-class areas might be by the river (upstream) or higher up a mountain, or near another natural resource like a glade or lakeshore, away from industry. Farmlands are farther out from the settlement. Otherwise, we have residential and commercial zones, but they tend to be near each other, just like they are in your town; this sort of zoning is often on a block-by-block basis because no one wants to travel far. For that reason, the wealthiest might live in the center of town.

SETTLEMENT TYPES

The difference between settlement types is largely physical, determined by population size, defenses, and the availability of resources. Magnitude affects everything, including the amount of territory covered to how much of it can be farmed or protected and how often the settlement is visited. Those with a lot of traffic, something to offer residents, or both, are likely expanding. Conversely, those with less to offer may be shrinking. Most of this chapter will apply equally to all settlement types, but here we'll look at specific considerations.

OUTPOSTS

These are structures or groups of them where the population is too small (or not perpetually present) to qualify as a village. Whether we call them outposts or something else, the smallest permanent dwellings are anything from a single building that might not be perpetually manned, like a tower, up to a larger fort more like a castle. An outpost might only be needed during certain seasons or conditions, getting overgrown during the absence of people, or just minimally staffed. It could be a refueling station or scientific observation post, particularly in SF.

This has practical consequences. Farming is unlikely if no one is there year-round, requiring residents to bring food with them, hunt for it, or be supplied from elsewhere, which is believable if the outpost is associated with a larger settlement that built or maintains it. We take for granted food and water supply or the presence of doctors/healers, repairmen (such as blacksmiths or mechanics), or police, but many of these may be missing from the outpost's staff. Decide which absences make sense or propel your story forward; wounded characters with no healers around adds tension, but a missing blacksmith is harder to make interesting or worth commenting on; in SF, those who can repair equipment are seemingly needed more often.

While it's typically known who built a larger settlement, an outpost might have been long abandoned and possibly used by someone other than its builder. This can offer mystery, such as hidden rooms or ones with disturbing contents and purposes. There's also the possibility that whoever (or whatever) normally occupies it will return and catch our characters making themselves at home. It's important to decide who, if anyone, has been using this place lately, its condition, and what we intend to happen to our characters while here. Do they know about this place and think it's abandoned, or do they know something bad is here but they need it for shelter anyway and come prepared for battle? Unknown outposts that are stumbled upon are the most nerve-racking if something seems "off" about the place, as though danger lurks.

Our less civilized species are likely unable to create buildings. This suggests they're the ones to take over somewhere abandoned or often unoccupied. They may even do so seasonally so that the regular inhabitants know this and prepare, either by laying traps, making it otherwise less desirable when gone, or coming back heavily armed for the yearly reclaiming of their outpost. The unsavory inhabitants might also leave behind a mess, including carcasses of food, enemies, or both.

CASTLES

In this section, we'll look at castles that have no village surrounding them.

Unless abandoned, castles are populated year-round and will be much like a village in which the residents live within the castle walls; there may be buildings scattered outside the walls, such as stabling for animals or guard houses, which are easily replaced if destroyed in a siege. The land around the castle offers farming and hunting opportunities, while the water source is typically protected (such as a well inside the walls). The castle is self-sufficient due to its defensive nature, and in times of peril, food may be stocked for a significant amount of time, but bear in mind that the ability to preserve foods is somewhat lacking in eras during which castles are widely used. Due to their self-sufficiency, castles typically have everyone they need, such as a healer or blacksmith.

Castles can be placed along important trade routes, at the opening to dangerous territory such as a mountain pass, or near valuable resources. They might take advantage of a natural fortification that is easily defended and be a general defensive/offensive location within a sovereign power. They can also protect borders, though these borders can and likely have changed at times, often with the castle being conquered and finding itself part of another kingdom. Decide if each castle is currently in the hands of those who built it (or their descendants). Changing possession can mean that two opposing kingdoms have each occupied it at times, both knowing its secrets; this is seldom discussed or utilized in fictional work, as occupants are typically portrayed as knowing the castle's secrets while their enemy has no idea.

VILLAGES

While there are smaller permanent settlements, like a hamlet, world builders don't typically need anything less than a village. There should be a reason the village exists there, such as good farmland or natural resources, or even just being the halfway point between two other locations that can't be traversed in less than a day, requiring somewhere to stay. If there's a water source there, what starts as a known resting/camping place can become a village when inhabitants or passers-through begin adding buildings. If this is the case, an inn or two is quite likely and might be the focal point of town. Naturally, such a place is likely welcoming of strangers.

By contrast, a village that a group formed in a remote location might be there to retreat from others, especially if the founders share a vision, like a religious creed. We don't need to state why our village exists, but a detail like this can make it easier to characterize the place. It also creates reputation, which one of our visiting characters might know. Or they might find out the hard way. Villages tend to have a population with a limited number of religious and political views, which our characters can run afoul of if wearing a talisman of a despised god, for example.

A village is unlikely to have a dedicated, official protector like a sheriff, but the most skilled warrior living there will probably take it upon himself to protect others and resources as needed, with help from the able-bodied. These individuals may not be formally paid, as it's not a full-time job, but receive perks like a free meal or two for an act of bravery. They could also be trouble instead of a protector, intimidating others.

A village usually lacks a surrounding wall or has a wooden one at best, and less durable materials like wood are likely to be used for buildings. The quality of craftsmanship might be poorer due to fewer trained carpenters or blacksmiths, but if such individuals are present, they may be prominent. If our visiting characters have skills a village needs, they may be able to barter their work for food and lodging. For example, the town's blacksmith died recently—just don't make his death yesterday (that's too convenient). If this was months ago, not only is this more believable, but it means more work is needed as a village falls into disrepair. This sort of thing works with wizards or healers, too, or mechanics and scientists in SF.

For map making, we seldom draw villages unless doing a close-in view of where the story takes place. A continent or regional map would have so many villages as to become unwieldy. This means we can often invent a village on the fly for our needs. We're less likely to care about its symbol, colors, slogan, or anything else, and can skimp on much of this until needing it. Unless the village is famous for something, we're unlikely to ever mention its existence unless characters are arriving there or originated from it. Villages seldom have zoning and are more likely to have buildings that are a combination of a store on the ground floor and a home above it. And everyone knows everyone else, for better or worse.

TOWNS

Towns are the smallest settlement that we're likely to create files of information about and draw on maps. They differ from villages not only in size but competition and backup resources; to use the example from the previous section, multiple carpenters or blacksmiths if one dies. Our traveling characters are unlikely to get away with bartering their services for fare and lodging, unless the skill is something rare, like wizardry, healing, or specialized engineering skills. The variety of people and skills tends to raise the quality of everything, including town walls, gates, tools, buildings, food, clothing, and other merchandise.

The amount of crime will depend partly on population size and character, and which species are here. While some diversity of species can exist, one tends to be a majority and others less well represented. Smaller towns mean less anonymity, so if someone steals something and tries to sell it to someone else or wears/uses it, this is more likely to be noticed unless sold to visitors who leave before wearing it. Conversely, a business can cheat people more easily with the lack of oversight, regulation, and laws found in a city. Corrupt officials might also hold considerable power, intimidating residents and visitors alike; the towns in Hollywood westerns come to mind.

A town often has formal guards who report to someone. This is one reason that taxes are almost a certainty, as these professionals need to be paid. We can imagine a skilled swordsman from a village wanting to be paid for his services and moving to a nearby town, maybe even to a city. In addition to guards (who act like police), specialized forces might be here and will depend on terrain; horsemen, knights, and archers are some skilled positions in fantasy, while sharpshooters and pilots are likely in SF, and we can invent others to go with technological weapons or defenses we create. The larger the town, the more likely a wall, and its height, materials, and the prevalence of archer towers, for example, also rises. Some buildings might lie outside the wall due to the town's continuing expansion after it went up. In a world where flight is common, newer walls might be rare, since they can be flown over.

A town will have considerable farming nearby and needs a larger source of drinking water, so these are often by rivers and lakes. They may employ irrigation. In our modern world, farmers don't get much respect, which is partly an effect of population size and industry making it easier to take our food for granted. In less civilized worlds, the importance of farmers and effects of floods or drought are harder to overlook. Especially in smaller settlements, any town council will likely focus in part on farming issues, and life will revolve around agricultural events like the planting or harvest. When inventing plants and animals for our setting, as covered in *Creating Life (The Art of World Building, #1)*, we may wish to decide if farmers can grow a crop and what the harvest cycle is.

A mayor and formal town council may exist, with individuals appointed by vote, reputation, or prominence, which could be influence, wealth, or land ownership. A family can hold sway over generations, too, for better or worse, and may be the ones whose name graces the town or areas of it. Larger towns are sometimes divided into wards, with each such neighborhood bearing a name and having a representative on a ruling council. Zoning also occurs, but this typically occurs as the settlement grows so that the oldest areas are more likely to be mixed use than later additions.

CITIES

Formality typically rules a large settlement. There are laws, regulations, police, a legal system, mayors, voting (in free societies), zoning, and even procedures like how to evacuate or handle certain emergencies. Everything is taken more seriously due to physical and population size and diversity. Otherwise, the chaos overwhelms, especially in times of conflict. This formality can become a problem, however, when groups are marginalized or taken advantage of, or when laws and regulations are unfairly and inconsistently applied, causing social strife that may boil over into protests, riots, and death. Congestion makes the spreading of disease an issue. Cities offer the best and arguably worst of everything due to competition and quality.

The population is likely to be diverse even if some wish this were not so. Even hundreds of years after a settlement began, newer species can face racism from factions that want a return to the old ways, when their majority ruled and made no concessions to other species. A stark difference between poor and rich can be common, and stricter separation of crime-ridden slums and clean, wealthy districts is common. Marginalized groups will have less sway in town affairs and may be prevented from holding office.

Cities may have the best fortifications and military to staff them, with entire garrisons of trained warriors, many with elite skills; formal ranks are likely and a subculture for these people will exist, with inns, taverns, and equipment shops catering to them. All of this is more likely with somewhat isolated cities as found hundreds of years ago; such places weren't yet surrounded by suburbs, and police, not military, enforce daily order and the military is reserved for civil unrest and actual wars or excursions into other territories, for example.

Zoning will prevent industrial, commercial, or residential from mixing but will result in more traffic from commuting, even if that's mostly pedestrian in fantasy settings. Such a scenario lends itself to pickpockets and people hawking wares to passersby, making for noise. Main thoroughfares are more likely to be paved; otherwise, the mess after a rain storm is considerable. In SF, all roads are probably paved and parking is another concern, though public transportation may have reduced or eliminated this.

Pollution is a major concern and taxes help pay for better infrastructure to minimize the risk of illness spreading. Sanitization is generally better unless the city is run down. Increased anonymity in the largest cities means people only know a small percentage of the population and can fall back on stereotypes and prejudice to judge those nameless masses with whom they share a city.

Rivers and lakes provide the needed water for cities, so we'll want to place our largest settlements along them, though in SF we can use technology to create drinkable water from sea water, for example, and make better use of irrigation and the divergence of rivers from their natural course. Dams can also create lakes that didn't exist before. There are also likely man-made reservoirs, particularly if the area lacks water.

In SF, public transportation is common and might include a space port. We should decide where this is located, but the answer is that it's typically near industrial areas and somewhat out of the way due to pollution, traffic, and noise; think of airports and all they provide in food, other transportation, and nearby lodging.

The largest type of city, a metropolis, is so large that it has often absorbed nearby villages and even entire towns. Individual towns may have retained their names and governments, but physically they've been absorbed into the metropolis, with no intervening gaps. These formerly independent settlements could have building styles unique to them and seem like neighborhoods of the larger settlement. If they had walls, those might still be there because in an attack, each walled area has its own fortifications.

IN SPACE

In SF that features space travel, additional considerations arise.

VACUUM SETTLEMENTS

Any settlement surrounded by a vacuum instead of breathable air has a multitude of issues. Everything which maintains life is artificial and can be arranged how we like for our needs. This includes the presence or absence of greenhouses for edible plants (and the oxygen they produce). Are food animals feasible in larger settlements? There seems to be no reason they can't be, given that we're inventing fictional technology, but one wonders how well animals would fare in such environments. Often characters are miraculously fed from things like replicator machines that can produce a sizzling steak to order, but this god-like ability is perhaps the most far-fetched in all of SF.

Aside from the fabrication of air and food (and possibly gravity), a vacuum settlement tends to be formal because it's not like anyone can wander over and make themselves at home. Space and resources are limited and it takes considerable effort to get here from there. Under most circumstances, laws, regulations, and agreement are essential because violation can result in immediate destruction and death for everyone. In particularly large settlements, visitors causing problems may be less of an issue due to redundant fail safes and the strict enforcement of arrival and departure procedures that greatly reduce accidents.

ORBITING SETTLEMENTS

There are many opportunities for settlements on planets, moons, or even asteroids, but settlements can also exist in orbit around any celestial body with the gravitational force required; this is a function of the mass of two objects—so as long as our settlement is smaller than the thing it orbits, we're okay.

We should decide if our orbiting outpost is tidally locked or not (see chapter 2, "Creating a Planet"). This might have been done on purpose, with whoever placed the settlement in orbit causing this with some maneuvering (preventing rotation). Real estate values may be better on one side, such as the one facing a nebula, resulting in "The Nebula District," for example. What if something causes rotation to begin, such as sabotage by disgruntled residents who wanted the good life, too? What if the side facing that nebula also dealt with more radiation and had infrastructure to counteract that, and now the poorer areas are facing it without protection because they never thought of that?

DEFENSE AND OFFENSE

Earlier parts of this chapter touched on what sorts of threats might be near from wildlife, species, and neighbors, and how this can impact a settlement's defenses. Let's look more at the sorts of protection that might be needed.

FORTIFICATIONS

A settlement without defenses is unlikely to resist capture. Here we look at the types of fortifications a settlement may need.

CLEARED AREAS

While not an actual fortification, a cleared area devoid of trees often surrounds a settlement to prevent opposing forces from approaching unseen. Decide how far out this region extends from the city or whether it's been done at all. Trees might have been left there as a trap and the locals know better than to set foot inside.

ARCHERY TOWERS

Whether towers for archery or another missile defense, lookout towers provide the opportunity to rain missiles down on approaching forces. They could be located all around the settlement, but we should establish what's going to attack and from which direction. An army can typically approach from only one side; if they can do so from all sides, then this settlement isn't in a good location for defense. The direction from which the primary threat comes will have more towers, as will major entrances. A city wall might also provide an inner walkway that means archers can be anywhere and move easily; in this scenario, actual towers might be mostly for lookouts.

CASTLES

In fantasy settings, the castle is a major part of many settlements and the center of life. In addition to a strategic position for firing upon attackers and making itself harder to conquer, castles are used to shelter locals in case of emergency or invasion. In a village or small town, the entire population might fit in the castle. They'll be overflowing the rooms, sleeping in halls, maybe even in the courtyard, but it's better than being in the path of an opposing army. However, in larger settlements, not everyone's going to fit. No matter the size of the community so housed, there must be enough food and water to outlast a siege or surrender is inevitable. In cities, the castle's fortifications will be augmented by the city wall, which can protect a larger population and the city itself.

THE WALL

Small settlements sometimes have a wall, which controls entrance and exit in addition to providing protection from attack. Some are only waist high and made of stones, which may seem pointless to us for being so easily climbed over, but limited material might be the reason for this. A settlement near mountains is unlikely to have such small walls of stone. Similarly, a low wall of timber when a forest stands near seems less believable.

We should decide what this wall is designed to keep out. Anything with the ability to control fire will burn down wooden walls, though this is a time-consuming way to remove one, but a wooden wall can still slow an attacking force, especially if it's comprised of less-intelligent creatures, such as animals or monsters.

WHICH ARMED FORCES ARE HERE?

In fantasy, most settlements will have some archers, swordsmen, knights, and others capable of armed combat, but what we want to look at now is whether large groups of these will exist in a settlement, and why that might be. The use of technology in SF might reduce the skill and training required to operate weapons or defenses, allowing more generalized troops. Training is often required; still, this training is often more mental than physical. We'll spend less time looking at this because those technologies and the skillsets needed to operate them are imaginary, meaning we can invent restrictions as needed for our story. Reading about considerations for existing military may give you ideas.

LOCAL GUARDS

A larger settlement will have its local guards, what we call police on Earth. These individuals will have some skill, but nothing like those of more specialized warriors. This can be a sore point with them. Their reduced privilege or standing may cause jealousy, especially if they are mocked by more experienced warriors. This is a good way to add tension that occasionally erupts in a brawl, duel, or disciplinary action. These guards deal with more mundane issues among the population and less so with threats from outside. Minorities might feel unfairly targeted by them.

CAVALRY

In fantasy, a settlement with open lands around it is likely to have a cavalry, whether this is actual knights or less armored horsemen. Unless we invent different animals, this is the fastest way to travel on land without machinery. A horse charge is a devastating tactical move. A settlement surrounded for many miles with open land is virtually certain to have cavalry (and a large one at that). But if open land is only on one side, the size of cavalry is reduced in favor of other skillsets. Horsemen still navigate forests, depending on density, and there are often trails or roads, but higher density reduces the number of troops that may pass. The same is true of mountains. Few settlements will lack horses completely unless self-powered vehicles have replaced them, so what we're looking at here is the existence of a specialized force: cavalry.

KNIGHTS

While knights are often part of a cavalry, they may work independently of the cavalry, in circumstances where horsemanship is peripheral. Our settlement is likely to have knights if warriors with the greatest skill set and armament are needed. A settlement in the middle of a stable sovereign power without natural enemies (like an animal or monster in a nearby forest) is unlikely to have many, if any, knights in full-time residence. But if there's a horde of something dangerous in the nearby mountain range, or the settlement lies along a contested border, we'll have knights, and lots of them. Active war zones can change the need for such individuals, as well.

FLYING FORCES

In fantasy, giant birds or dragons are two options our settlement has for an airborne military. If we decide to include creatures which are tamable to this degree in the settlement's defenses, we need to work out their capabilities, including range. These airborne forces are more plausible in mountainous areas, due to flying creatures' greater ease of movement there. Forests prevent them from flying, and therefore seeing, below the tree cover, but they offer an advantage even when plains or deserts surround a settlement. We might have invented flying creatures that are too small to be ridden but which can fly beneath the canopy, but this is still perilous due to the ease with which they can be shot down from hidden archers, for example.

In SF, an air force is virtually a given, with machines replacing creatures, but not always; nothing says we can't have such exotic animals, too. This defense might have replaced cavalry and other land forces or augment them. Ships ranging in size from single-rider craft to troopships are options that give us great flexibility in what we decide is available and in what quantities, and what sort of training, if any, the riders need. It can be attractive to decide that little training is needed for one simple reason: our characters could arrive on a world which requires them to operate one of these and do so with a modicum of success, resulting in a hopefully thrilling chase on slightly unfamiliar machines through strange territory.

Consider the impact of such machines on the ability to defeat or bypass threats on land, such as creatures capable of interfering with them. A dragon that blasts fire or ice into an engine comes to mind, but any creature able to hurl a projectile a short distance into the air can bring down a low-flying, small craft if done right. There's a tendency to make machinery impervious to such threats; avoid this trap and your work might stand out in a good way.

NAVY

The navy is easy to overlook in fantasy, as so much is focused on land and even aerial threats. In SF, the battle is typically in space, making this ignored. Regardless of genre, consider using the details found in Chapter 8, "Travel by Water," to create a robust presentation of naval issues. Lake-side settlements will have a decent number of ships, but their focus may be commercial rather than conquest.

The settlement's access to lumber, if that's the primary material for ships, will limit its shipbuilding capacity. To be a seafaring power, the country requires both sufficient wood and access to the open ocean; by contrast, if they're located on a sea and must get past other navies to reach open water, they might be restricted to a smaller fleet. They might also become allies with a power that has a bigger navy. A settlement on the coast might be at risk for attack by ships that have cannon or a replacement for such firepower. This will mean fortifications like lighthouses, a castle, and a battery to repel an attack. Their own fleet is the best defense and keeps the fighting at sea.

DETERMINE HISTORY

To create a settlement's history, it can be beneficial to have already decided the history of the sovereign power to which it belongs. Is it part of one now or has it been part of different powers? Understanding where this settlement lies in relation to powers makes this easier to decide. Anywhere near a border has likely endured changes, but even places many days' travel from the nearest border could've experienced change. This is especially true if an empire has ever spread over it.

A city a thousand years old has likely changed hands, but one only a few hundred years old might never have. Decide how long ago this settlement was founded. If large scale wars are rare in that area, it might've only changed hands a few times, but more tumultuous places might have experienced this every generation, or more frequently. What matters is how much of a melting pot experience the community has had. This can cause a mix of building styles, materials, customs, and certainly population. And if a different species is the conqueror, we'll almost certainly have a more varied atmosphere than the mono-human one often shown in fantasy.

We don't need to identify or discuss these wars. All we need is the fact of the settlement having been embroiled in one, and the resulting damage or destruction. There can still be toppled buildings around. There might be monuments to individual soldiers or generic ones who represent a conflict. If a power conquered the settlement, erected such statues or buildings, and then disappeared, are these items still pristine, gone altogether, or defaced? Have some been repurposed, with their original meanings and inscriptions redone or removed so that the source is no longer apparent? Is a building abandoned? A tourist attraction? Such a building could be one native to the population, abused by conquerors, and still standing but unused, or taken over by vagrants. Sometimes these are an eyesore and sometimes they're a source of pride.

On a practical level, we don't need details about which power it's been a part of, because in most cases we'll do little more than mention the fact in passing. We can just decide that it's changed hands to this one or that one a certain number of years ago, and various relics are around town as a result. But it isn't just structures but people who are affected, and their memories and attitudes about other places. Two places that were once enemies won't always be, nor will two that are friendly always be. Persistent strong sentiment is rare and is usually fueled by something like religion or ethnicity. Opinions and sentiment change over time, provided that situations have changed, and what remains is subtler lingering dislike or prejudice.

We can also have events that took place within a settlement, such as discoveries, inventions, accidents, and failures. Great fires, droughts, earthquakes, and other natural disasters sometimes leave a mark on not only the topography, but the living memory of a population. In a world with magic or technology, good and bad acts are likely, the number of them dependent partly on population size and settlement longevity. Is our settlement famous for anything having occurred here? Will it be?

LOCAL LORE

Settlements sometimes have local stories or legends. In a fantasy setting, this is arguably more common in villages and towns than in cities due to their lower education and worldliness, leading to myths. In fantasy, these may center on supernatural phenomena, such as magic or ghosts, even the appearance of gods. But in SF, these may be more technological in origin, such as first contact with alien species. Events are one way to create these, with a story surrounding those events. These stories often have missing details that could alter their interpretation, which also lends itself to there being misunderstandings about what really took place. Any unusual place or character, past or present, can cause lore. World figures who originated from here are good examples, and we can decide this person has unusual talents or skills that this settlement claims some responsibility for, though that's only likely in the event of a hero, not a villain.

HOW IT IS KNOWN?

Every settlement tends to be known for something, such as a product, event, or population skillset, like excellent archers. Do they make great wines? Weapons? Are their knights amazing? The wizards? Pilots? Or is the place run down and a haven for bad people like pirates? The reputation can help us craft a viewpoint that adds character.

REPUTATION

The larger the community, the more likely we are to think of the settlement's reputation. This status is as much about the population's makeup, beliefs, or acts, as about what the settlement represents, though these are intertwined. We need a sense of what this place is like, and how we intend to use it, to form this reputation. Do we want it feared or a haven? Frequently or rarely visited? Humble and easily conquered or aggressive and out to dominate life around it? Are the warriors or rulers famous? For what? The amount of danger a settlement experiences can influence this.

COLORS

A settlement's colors will figure in our work in two major ways: characters might use them for personal or structural decoration, and flags, banners, or symbols are likely to incorporate them. During battle scenes, we're almost certain to mention the flags of the opponents. When characters arrive at our settlements, they may notice the pennants, and local colors may figure in awnings and other functional fabrics. Ships may use the colors on their sails or trim, while more technological vehicles could feature them on the designations painted on the vessel, and the interior.

The colors can be arbitrary, in which case it's recommended that world builders delay on a decision. By the time we need to be specific, maybe we'll have thought of a justification. If we'd like a reason, which is optional because we may never explain it, we can associate colors with something. Red makes sense for a settlement with a violent history, for red's association with blood. Blue might work for port towns, green for forest ones, and yellow for deserts or plains. Or we can use a suggestion of wealth, like gold and silver, whether the settlement has mountain mines for these minerals or just fancies itself wealthy (whether it is or not). A port city with a marauding navy that plunders other towns might also choose gold to show its wealth. Humility might figure in a settlement's sense of self, resulting in muted browns. A justification can be simple. And in a more primitive or isolated society, colors might be limited to what dyes can be created from plants.

We might want a sovereign power to have a primary color that is incorporated in all symbols by settlements. For example, the Kingdom of Antaria's color may be blue, and the capital's colors are blue and gold, while a sister city is blue and silver. A nearby town is blue and brown, etc.

Symbols

Many settlements have a symbol that's a source of pride, identity, and possibly fear among opponents. This symbol might represent the population's values and be humble for a peaceful place, or aggressive for a warlike or barbaric one. The settlement's colors might be part of it or even derived from it, so we can create this first. A wolf symbol suggests white. A raven suggests black. These can give us one of our two or three hues.

Symbols are often simple so they're easy to remember and therefore more powerful. Ones that don't require an explanation are better than those that do. Being easy to draw allows commoners to reproduce them, not just skilled artists. We can use animals associated with peace, war, or strength, or staple plants may suggest prosperity, though these won't exactly intimidate someone on the battlefield. Decide how often and what sort of hostilities a settlement faces before going with something warlike. A backwoods farming community probably favors tools of their trade. If a "first" happened somewhere, like the first launch of a ship into space, the silhouette of a vessel lifting off can become a new symbol. Crafting symbols isn't always easy, so consider saving this for when you really need one, and use the most obvious ones, which are often the best ones, first or on your most important settlements; there's a higher chance you'll be mentioning it.

Slogans

We seldom have reason or opportunity to mention a settlement's slogan, if it exists, but this may result from world builders not taking the time to invent them. Sometimes one doesn't exist until an event, like "Boston Strong" emerging after the Boston Marathon bombing. We can leverage this by tying our slogan to an event, recent or not. What is on the minds of the residents in the aftermath? Strength in the face of adversity led to the above example. Resistance might play on the minds of those in war-torn areas. We don't need a slogan for everywhere in our world and it could be difficult to conjure up so many, so focus on what you need for a given story. More can be added later; this is a prime subject to skip.

PRODUCTS

Every settlement has products it consumes or produces (or wants to). The population might be known for adoring particular wines, sweets, meats, or vegetables. Some will be delicacies due to rarity there. Others might be local and preferred for that, or coveted in various other locales far and wide. Locals might also have disdain for other products, particularly those with which they compete, or those from despised sovereign powers or regions. They might even enjoy such products while having contempt for those who produce them: "I hate elves but they sure do make good wine!" This sort of world building can be quickly mentioned in scenes to give an impression of a wider world than what we're seeing.

Forests provide plants for medicines and wood for furniture, tools, and building materials, including wooden ships, if the right kind of forest or trees are here. Mountains provide for gems and other minerals, even stone. The sea can be a product source for locals and an export to landlocked settlements. An import can be desired because it *isn't* found here. What if a port city doesn't have access to the trees needed to build ships? This sort of consideration can lead to trade with friends and enemies alike, helping inspire conflict. Inventing products doesn't seem glamorous, but much world building can be achieved by deciding what's available in a given region, and who they can sell to or get things from. Creating our own plants, animals, and resulting products gives us more options.

SECRETS

Inventing secrets for our settlement can be fun but is optional. Waiting until we have a need for a secret is recommended because a secret is, by definition, unknown, and we'll have no reason to mention it unless characters uncover it. Secrets can be incorporated into city layout, such as there being a building off limits to most people, for a reason that's a lie or which isn't admitted to at all. Maybe a building's location seems inappropriate, and the explanation lies underground, such as an entrance to secret catacombs, or a supernatural phenomenon, whether sinister or helpful. If we've created gods, world figures, and undead, the events of their existence can result in such places.

Secrets can be more mundane, such as benevolent or nefarious groups operating in the shadows; they might have influence over settlement leaders. Hidden doors or places are less exciting unless there's something truly interesting there, such as a portal. We can have landmarks like statues that have an unknown feature that is activated under the right circumstances. Maybe a statue is a being that can be reanimated, either as a stone golem, a living person, or undead. Religion is good for creating places with unknown (or largely unknown) features. See chapter 11, "Creating Places of Interest," for additional ideas.

HOW MANY PLACES TO CREATE

If we're creating a world, or part of it, to tell one story, our focus is on those locales where events happen now or in the past, and which influence our work. Creating full details is advantageous for these places. Other settlements mentioned in passing can have little more than their power, location, climate, terrain, reputation (including defensiveness), population type and disposition, major products, and a few identifiers such as symbol and colors decided.

If we're creating a world we intend to use often, we can become overwhelmed with scores of settlements to invent. There's a way to manage this. Full details on a place are still only needed when we're going to use it in a tale, or if we happen to have ideas. For the rest, a master spreadsheet with high-level details on every settlement can make it easier to invent that information. We'll avoid creating the same symbol for two places, because we can see, in one file, all the ones we've already done. We can also more easily find this information when we need it.

A spreadsheet with columns like the following helps:

- Name
- Sovereign power
- Location
- Population size
- Species here (and percentage of overall population)
- Products
- Symbol
- Colors
- Military

Despite this information being in a spreadsheet, we'll probably want a file for each settlement, where this information is potentially duplicated, and get in the habit of updating both file and spreadsheet when we make changes.

Why would we want to create this high-level information for everywhere? We might want to remark that a character is drinking one of the fine wines from a place, or wearing clothes from there (or in their fashion). Maybe they're sitting on chairs from another place, evident in its design. Or they're sailing on a ship with a distinctive style. These little touches add realism and are easy to accomplish, but, as mentioned under the previous section about products, animosities and friendliness can result in added tension on regional levels.

WHERE TO START

It's wise to start with the settlement's location, as this affects everything about it, including layout, climate (and therefore dress), and neighbors, which can include not only other settlements and sovereign powers, but nearby species that live in adjacent terrain. The settlement size, and therefore population, is a second area to consider, as this affects the society and its world view. We might next consider the defense needed due to nearby threats. What it's known for can either be a starting point or a minor detail we add toward the end of our conception. Above all, start with whatever strikes you as a solid idea you won't change your mind on later, as this inspiration often colors much else about our invention.

CHAPTER SEVEN

TRAVEL OVER LAND

On Earth, motorized vehicles come with a speedometer to tell us how fast we're going. Using navigation systems, which are typically connected to GPS, we can even learn how long a trip will take and get continual updates on that. In a SF world with even more advanced technology, we can likely assume the same convenience, but in fantasy worlds, none of this exists. Few of us know how long it takes to get any significant distance by walking or riding various animals. This chapter focus mostly on a fantasy-like setting, where help determining speeds, capabilities, and the impact of terrain on non-magical travel is needed.

Most of the Earth uses the metric system. If releasing products, it's wise to state measurements for the culture where the product is released. Despite this, miles were used instead of kilometers while writing explanations in this chapter because theories apply regardless of the measurement used and explanations are clearer with consistency. Conversions to kilometers are included for formulas.

Writing "Not drawn to scale" on any maps we create is recommended. This provides some leeway in regards to stringent accuracy. A map is not needed for understanding this chapter, but the guidelines are written assuming that you have a map and now want to determine distances and corresponding travel times.

MODE OF TRAVEL

WALKING

Depending on the level of prosperity and technology in our world, most people will only have walking as an option. This is one reason people traveled less on Earth long ago. A trip can be arduous and fraught with peril from thieves and other bandits. Add to that the nefarious creatures in fantasy worlds and people will often stay put. Generally, in a world with poor medicine like in most fantasy settings, those walking are more likely to be between the ages of ten and forty. Those younger or older than this tend to suffer more from long walks. Their fitness level and our world's standards of health impact this. On Earth, few people lived past forty long ago, a problem that modern medicine has reduced. Now people are generally healthier, but if our invented society is based on a medieval one, our inhabitants might be somewhat frail by forty.

When traveling by foot, most people will walk the entire way—only trained warriors or messengers will run any meaningful distance. The ability to run for long distances requires conditioning and practice and is therefore not for the average person unless they happen to love doing it.

Armor, weapons, and supplies will encumber warriors, slowing them and reducing endurance so that they cannot travel as far in a day. A messenger might be less encumbered, but that depends on their location. If traveling in fairly safe lands, they need fewer protections and might carry less. A messenger for the royalty might receive free room and board, and need few supplies. Molesting one might be a capital offense so that they have little to fear. By contrast, in a dangerous wilderness or sovereign power, death from other species or animals (even plants) can happen at any time.

Most of our humanoid species will be close enough in height to humans for there to be no measurable difference. Those much smaller or taller have a shorter or longer gait. This can mean more or fewer steps to accomplish the same journey. This could, in turn, have them tired upon completion. They might also take more or fewer hours to complete the trip. We can alter them to compensate if desired. For example, perhaps our short species has better endurance and travels for more hours without fatigue, reaching a destination in more hours but still making it.

While carrying minimal supplies, the average human can reliably walk twelve miles a day, day after day, without needing to rest or be exhausted. A Roman legion could do fourteen to twenty miles per day. Someone could conceivably do over twenty miles in a day but be exhausted. A marathon of over twenty miles can be done in a few hours, but those people must train for it and must recover for days afterward. In other words, we can fudge travel times in our world based on story needs, but we should first understand a baseline.

Caravans are a special case wherein the entire group moves at the speed of the slowest traveler, unless that person can be placed in a wagon or on a steed. This often means that the slowest mover is an animal, so first we'll need to decide which ones are in the caravan and how encumbered they are, as this may reduce speed.

RIDING ON LAND

There are arguably three scenarios for ridden animals and their encumbrance—light, medium, and heavy. A horse outfitted for a casual ride and ridden by someone with minimal gear (spare clothes, a sword, some utensils and water) has the lightest load and will be able to travel farther in a day, thirty or forty miles. By contrast, a fully armored knight (plate armor, with multiple swords and a lance) on a war horse that's also fully armored (plate armor) will have less endurance and speed. This will reduce the distance traveled in a day. A less armored warrior (chainmail, shield, one sword) and a lightly armored horse (just leather) will be able to travel father. This also relates to elephants, camels, and our custom animals.

Specialized horses can go over one hundred miles per day for several days in a row. The Pony Express riders could travel many miles, but they nearly rode a horse into the ground between stations, when they mounted another and kept going at the same breakneck speed. Horse-pulled wagons travel about fifteen to twenty-five miles per day without roads. Other animals like oxen, giant lizards, and elephants will have different speeds and endurance. We can use any of them as analogues for our invented animals.

FLYING

While flying can generally be assumed to be done in a straight line, factors change this, though this depends on the mode of travel, as what affects a dragon wouldn't affect a Boeing 747. Mountains can be tall enough that they must be circumnavigated. Real birds struggle to get over the Himalayas, for example, because the air is thinner. Dragons are often depicted as all-powerful, but describing their difficulty in climbing over mountains is one way to make them more realistic. This is one reason, along with rain shadows, for characterizing any land features we've created; in this case, we'll decide which mountain ranges are this tall (hint from Chapter 4: the tallest peaks are in the interior of a continent, not on its coast).

Hostile territories can also change flight patterns, whether that hostility derives from other animals or sentient beings like humans with missile weapons. A lone dragon might fear to fly through an area inhabited by other dragons, if the latter are territorial or of a hostile variety. If the dragon is unafraid, his rider might be more cautious.

Politics can also cause hostility. A dictatorship might have outlawed all dragons, for example, that aren't ridden by its own military so that borders are closely watched. Being caught could be a problem. While some might attempt passing over the territory using flight or subterfuge, some will simply go around. In such cases, we'll need to figure out the shortest path that is not a straight line.

ANIMALS

All flying animals that are depicted as being ridable are imaginary. The likelihood is that none would get off the ground with a rider, but there's no fun in that. We must take being realistic with a bigger grain of salt than normal, but the useful details and considerations that arise from trying to be realistic can make our work more believable.

Except for mountains, flying animals are unaffected by the terrain, whether that's roads, forests, rolling hills, or deserts. Flying low changes things a little, as foliage may hide threats, but we're focused on speed here, not dangers except as those that affect flight paths.

When deciding how far (and fast) invented animals can travel in a day, it can help to start with understanding what real Earth birds can do. A carrier pigeon can fly about fifty miles per hour and cover seven hundred miles in a day. Hawks reach twenty to forty miles per hour during migration. These guidelines can help us determine the speeds and distances of our invented fliers. If we have a species that is humanoid with wings, aerodynamics will ensure they fly more slowly than birds. Their maneuverability is also reduced so that a giant bird should have little trouble catching and killing our species, unless the latter is well armed with missile weapons. For these reasons, flying low and hugging treetops and mountains is wiser for our humanoid character than open air unless they have no reason to suspect such a foe. The sight of such a threat should prompt one to seek shelter.

AIRSHIPS

Whether we call them airships, blimps, or dirigibles, these aircraft use buoyancy to stay aloft. This chapter won't focus on the differences between them but rather how fast they can travel. The larger airships like the Hindenburg have higher speeds and other capabilities. The Hindenburg before its demise could reach 84 mph (135 k/mph), but smaller blimps are a bit slower—their maximum speed is 70 mph and with a typical cruising speed of 30-50 mph. The limitation is inherent in the shape and design; using a bigger or more powerful engine won't change this.

As opposed to a balloon, they are maneuverable. The large ones can ascend as high as 24000 feet (7300 meters), which means they can theoretically fly over any mountain range on Earth. However, their payload is reduced when that high and they mainly operate between 1500-8000 feet (460-2500 meters), though the Hindenburg typically did so under 650 feet to stay below clouds and monitor them for storms. The purpose of the flight will determine their altitude, as a passenger ship might sail lower to provide views while a surveillance blimp might be higher to avoid detection.

Figure 33 Zeppelin Airship

When planning a trip for our characters, we can assume a straight line unless we have some reason not to do so, such as the avoidance of a storm or hostile territory. Airships must refuel and this could restrict their uninterrupted flight to 24-50 hours, but the Hindenburg could fly over 100 hours, typically when crossing an ocean.

BALLOONS

Hot air balloons drift with the wind. They cannot be propelled through the air and their flight path cannot be controlled beyond a limited degree. Their speed is also rather slow, such as 3-6 mph for commercial flights, which range from 3-10 miles long and take roughly an hour. Longer trips are possible as the Earth has been circumnavigated in a single trip more than once; fuel, supplies, assistance, and navigator skill are the requirements for such a feat. For world builders, we mostly need to know the balloon's air speed and what sort of trouble our characters might get into if the flight doesn't go as planned, but this will depend on landscape.

AIRPLANES

There are many variations to planes and engine types that will determine how long it takes to travel between two locations by aircraft. This includes fuel capacity, wind, and the plane's purpose, as a passenger jet is slower than an F-16, but also faster than a crop duster. The variety is extreme enough that trying to summarize this may not serve a world builder well and has been omitted from the book.

What we need to first do is decide on the tech level of society and what sort of plane we need (passenger, fighter). What's the purpose in our story, and do we want our characters to have a plane that suits that purpose or not? Perhaps only a two-seat propeller plane is available but they'd prefer a fighter jet. We'll also need a sense of how far they need to go. From here, we'd Google the plane type, learn its speed and fuel capacity, and get a sense of how long a trip might take if done in a straight line.

OBSTACLES

THE IMPACT OF TERRAIN

The terrain we travel over impacts our speed and even reliability. Sand will impact a two-legged species less than a wagon, with wheels that are bogged down, but remember, from Chapter 4, that most deserts are rocky rather than sandy. A forest with thick underbrush slows everything. A light forest will have less impact. The density of under-brush in a forest is a moot point if there's a cleared road through it. Rolling hills, foothills, and mountains will slow everyone whether there's a road or not; it takes time to go up and down and this is worse on the legs of humanoids or animals, increasing fatigue.

Roads paved with cobblestones aren't very smooth and can not only slow travel but fatigue feet and even wagons, where the bumpy ride strains construction. Such roads are more common near a city, extending only a short distance from the walls. Very dry, hard ground is tough on feet, which is why horses will prefer the grass. An unpaved roads means potholes and potentially mud.

Paving, when present, seldom extends far from a set-tlement due to expense. This is one way to indicate wealth, such as in an empire. We may want to decide that most roads are unpaved for most of their length.

Rivers can require traveling to a known crossing, which might be guarded by creatures or species who charge a toll or simply won't let others pass without a fight. Given fords' importance, such a crossing might be controlled by a city, sovereign power, or band of opportunistic thugs. But our main concern is to decide where a river crossing is between two settlements and measure the distance to it from both places, unless the bridge happens to be directly between them.

THE IMPACT OF LIFE

Wild animals and sinister species make traveling more perilous. On a wide open plain with low grass, one could see trouble coming from a long way off, but tall grass or a thick forest could slow our travelers even if there's a road through the terrain. Due to this, there's a difference between the theoretical travel time and the actual. This is another way to slow our characters.

CALCULATION PREPARATION

Multiple steps are needed to calculate distance and travel times. The existence of a map is assumed but not necessary. Just ignore those steps if you don't have one. If you're familiar with Excel, some of this might easier to absorb.

GET ORGANIZED

If we're calculating distances for multiple journeys, we'll want to keep a list somewhere, like a spreadsheet. We'll need to write down the names of each place, of course, but this causes a minor problem with alphabetizing the list. If we write down Washington to Baltimore, then when scanning the list for Baltimore to Washington, we won't see it. We might think we forgot to write it down. It's recommended to alphabetize left to right, too, not just up and down in our list. It might be better to organize by geographic regions or kingdoms, too, if we have a large list of a hundred locations, for example.

What we're after is a listing like this:

Start	Destination	Distance in Inches
Kingdom of Illiandor		
Arycndl	Illiandor	.5
Arycndl	Talendor	1
Illiandor	Talendor	.75
Kingdom of Kariah		
Cree	Kharlan	.25
Kariah	Kharlan	.25

Figure 34 Sample Distances

MEASURE

It's time to measure. We can print our map and do this in the physical world, or import a digital map into a drawing program that has rulers above and to one side of the image. Or we can just eyeball everything. Adding a note to our map—"Not drawn to scale"—is also recommended to provide leeway.

We might decide to only include the distances between settlements, but we can also measure distances to nearby land features if those places are of interest to our story. A forest or mountain range frequently traversed or skirted can impact character decisions and travel times.

If characters go through a terrain, we might want to measure how far that extends. For example, if Arycndl to Illiandor is an inch overall, but a quarter inch is heavy forest and another quarter inch is rolling hills, we might want to indicate this. Each terrain will cause a different travel speed. This might be more detailed than we want, but it adds realism. It can be useful in stories as we remember to observe how much time will be lost on parts of the trip.

This example shows what we're looking to do. The numbers are inches (modify for metrics if needed).

Start	Target	Road	Forest	Hills	Total
Arcyndl	Illiandor	.5	.25	.25	1
Illiandor	Talendor	.25		.25	.5

Figure 35 Sample Measurements

To those columns (road, forest, and hills), we should also add plains, mountains, deserts, and swamps.

SCALE

Determining our map's scale is easy. Just pick a number. Maybe .25 inches equals twenty miles. Based on this, we can calculate that one inch is eighty miles. Changing our minds about scale can become a problem unless we use a program like Microsoft Excel's spreadsheet feature. If we set it up correctly, we can change our scale at any time and have all our miles re-calculated for us. This book provides a free template that already does this, and a lot more, for you. See the "Template" section later in this chapter for more details.

Before choosing our scale, we should get an idea how far apart we imagine these places to be. One way is to reference familiar places on Earth. We might have the impression that two locations are as far as apart as our home and job are, or two cities we frequent. Use online mapping websites to learn how many miles separate them.

We might have a continent that we imagine to be as large as Australia, whether we've ever been there or not. Online maps can tell how far apart cities there are, giving us a sense of scale. Choose two cities and ask a mapping app for directions to learn the miles. If two similar locations on our map are that far apart, this gives us scale. For example, Melbourne to Sydney Australia is 867 kilometers. Then 867 divided by 4 is 216 kilometers per inch. Sometimes such a number might surprise us and we might have to decide our continent/location is smaller or bigger than we'd thought.

With our scale chosen, we can calculate how far away all locations are and fill in a list of this information. In the example below, this has been done with two rows, using a scale of 1 inch equaling 20 miles:

Start	Target	Road (inches)	Road (miles)	Hills (in.)	Hills (mi.)	Total (in.)	Total (mi.)
Arcyndl	Illiandor	.25	5	.25	5	.5	10
Illiandor	Talendor	.5	10	.25	5	.75	15

Figure 36 Sample Terrains

There are better ways to organize this information, as found in the template, but this demonstrates the idea.

BASE MILES PER DAY (BMPD)

For simplicity, I'll use miles instead of kilometers for the acronym BMPD, but these guidelines may be easily converted to kilometers. We need to know or decide how far humans, wagons, dragons, and other species can travel in a day. We have leeway with invented species but should base them on something similar. Humans can reliably walk twelve miles a day without having to rest or recuperate.

Faster or longer travel is possible with consequences, but we're first looking for a reliable base miles per day.

Horses do better on softer ground, making that their ideal terrain. This will be true of other hooved animals, too, regardless of what protections we put on their feet. In the next chart, we'll see that the ideal terrain is indicated by a zero in a column. The zero means that the terrain, such as a road for walking, has no negative impact and does not modify the base speed.

Research is the best way to determine the BMPD for our life forms. You can use the values I chose (in the next chart) or research humans, riding horse, wagon, and carrier pigeon BMPDs yourself.

TERRAIN MODIFIERS

As mentioned earlier, the difficulty of the terrain will modify the base miles per day (BMPD). You'll have to decide for yourself how much speed and distance is lost. Or you can take my current estimates as being plausible if not entirely scientific. My judgement calls are subject to change as I get smarter about all this. Either way, I don't worry over it too much for one simple reason—no one from the planet I've created is going to show up on Earth and announce to everyone that I was wrong about how long it really takes to travel between two places. Besides, my map is not drawn to scale!

Here is my chart of BMPD and the number of miles *lost* per day due to terrain.

Travel Mode	BMPD	Road	Plain	Forest	Hills	Mountain	Desert Swamp
Foot	12	0	0	1.8	3	6	4
Riding Horse	35	3.5	0	3.5	9	18	12

Travel Mode	BMPD	Road	Plain	Forest	Hills	Mountain	Desert Swamp
War horse (light)	28	2.8	0	2.8	7	14	9
War horse (heavy)	21	2.1	0	2.1	5	11	7
Wagon	25	0	2.5			17	
Dragon	500					160	
Carrier Pigeon	700					10	

Figure 37 Terrain Modifier Example

Looking at the first row, this means that humanoids travel 12 miles per day over level terrain. This speed isn't impacted by road or plains for the worse (as indicated by the zeroes). A light forest, without road or trail, slows humans 1.8 miles per day, travelling only 10.2 miles per day. In a heavy forest without road or trail, we lose 8 miles per day, due to thick underbrush we must hack through, moving only 4 miles. On rolling hills or foothills of mountains, we lose 3 miles per day, and mountains reduce speed by half, to 6 miles per day. A sandy desert or swamp reduces distance covered per day by 4 miles, to 8.

The greyed-out sections don't apply. A flying dragon is unaffected by roads, plains, forests, hills, deserts or swamps. Mountains' effect will depend on their height. Similarly, a wagon cannot typically pass through a forest, sandy desert, or roadless swamp. The presence of a road means that the existence of a swamp or other impediments can be largely ignored because the road bypasses the difficulties inherent in an untamed swamp, unless flooding has taken place.

You'll note that the ideal terrain for horses is plains, indicated by the zero for plains. They lose distance on roads instead, because stones are hard on their feet, reducing endurance and therefore distance traveled per day.

Calculations were used to create the modified values. BMPD is reduced by a percentage. For example, mountains cut the BMPD in half. I used 25% for hills, 66% for heavy forests, 33% for desert, and only 15% and 10% for light forest and roads/plains. You can use my values or your own. Below are all my modifier calculations in the same chart as above, showing what I multiplied BMPD by. BMPD * Modifiers = Miles Lost.

Travel Mode	BMPD	Road	Plain	Forest	Hills	Mountain	Desert Swamp
Foot	12			.15	.25	.5	.33
Riding Horse	35	.1		.15	.25	.5	.33
War horse (light)	28	.1		.15	.25	.5	.33
War horse (heavy)	21	.1		.15	.25	.5	.33
Wagon	25		.1		.25	.66	
Dragon	500					.2	
Carrier Pigeon	700					.2	

Figure 38 Terrain Modifiers

OTHER MODIFIERS

What we're calculating is typical conditions. We can speed up a journey in ideal conditions or slow it down with poor ones. If desired, we can use additional modifiers, such how much people are slowed down in darkness, rain, or snow (of various depths). Danger along a route might also slow travel. I chose not to include these in my charts to avoid overkill but you can. For me, it's enough to know what's typical and modify an actual journey's time based on story needs or even whim.

CALCULATIONS

Now we need to calculate the number of days it takes to travel between two points on our map. The formula is distance divided by speed. First, we need to calculate speed by taking the BMPD and subtracting the amount of time lost by the terrain traveled over. The resulting formula is:

Distance / (BMPD—Terrain Modifier)

For example, traveling by foot is 12 miles per day. According to my chart, if traveling through light forest without a road, we lose 1.8 miles per day, resulting in a speed of 10.2 miles per day. If our map's scale says that a quarter inch is 20 miles, and our journey is 1 inch, then 20 * 4 is 80 miles. Eighty (80) miles divided by 10.2 miles per day gets our answer: just under 8 days.

80 / (12—1.8)

Calculating speed for every mode of travel, through every type of terrain, for every two locations on our world, can be time consuming. Doing so has an advantage: once the calculations are done, we don't have to do them again. If we change our mind about scale and have used the provided spreadsheet to track our data, then our calculations will automatically update. This method might be more suited to those intending to use a world over many stories.

By contrast, there is a more manual method, discussed in the next section, that avoids using formulas to change things. Its chief disadvantage is that if we change our mind on scale, calculations we've logged before must be redone. Those using a world once or twice might find this is the most suitable approach.

Pre-Set Calculations

The easiest approach to calculating travel between two places is to be generic about it. Looking at the chart below will make the explanation clearer. This chart states in line 1 that everything on it is for traveling on a paved road. Column A shows inches on our map, while columns B and C shows the corresponding number of miles or kilometers; which we use is irrelevant for determining speed. Columns D through J are the number of days to travel each distance from the first three columns by foot, riding horse, etc.

This chart, and others for different terrains, is included in the free template given to newsletter subscribers. The file allows you to change the scale so that .25 inches could be 25 miles instead of 20, for example, and all the chart's data will change immediately.

Using these pre-set calculations, we never need to use formulas to determine travel time. Instead, we can take our measurement between two places, like Illiandor and Talendor, and see that it is 2 inches. Line 11 above shows us how far that is and how long each travel mode is..

	A	B	C	D	E	F	G	H	I	J
1	Traveling on a Paved Road (or Flying Straight)									
2	Inches	Miles	Kilometers	Foot	Riding Horse	Warhorse (light)	Warhorse (heavy)	Wagon	Dragon	Carrier Pigeon
3			Distance			Days by Travel Mode				
4	0.25	20	32.2	1.7	0.6	0.8	1.1	0.8	0	0
5	0.5	40	64.4	3.4	1.2	1.6	2.2	1.6	0.1	0.1
6	0.75	60	96.6	5.1	1.8	2.4	3.3	2.4	0.1	0.1
7	1	80	128.7	6.8	2.4	3.2	4.4	3.2	0.1	0.1
8	1.25	100	160.9	8.5	3	4	5.5	4	0.2	0.1
9	1.5	120	193.1	10.2	3.6	4.8	6.6	4.8	0.2	0.2
10	1.75	140	225.3	11.9	4.2	5.6	7.7	5.6	0.2	0.2
11	2	160	257.5	13.6	4.8	6.4	8.8	6.4	0.3	0.2
12	2.25	180	289.7	15.3	5.4	7.2	9.9	7.2	0.3	0.3
13	2.5	200	321.9	17	6	8	11	8	0.3	0.3
14	2.75	220	354.1	18.7	6.6	8.8	12.1	8.8	0.4	0.3

Figure 39 Travel on Paved Roads

But what if the two inches between these locations are over different terrain? Maybe 1 inch is a road and another inch is rolling hills. We need to grab line 7 from both charts (the line for 1 inch). Now we have realistic data with thought behind it.

In the included template, I've added an area for you to add up these values. It looks like these screen shots. What I did here was take the inches by road and hills and typed them into the chart. Then I add the miles by looking at the other charts. I also added the values for a riding horse, in this case. It shows my final results for a particular journey.

The main problem with the above chart is that our data is not preserved. When we want to do a second journey, we'll have to replace that data, unless we save it somewhere. Also, if we change our mind about scale, that saved data must be redone. For this reason, some world builders might want to follow the steps in the next section.

Inches By	Distance			Days By Travel Mode						
	Miles	Kilometers	Foot	Riding Horse	Warhorse	Hy Warhorse	Wagon	Dragon	Pigeon
Road	0.25	20	32.2		0.6					
Plain	0									
Light Forest	0									
Heavy Forest	0									
Hills	0.5	40	64.4		1.6					
Mountains	0									
Swamp/Desert	0									
Total	0.75	60	96.6	0	2.2	0	0	0	0	0

Figure 40 Travel Sample

CUSTOM CALCULATIONS

World builders who intend to use the world for many years to come might want to preserve travel times between many places in a single database. Doing this requires a time investment and familiarity with formulas that will scare away many people. This section is designed for the brave. I did this once for my main world, Llurien, and will likely never do it again, even for new continents, because it's too much work. There's also a significant risk of making a formula mistake. A major advantage of doing it is that, once done, it never needs repeating. A change of scale updates the entire spreadsheet.

The details of these custom calculations are discussed in the following template section. Explaining how to do it without the template as a visual guide is unnecessarily challenging. And setting up that template yourself is more pain than you likely want.

THE TEMPLATE

Most templates for this book are Microsoft Word documents that are downloadable but also printed in an appendix. For the travel calculations, there is a Microsoft Excel spreadsheet instead, which I discuss here. You can join the newsletter and download the "Travel Template" for free at http://www.artofworldbuilding.com/newsletter.

I'm not going to provide instruction on spreadsheet basics, just how to use my template, with caveats and tips. You will need to read this carefully and study the template. I suggest downloading it first, looking it over, and then reading along while keeping the template open to refer to. Those familiar with Excel and spreadsheet technology will find this much easier to follow and use.

The spreadsheet template has multiple sheets, which are discussed next. An additional sheet for calculating travel at sea is included and discussed in the next chapter.

SCHEMA SHEET

The first sheet in the template we'll look at is called "Schema." The screen shot below shows two columns, "Inches on Map" and "# of Miles", or how many miles to the inch. This sets the map's scale.

	A	B
1	Inches on Map	# of Miles
2	0.25	20
3	0.5	40
4	0.75	60
5	1	80
6	1.25	100
7	1.5	120
8	1.75	140
9	2	160
10	2.25	180
11	2.5	200
12	2.75	220

Figure 41 Inches and Miles

The value in cell B2, highlighted in green, is the only one you need alter. Cells B3-B12 contain formulae to calculate distances based on the value in B2. In other words, B2 is the number of miles for a quarter inch. For example, half an inch is twice one quarter of an inch, so the number of miles is doubled. You can change the value in B2 right now and see how it changes this section of the "Schema" sheet. It also causes all the values on the "Travel" sheet to change. This is what we *want* because we don't need to ever recalculate a value.

The second area of the "Schema" sheet, pictured below, is the BMPD and miles lost due to terrain. This should look familiar because I covered this earlier in this chapter. You don't need to change this unless you disagree with my formulas or the "Base" value I used. The green cells do not have formulas, so you can just type a new value. For the other cells, you'd need to modify the formulas if you don't agree with them. You'll notice that some cells have a little red triangle in the corner. This means I have a note, usually explaining my rationale for the formula, and you can see this comment by hovering your mouse over the red triangle. A right-click on the cell will open a menu allowing you to edit the comment.

14		Base Miles Per Day and # Miles Lost Due to Terrain							
15	Travel Mode	BMPD	Road	Plain	Forest (light)	Forest (heavy)	Hills	Mountains	Desert
16	Foot	12	0	0	1.8	8	3	6	4
17	Riding Horse	32	3.5	0	5.25	23.1	9	18	12
18	War horse (light)	28	2.8	0	4.2	18.5	7	14	9
19	War Horse (heavy)	21	2.1	0	3.15	13.9	5	11	7
20	Wagon	25	0	2.5			6	17	8
21	Dragon	600	0					120	
22	Carrier Pigeon	700	0					140	

Figure 42 Base Miles Per Day

TRAVEL SHEET

The travel sheet utilizes the schema sheet. I've provide sample data so you can see how this works. This sheet gets a little complicated so digest this in pieces and study what's happening closely. It is divided into sections. In general, the grey columns should never be altered as they are counting other areas of this spreadsheet for you, using formulas you'll never need to alter.

The first section, pictured below, is just two columns, A and B, which are the Start and Destination locations. This is the easiest part to fill out. Just add all your places here, organized by region or sovereign power.

The second section, "Inches over Terrain Type," is pictured below and is columns C through J. This is the measurement of how many map-inches separate two places. If the total distance is one inch but half is on roads and half is over rolling hills, you would enter .5 in column C (roads) and .5 in column G (hills). The grey-colored J column, "Total," totals the inches for you, and should not be altered. This section is also easy to fill out. Measure your map and type in your values.

	A	B
1	Start	Destination
2	Free Cities	
3	City 1	City 2
4	City 1	City 3
5	City 3	Town 1
6	City 3	Town 2
7	City 4	Wizard Tower
8		
9	Kingdom of Wherever	
10	City 1	City 2
11	City 2	City 3
12		
13	Kingdom of Nowhere	
14	Town 1	Town 2
15	City 1	Town 1

Figure 43 Start and End Locations

The third section, "Miles over Terrain Type," is figure 45 and is columns K through S, with the last two columns adding up both total miles and total kilometers from the columns to the left (K through Q). For the other columns, we're getting the number of *miles* that corresponds to the number of *inches* from the second section. In the sample data, column C3 shows .25 miles over road. That means

240 | RANDY ELLEFSON

that column K3 should show "20" miles, because that's the scale we have set on the Schema sheet.

K	L	M	N	O	P	Q	R	S
Road	Plain	Forest (light)	Forest (heavy)	Hills	Mountains	Desert - Swamp	Miles	Kilometers
			Miles over Terrain Type				Total Distance	
20							20	32.2
	80						80	128.7
40	100						140	225.3
	20	80	60				160	257.5
				40	40		80	128.7
40	120						160	257.5
20						100	120	193.1
20	60						80	128.7
120							120	193.1

Figure 44 Inches Over Terrain Type

Instead of manually looking at the Schema sheet, seeing that we want 20, and typing that into K3, we're using a formula to automatically grab that value from Schema for us. The reason for this is that, if we change our scale on the Schema sheet, the new value would appear in K3 without us having to alter K3. This takes more work to set up but will save you eons of time if you change your scale, as you probably will. Using formulas like this frees us from worrying about getting our scale "right" the first time and allows us to change our minds later without having to redo everything. If you click K3, you'll see the formula above that:

=ROUND(Schema!B2,0)

The text "Schema!B2,0" is grabbing the value out of B2 on the Schema sheet and inserting it here (in this case, the value is "20"). The value is also being rounded to a whole number, which is what the black text is doing. There's no automatic way to grab the part in parenthesis. Copy and paste this formula into every cell that needs it, to complete this section of the Travel sheet. The same principle applies to .5 inches, except that you'd change the formula to use cell B3 instead of B2 from Schema sheet. And so on.

You can experiment with this right now. Go to the Schema sheet and type 10 into B2 and then come back to Travel and see the new numbers.

T	U	V	W	X	Y	Z
Foot	Riding Horse	Warhorse (light)	Warhorse (heavy)	Wagon	Dragon	Carrier Pigeon
Days by Travel Mode						
1.7	0.6	0.8	1.1	0.8	0	0
6.7	2.3	3.2	4.2	3.2	0.1	0.1
11.7	4.1	5.6	7.4	5.6	0.2	0.2
24.5	8.3	10.4	13.9	6.5	0.3	0.2
11.1	3.9	6.5	6.5	7.1	0.2	0.1
13.3	4.7	5.9	7.8	6.9	0.3	0.2
4.2	5	6.1	8.2	6.7	0.2	0.2
6.7	2.3	2.9	3.9	3.5	0.1	0.1
10	3.8	4.8	6.3	4.8	0.2	0.2

Figure 45 Miles Over Terrain Type

The fourth section, "Days by Travel Mode," is pictured next; columns T through Z are what we're after. This is the most difficult part. We want to take the number of miles from the previous section and divide it by the BMPD for that travel mode, minus the modifier for that terrain. In other words, if it's 20 miles, we divide that by our BMPD speed, such as a walking human (12), except that we first need to modify this BMPD by subtracting the number of miles lost due to the terrain. In the case of a road, a walking human loses no speed, according to our Schema sheet. We'd divide 20 by 12 to get 1.7 days. However, a riding horse moves at a BMPD of 35, and on a road, it loses 10% of its speed, or 3.5 miles, resulting in a speed of 30.5 miles per day. When we divide 20 miles by 30.5 per day, we get .6 days for a riding horse to go 20 miles. In other words, it will take just over a half day to go twenty miles under ideal conditions and without hurrying. You need to know this for storytelling.

T	U	V	W	X	Y	Z
Foot	Riding Horse	Warhorse (light)	Warhorse (heavy)	Wagon	Dragon	Carrier Pigeon
Days by Travel Mode						
1.7	0.6	0.8	1.1	0.8	0	0
6.7	2.3	3.2	4.2	3.2	0.1	0.1
11.7	4.1	5.6	7.4	5.6	0.2	0.2
24.5	8.3	10.4	13.9	6.5	0.3	0.2
11.1	3.9	6.5	6.5	7.1	0.2	0.1
13.3	4.7	5.9	7.8	6.9	0.3	0.2
4.2	5	6.1	8.2	6.7	0.2	0.2
6.7	2.3	2.9	3.9	3.5	0.1	0.1
10	3.8	4.8	6.3	4.8	0.2	0.2

Figure 46 Days by Travel Mode

If this is confusing, just go through it slowly.

The formula is: =ROUND(SUM(K3/(Schema!B16-Schema!C16)),1). What this says is round (to the nearest tenth) the sum of a calculation, which is the number of miles to travel (K3) divided by the BMPD (Schema!B16) minus the modifier (Schema!C16).

For part of it, we could just write B16—C16, but those two cells are on the Schema sheet, which requires us to add "Schema!" in front of it, resulting in Schema!B16, for example.

It gets more complicated when our travel distance goes over more than one kind of terrain. In this case, we need to calculate each of them as explained above, and then add them together. In that sense, it's not that hard, but if you're not used to looking at Excel formulas, it becomes confusing. Study this one:

```
=ROUND(
SUM(L11/(Schema!B17-Schema!D17))+
SUM(M11/(Schema!B17-Schema!E17))+
SUM(N11/(Schema!B17-Schema!F17)),1)
```

This is for riding horse and basically says 1) divide the distance over plains (L11) by BMPD for riding horse—Modifier on plains, and add it to 2) divide the distance over light forest (M11) by BMPD for riding horse—Modifier on light forest, and add it to 3) divide the distance over heavy forest (N11) by BMPD for riding horse—Modifier on heavy forest.

I'm also using a rounding function so that we get results like 4.1 miles per day instead of 4.11341 or something equally annoying. The round function looks like this: ROUND(our calculation, 1), the 1 being how many places after the decimal we want.

You may find this spreadsheet to be a lot of work. Consider doing this in small stages instead of all at once.

MANUAL TRAVEL

This sheet on the template is discussed in section, "Pre-Set Calculations." Each mode of travel has its own section. The numbers of miles, kilometers, and days needed to travel are based on the Schema sheet. No changes to this page are required.

AREA SIZING

	A	B	C	D	E	F	G	H	I
1	Area	Inches	Miles	Kilometers	Inches	Miles	Kilometers	Sq. Miles	Sq. Kilometers
2			Length			Height			Total
3									
4	Continent Name	15	1200	1931.2	12	960	1545	864,000	2,237,778
5									
6					Kingdoms				
7	Kingdom #1 Name	2.25	180	289.7	2.5	200	321.9	28,800	74,604
8	Kingdom #2 Name	1.5	120	193.1	2	160	257.5	17,280	44,751
9									
10					Features by Region				
11					Kingdom #1 Name				
12	Forest #1	1.5	120	193.1	1.25	100	160.9	12,000	31,070
13	Mountains #1	0.75	60	96.6	1	80	128.7	4,800	12,432
14									
15					Kingdom #2 Name				
16	Forest #1	1.25	100	160.9	1	80	128.7	7,200	18,637

Figure 47 Region Sizing

On the template, there's another sheet called "Regions." This sheet allows us to figure out how many miles (or kilometers) long and wide our land features are, and the total square miles or kilometers. Though this has nothing to do with travel, this chapter's subject, it's on the same template to make use of the Schema sheet. Most of us likely won't care about the total square miles of land in a region or sovereign power, but for those who do, this sheet calculates it for you.

Measure the length and height of each sovereign power or land feature on a continent. This will help you learn how big everything is. With the inches columns filled in, we can once again use the Schema sheet to determine how many miles and kilometers everything is by referring to the appropriate cells. In the image above, you can see "Continent Name" is fifteen inches long. Since I don't have fifteen inches on Schema (I stopped at 2.75), I used math to get my fifteen inches. In other words, the calculation is for two inches multiplied by seven (to get fourteen inches), then one inch added to it. For example, =ROUND((Schema!B9*7)+(Schema!B5),1). The same was done for height. Doing it this way once again means that if I change the scale of my map, the numbers change for me.

The calculation for square miles/kilometers is done by multiplying the values for length by height. However, this assumes our land feature is a square or rectangle when it probably isn't. The solution for this is another multiplication, this time by a percentage represented by a decimal value. For example, if we have a forest that is 100 miles by 80 miles, the square miles would be 8,000 (100 * 80). However, maybe it's not an actual rectangle, so we decide ten percent of that area is not included in the territory. We'd change the calculation from 100 * 80 to (100 * 80) * .9, resulting in 7,200 square miles. The same modification is done to kilometers. This example is in the spreadsheet for "Forest #1 Name" under "Kingdom #2 Name."

LASTLY

When experimenting with this spreadsheet, be careful of the way Excel works. We can accidentally change the formula in a cell if we click elsewhere. It's best to use the tab key to navigate out of a cell with a formula.

WHERE TO START

Determining the distance between locations for which we want to calculate travel times should be an early decision. Take terrain changes between each pair of locations into account. Then decide which travel methods will be used in your books; there's no sense in calculating dragons' travel time if they don't exist in your world. Review the base miles per day that this book provides and alter them to suit your judgment. Do the same for terrain and other modifiers. Now you're ready to calculate the travel times. The easiest method is to use the pre-set ones provided. Otherwise, carefully study the equations in this chapter and the Excel spreadsheet and apply them as needed.

CHAPTER EIGHT

TRAVEL BY WATER

If you're a landlubber like me, you have little to no idea how long it takes a ship to sail from one place to another. That will change by the end of this chapter, but we have considerable leeway in deciding the length of any journey. Much of what follows here is about travel under sail, or by rowing, not by engines. In fantasy worlds, those engines are implausible. In SF, travel is typically through the air. The speed calculations in the section on ship speeds can apply to engine-powered ships as well, since a knot is a knot and it doesn't matter what's causing this speed, with the caveat that winds and oars cannot produce the constant speed of engines.

Several factors influence the difficulty of sailing between locations. The wind direction is chief among them. The ship building skills and seamanship of various countries also impacts this. All of it influences trade routes and which nations can conquer others. A ship would not be able to sail directly into a headwind. Taking an alternative route might force a ship closer to an enemy coastline.

There are several reasons we have leeway in determining the duration of a ship journey:

1) Our map, should one exist, is not drawn to scale
2) Oarsmen cannot row indefinitely and might have different levels of endurance and training from ship to ship
3) Wind speed is not constant even in the open ocean, affecting both the ship itself (if sail powered) and the height of waves that could further impact speed
4) Wind direction is also not constant, affecting the angle at which wind fills sails
5) Different types of ships sail at different speeds under the same conditions
6) Our ship is weighed down by people, cargo, food, and weapons/ammunition, any one of which can change in quantity during a voyage. A ship that just left dock is heavier than one at sea for six months, unless the latter is laden with treasure
7) Our ship might be damaged
8) Our ship is sailing on a fictitious planet, with possibly a different number of moons and whatever else might affect the seas

Maybe it comes as no surprise that we aren't sure how long a trip will take. What we're looking for is a reasonable approximation that a ship will take between X and Z number of hours to travel Y number of miles/kilometers, depending on conditions. But we don't have to do this. We can just invent numbers and not worry about it. Never stating the distance between two places helps. Grounding our numbers in some real-world knowledge is an approach that more serious world builders might want to employ, especially if we intend to reuse the setting. Otherwise, we might be inconsistent. Regardless of our choice, the knowledge can help inspire believable details in our work.

For example, let's say that for our story, we need a trip to take 24 hours, but our calculations reveal that a ship usually takes 24-30 hours. We're in luck and can do it. When describing that journey, we could state that our sailors enjoyed nearly ideal conditions. This could allow for characters to undertake sword practice on deck or another activity requiring surer footing. A wizard could have time to mix materials needed for spells.

In another scenario, maybe we want our characters to feel confident they'll make that trip in time. But we want to surprise them and make them arrive late, in 34 hours. We can throw up a storm to slow them, making a character sea sick and preventing others from doing much of anything. Or maybe they battle a ship or sea monster and in so doing lose a mast despite their victory.

We don't have to do these things, but stories always need unexpected challenges, and if the sea isn't hard to predict, nothing in our world is.

SHIP TERMS

A few basic terms are helpful to know. This is not an exhaustive list of nomenclature, just what we need to know to understand the differences between vessels.

MASTS

A mast stands vertically from any ship that has sails. There can be more than one, depending on ship size and type. The center mast is the tallest and called the main mast. The mast at the bow (front of the ship) is the foremast and is shorter. The rear one, should it exist, is called the mizzen mast, and is the shortest. In a two-masted ship, the mizzen mast is the omitted one; however, the other two masts are farther back in the ship's body.

Figure 48 Ship with Three Masts

YARDS

Each mast will have at least one yard, to which the sails are attached. In many ships, the yard is horizontal. If perpendicular, or square, to the ship's length, the ship is "square-rigged". Most ships have from one to three yards of different lengths and thicknesses. By contrast, in lateen-rigged ships, the yard is sloped, running parallel to the ship's length, one end pointing at the sky, and there's only one per mast. The yards have names but these aren't needed to understand this chapter.

Figure 49 Horizontal Yards

Some ships have a combination of square and lateen rigging. This usually means the main and foremast are square while the mizzen is lateen. This will be mentioned further when looking at actual ship types.

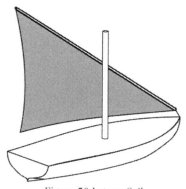

Figure 50 Lateen Sail

SAILS

In square-rigged ships, the sails are a trapezoid, being wider at the bottom than the top. On a lateen-rigged ship, a triangular sail is used. This is sometimes called fore-and-aft rigging because that's how the yard is aligned (forward and aft, or rear). This rigging allows for a closer point of sail on the wind, being more maneuverable. It takes advantage of rapidly changing winds such as in the Mediterranean, but in the open ocean, winds are more constant and a square-rigged ship does not suffer a disadvantage. Sails can be configured in many ways, most of which will confuse anyone not familiar with them, but this resource goes into more detail: http://www.artofworldbuilding.com/sails.

SHIP RATES

In the British Navy, ships were rated based on the number of guns and personnel. This is something authors can mention but screenwriters might find hard to work into a conversation without being obvious about it. In either case, if we have a character say, "That's a first-rate ship," people will assume that means "it's a quality ship," not that it means the ship has over a hundred guns and more than eight hundred crew and is therefore in the biggest class of ships. The same applies to "second-rate" and so on, with many audiences assuming the ship is inferior when this isn't true. The ratings are not a judgement of quality, though in the "bigger is better" mentality, it is. Beware of this when writing about it.

Whether we emulate this or not, here is a basic rundown, according to *Men-of-War, Life in Nelson's Navy* by Patrick O'Brian:

"First rate: 100-112 guns, 841 men (including officers, seamen, boys, and servants)

Second rate: 90-98 guns, 743 men

Third rate: 64, 74 and 80 guns, 494, about 620, and 724 men

Fourth rate: 50 guns, 345 men

Fifth rate: 32, 36, 38, and 44 guns, 217-297 men

Sixth rate: 20, 24, and 28 guns, 128, 158, and 198 men."

Anything with fewer guns wasn't rated and all the above had three masts. Not including the forecastle and quarterdeck, the first and second-rate ships had three full decks for just the guns. Third and fourth rate had two gun decks and the rest had one gun deck. With multiple gun decks, the guns on the lower decks were the biggest and this was where crew slept and ate. High decks had increasingly smaller guns and cannonballs for the obvious reason of not making the ship top heavy. Weaponry is discussed later in this chapter.

This large image of a third-class man-o-war gives a great view of the rigging and even interior of a vessel: http://www.artofworldbuilding.com/warship.

SHIP TYPES

While we could invent a new ship, there's little reason to, for several reasons. We aren't likely to engineer something that would stay afloat if constructed, but a large variety of ship types are available to us already. Within each type, even more variety is to be found. This means we once again have leeway to make alterations of our own if we need to, provided we get the basics right. Naval terminology regarding ships was somewhat flexible at times, but settled into more definitive terms. This works to our advantage because we can get things approximately correct and fudge details. In addition, audiences seldom know about existing ships and probably don't thirst for something new. For these reasons, we'll look at the more prominent, existing ships, not learn how to build new ones.

Vessels comes in two groups: long ships and round ships. The latter aren't circular, of course, but are called this because they are wide when compared to the narrow and streamlined long ships like those used by Vikings.

LONG SHIPS

The earliest vessels are the long ships, which are largely powered by oars but also have sails for additional propulsion. The galley is the primary type, and there are variations on it. All were designed for war or swift transportation, as opposed to carrying cargo.

GALLEY

Synonymous with Vikings but used elsewhere, the galley is the basic vessel powered by strong, highly trained rowers. It often includes a single mast and a metal-shod prow for ramming, an act followed by boarding. It is highly maneuverable but has a wide turning arc and requires calm weather. It is also not for open seas (despite being occasionally used this way) and is consequently found along coastlines. The invention and addition of firearms to ships caused this type to fall into disuse on Earth, but if our world doesn't have gunpowder or similarly powered gunnery, the galley might still be favored.

Figure 51 Galley

The later, 17th century galley on Earth had two masts and a captain's cabin at the rear, which adds usefulness to us as storytellers simply because a room exists in which conversations or acts not for others to witness may take place. If using this type of galley, we need another name for it, such as naming it after a sovereign power from which it's thought to have originated.

The galley type known as a galleass is quite large, having both a rear and forecastle for artillery and soldiers, and up to twenty-five oars per side, each oar rowed by five men. Above the rower's heads might be a deck for soldiers and operation of sails and gunnery. This ship wasn't as fast and often served in the vanguard of an armada as a commander's vessel.

ROUND SHIPS

Designed for carrying cargo and passengers, the round ships are also used for war and are what we've seen in every pirate movie. The round ships primarily use sails for power. When there's no wind, or an unfavorable one, oars can assist the smaller round ships (up to a frigate in size).

Later ships are more maneuverable than long ships like the galley except in calm weather. The round ships mentioned in this chapter are square-rigged on all masts unless otherwise noted.

The man-o-war is not a specific ship type but a generic English name for a three-masted war ship outfitted with soldiers and cannons. This includes the frigate and ship-of-the-line, among others. On our invented world, we can apply the term to similar ships even if an Earth equivalent is not deemed a man-o-war.

While there are many specifications about round ships, the ones listed in this chapter offer a quick comparison regarding ship length, guns, crew, and maximum speeds. Finding definitive answers for each proves somewhat challenging due to conflicting specs cited in various sources. One source might say frigates are from 135-175 feet while another might say they range up to 200. Such details might be insignificant, especially given that, as world builders, we'd be discussing ships on our imagined world, where anything is possible and details could differ at our whim. Still, some effort should be made to know the guidelines before going so far outside of norms as to strain credibility.

To that end, the approach used to compile these specifications was to find reputable sources stating the range of widely accepted possibilities. Further, specific ships of each type with known stats were also considered. In the end, if two sources provided similar numbers, such as 24-40 and 24-44, the larger range is indicated on the chart. If one source provided a number far higher than others, such as 24-40 vs. 24-60, then the higher number was added in parenthesis with a question mark, such as the frigate gun count below, where it reads "24-40 (60?)."

Note that the maximum speed in knots is in ideal conditions with a strong wind on the optimum point of sailing (which direction the wind is blowing in relation to the ship's heading). No ship experiences such conditions throughout a journey, making the number somewhat useless for determining a trip's speed. These numbers are mostly for understanding a ship's capability.

Ship Type	Length in Feet	Guns	Crew	Max Speed (knots)
Brig	123	10-18	155	11
Frigate	135-212	24-40 (60?)	217-345 (815?)	14
Galleon	140-160	30-74	200-400	10
Gunboat	49-72	1-3	12	14
Ship-of-the-line	150-250	64-140	494-1280	11
Sloop	60	14	75	11
Sloop-of-war	60-110	8-24	112-125	11

Figure 52 Ship Chart

What follows are some of the more well-known ship types of Earth.

BRIG

The brig is a two-masted, square-rigged ship that has a single gun deck. It is fast, highly maneuverable, and can be used as a merchant ship, war ship, or scouting vessel. Pirates frequently employ them. A brig is arguably different from a brigantine but even sailing enthusiasts might disagree over any differences, and historically the names were interchanged; we can use either term. Early brigantines were often outfitted with oars, allowing for movement with poor winds or in and out of harbor more easily.

Figure 53 Brig

FRIGATE

The frigate is a fast and highly maneuverable, fourth or fifth-rate ship with one gun deck. These are attack ships and often used as scouting vessels for a fleet, escorting, patrolling or acting independently. They are the largest ships used independently because bigger ships are deemed too valuable to risk being captured or destroyed, which is more likely when sailing alone. Some frigates have two gun decks and are called heavy frigates. The term "frigate" is sometimes used generically to refer to quick ships.

Frigates are the same length as higher rated ships but have fewer decks. They carry supplies for six months. Any areas like a forecastle aren't as tall as ships-of-the-line. They avoid fights with ships-of-the-line due to being out-gunned. During a line of battle, they do not join the firing ships but are in another row behind them, relaying signals up and down the battle line, as ships-of-the-line can see only the ship before and behind them, making communication difficult. They also aren't fired upon by the enemy unless they fire first, as it is bad etiquette; they are not only smaller but are present to relay messages, not fight.

Fregate a la Voile,

Figure 54 Frigate

FIRE SHIP

Any ship can be turned into a fire ship, but as this means certain destruction to the ship in question, ships that have little to no value are used. The ship is rigged to burn from within the hold, where specially designed tubes vent the flames toward enemy ships and the rigging. The ship is sent floating into the general melee of a sea battle during engagements between fleets; it isn't something we'd see sailing around by itself. We might assume that something as valuable as a ship-of-the-line is an unlikely fire ship even if damaged beyond any other use; too many men would be required to sail it into position and then abandon it for other ships, but it could be done.

GALLEON

The galleon has two features that distinguish it from other round ships: masts and prow. Like other round ships, it has a mainmast and foremast, but the rear mizzenmast is lateen-rigged. It sometimes has a fourth, even smaller rear mast. This lateen style allows superior sailing that could save days or weeks over long voyages in the open ocean. An instantly recognizable feature is a long beak jutting forward from the prow.

Figure 55 Galleon

For authors, these features require explanation that may gain our audience little in understanding. This is especially true of the beak, which has no functional benefit aside from helping sailors tend to sails, which few readers will care about even if we understand the details of such things and wish to convey them. The beakhead is where sailors crapped, the waste falling directly into the sea, but this is true of all round ships, not just the galleon; oddly, it is the rear of round ships that has an area called "the poop." This is also from where the expression "I gotta hit the head" originates, as the latrine is at the head of the ship and therefore downwind.

If we wish to explain what a galleon is and how it differs from other round ships like the frigate, the difference between square and lateen-rigging and the possible impact on maneuverability and speed is what to mention.

GUNBOAT

Since our world might not have guns, a new name might be needed for this small vessel that carries one or more large cannons (or whatever missile weapon we invent). They are cheap and easy to build and therefore more expendable. Used in coastal waters, they are no match for large ships, but a score of them can do horrific damage to a lone ship, which can't sink them all fast enough. This boat is either powered by sails or oars.

SHIP-OF-THE-LINE

A ship with sixty or more guns, which includes all first, second, and third-rate ships, the ship-of-the-line acquires its name from being designed for the line of battle when two fleets fight each other in two parallel lines. This allows for firing broadsides at each other without fear of hitting their own ships. Smaller ships are not considered strong enough to withstand such a barrage from these vessels, the largest ships afloat, and therefore aren't part of the line, if present at all.

Figure 56 Ship of the Line

For an interesting cross-section of the interior of such a vessel, view this diagram:
http://www.artofworldbuilding.com/warship.

SLOOP

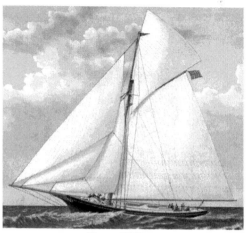

Figure 57 Sloop

To most of us, a sloop is basically a sail boat, having a single mast that is fore-and-aft rigged. If there are two masts, it's called a cutter instead (and is typically larger). There are other minor variations on this, each with a different name, but they are not ships of war and therefore might only figure in our work if our characters need a small, wind-powered vessel. Another option would be the galley (oar-powered long ship).

SLOOP-OF-WAR (CORVETTE)

This ship is not to be confused with a sloop. As its name implies, it's a warship, having a single gun deck with eighteen guns. It is considerably larger than a sloop and often has two masts. Eventually, three-masted versions were built and then resembled a small frigate. However, a frigate is square rigged; sloops-of-war have varying sail configurations, from all square-rigged to ketch riggings or snow riggings (googling this will reveal familiar images). The name corvette was later applied to them. The ships are not rated, having too few guns for the rating system of Britain, but we can rate them as we like on our world (i.e., seventh rate).

Figure 58 Corvette

PRIVATEER

A privateer is not a ship type but any ship operated by private individuals, or a group of them, for profit. They are given the right, via a letter of marque, to engage in acts of war on the seas by their sovereign power, which takes a percentage of any captured prize. Profits are otherwise split among crew and owners. The possession of the letter of marque, and the return and sale of prizes to the sovereign power, is what distinguishes a privateer from a pirate.

Not surprisingly, some pirates sought the letters (often illegally) to absolve their actions. Others acquired letters from opposing countries at war (not admitting to this, of course). They then attacked both sides as desired. For example, a privateer might have letters of marque from England and from France, using the former against French ships and the latter against English. Only he and his crew, and possible owners, might know this.

Privateers who didn't return captured prizes, or who otherwise violated their agreement, could be declared pirates. Some countries refused to recognize the letters of marque from their enemies and hanged captured privateers as pirates, or at least threatened to, leading to negotiations for an exchange of prisoners, for example.

As for the ships, they were heavily armed, fast, and highly maneuverable, as they were intended purely for assault. Since they captured ships and sailed them back (treasure inside), there was arguably less need for their own cargo space beyond provisions. Anything larger than a frigate was unsuitable (i.e., no ships-of-the-line).

SHIP SPEEDS

BY OARS

The top speed when using oars for propulsion doesn't matter much for travel because crews can't sustain it for long, despite one trip being done at 8 knots (which we can have our swaggering hero achieve because he's awesome). Ships would travel under sail for a trip of any length, with the oars being saved for a battle or a crisis. With favorable winds, a ship can do 2-3 knots while an unfavorable wind is half that (1-1.5 knots). For more details on calculating travel times, consult the next section.

By Sails

Now comes the challenging part—figuring out how fast our characters can get from one place to another on a wind-powered ship. This depends on where the ship is sailing. Not only are ocean winds more constant in direction and speed, but with sufficient crew to rotate duty through the day/night, ships sail around the clock. By contrast, sailing along a coastline or island means variable winds, requiring an adjustment to the rigging with each fluctuation. On such a trip, ships dock for the night at a port; the port has to exist and be friendly to them.

Note that explanations in this section are done using miles. Calculations for both miles and kilometers are included when we reach that point. Also, there's technically no such thing as nautical kilometers and any reference to this is only for those world builders more familiar with using kilometers than miles.

Speed is measured in knots. A knot is one nautical mile per hour (mph). A nautical mile is 1.151 land miles. Why the difference? The nautical mile accounts for the curvature of the Earth while the land mile does not. What this means for us is that if we've decided two ports on the same coast are 25 miles apart by land, divide this number by 1.151 to learn how many nautical miles this is (just under

22). If our ship has to go around a peninsula, for example, we'll need to measure that and take it into account.

Whether we measure in miles or kilometers has no effect on the time a trip takes. It only affects the numbers we use for our calculations.

Most ships have an overall speed of between 4-6 knots during a long voyage over open water, and 3-4 knots along coasts or along islands. This is not to say that ships cannot go slower or faster. Any ship can be becalmed or sail at its maximum speed under ideal circumstances, which is usually around 11 knots, depending on the ship (see the chart above). But it's rare for a ship to sail in ideal conditions for long.

Remember that some journeys might begin along a coast before using the open ocean, so we'll want the distance for the coastal leg, the oceanic leg, and then possibly another coastal leg. During coastal legs, a ship might put in to port overnight and therefore lose however many hours we decide they're docked or moored. If we assume a 24-hour day, for example, and one stop of 8 hours for the night, then a trip of 22 hours is extended by 8 hours and now takes 30 hours.

To calculate the hours needed to traverse two locations, follow the steps below. We'll use hours (instead of days) because our world might not have a 24-hour day. This also makes it easier to reduce travel time by the number of hours we decide that a ship is in port or is repairing damage while at sea.

1) Measure the sailing distance on the map. If using miles, skip to step three.
2) Optional: if using kilometers, convert the kilometers to miles by multiplying the distance by 0.62137

3) Divide the number of miles by 1.151 to learn nautical miles

4) Assuming average conditions (wind, cargo, personnel, etc.), find the range of hours your ship needs while traveling:

   a. At 6 knots: nautical miles divided by 6 knots = hours of continuous sailing needed

   b. At 4 knots: nautical miles divided by 4 knots = hours of continuous sailing needed

   c. At 2 knots (oar-powered): nautical miles divided by 2 knots = hours of continuous sailing needed

Here is an example, following the numbered steps above, starting with kilometers:

1) 125 kilometers from X to Y (along a coastline)

2) Optional: 125 x 0.62137 = 77. miles (rounded up)

3) 77. miles / 1.151 = 67 nautical miles

4) Speeds

   a. At 6 knots: 67 nautical miles divided by 6 knots = 11 hours (rounded up) of continuous sailing (no stops)

   b. At 4 knots: 67 nautical miles divided by 4 knots = 17 hours

   c. At 2 knots: 67 nautical miles divided by 2 knots = 33.5 hours

For the 33.5 hour trip, the ship could stop for the night. If we assume 8 hours each time, this results in 41.5 hours.

If you'd rather not make these calculations, join *The Art of World Building* newsletter to gain access to an Excel spreadsheet template that lays out the travel times for you.

ON RIVERS

Surface currents on rivers are arguably stronger than those on larger bodies of water due to the narrowness of the channel. The narrower the river, the faster the current, but depth can also make it faster. A river is not uniformly wide or deep and will become wider, and therefore slower, the longer it flows. This means river speeds farther inland are faster. A river's course also affects speed. Water flows faster in the center of a straight channel, but when it curves, the outer corner is fastest and the inner one slowest. Characters who are inexperienced sailors might be unable to utilize the currents well unless they happen to be keen observers and figure this out. How fast do rivers typically flow in knots? The extremes are almost 0 knots to 6 knots, but we'll typically want to aim for 1-4 knots. Faster than 4 knots on a river might mean it is treacherous.

WEAPONS

On Earth, if a ship in the Age of Sail has weapons, it has cannon, which requires gunpowder, which in turn means our world almost certainly has guns. If we don't want guns on our fantasy world, then no cannons either. That means a ship with no fire power and hence a lack of drama. Where's the fun in that? We can either keep the cannons or replace them, the latter requiring some understanding of what we're replacing. We'll need some details on how fast cannons fire, how far, and how many people are needed to do this. Then we can consider alternatives. For example, wizards may provide an equivalent to gunpowder, but if that alternative exists in enough quantity for cannons to exist, then wouldn't guns, too?

THE CANNON

A 36-pounder, meaning a cannon that fires balls weighing thirty-six pounds, is among the largest cannon aboard ships and requires fourteen men. A powder boy brings gunpowder from below decks; gunpowder is wisely stored somewhere less prone to explosions. This role is eliminated in a world without gunpowder. If we invent an alternative to the cannon, and there are a hundred such weapons, we'd have a hundred fewer crew aboard, which in turn reduces supplies needed.

A chief gunner aims the gun and primes it for firing, but does not fire the cannon; one of the other gunners does this. This role would still require an alternative, but the role would likely need a different name. The chief gunner is in charge of the crew, who practice together but seldom do so with live shot due to the cost. Not practicing with live shot affects the chief gunner's ability to practice aiming, but the rest of the crew can at least become efficient, affecting speed of firing, which is two to three shots in about five minutes.

The rest of the men are called gunners. Some prepare the cannon for firing, as follows. One gunner shoves a wet cloth down the barrel between shots to put out any sparks before more gunpowder is loaded. One man inserts a cannonball while another rams it in. This is followed by another wet cloth wad to prevent the ball from rolling out if the cannon is aimed downward. These various details and personnel are specific to the firing of a cannon and might be replaced by a different number of personnel depending on what replacement weapon we devise.

Cannons require men whose primary job is moving the cannon back and forth. Prior to firing, it must be pulled away from the hull because it is loaded from the barrel, but must be fired with the barrel protruding from the hull. This means men pull the cannon back, several people perform various loading operations, and then the cannon is shoved against the hull before firing. Cannons have huge recoil, meaning they leap backwards when fired. This means several crew are needed to shove the thing back into place. We might not need these men with an alternative weapon that lacks recoil.

Smaller cannons still have the powder boy, chief gunner, and at least two other gunners for cleaning, loading, moving, and firing a cannon, so the number of men depends on cannon size due to how heavy it is to move around between shots.

ALTERNATIVES

When looking for an alternative to the cannon, we can look to siege engines used on land for inspiration. The trebuchet flings stones high into the air but can only be fired from the top deck of a ship due to the firing action. This would significantly reduce their numbers and interfere with sailing, crew movements, and melee. The catapult and similar weapons aren't much better.

Our best bet might be the ballista, which is like a giant crossbow mounted on a frame. Like the cannon, this fires in a straight line rather than hurling a projectile high into the air, meaning this could be located where cannons are instead of only on the top deck. It one were sized correctly for the space, it could function in much the same manner, though its firing action is quite different. Even so, it seems to be the only logical replacement. A ballista is highly accurate and can be aimed at a single person and hit them.

The main issue with a ballista is power and range. The Roman ballista fired over five hundred yards and was made of wood, but if we construct ours from iron for the frame and metal for the arms, this gives us greater power. Our world might have a fictional alloy of greater strength, like adamantine, providing even more thrust. Use of a fictional alloy gives us leeway to claim it fires much farther than the Roman ballista. A 12-pounder cannon could fire fifteen hundred yards, and while the practical range was far less, we can claim nearly similar distances for our ballista. Being plausible is the bar we need to get over. Creative license helps us.

Ballista are strong enough to fire straight through an armored knight and pin him to even a living tree, the projectile embedding itself halfway into the trunk. Could one blow a hole in the side of a ship? Certainly. The missiles can also be topped with our special alloy for superior strength and piercing ability.

Ballista can be easily modified to fire balls, which would be smaller than cannonballs. This further means that they could fire chain shot: two balls connected by a chain. This is used to destroy rigging. Grape shot (many small balls) to slaughter crew on deck is unlikely to work due to the firing mechanism being unable to contain it as a cannon barrel would. An alternative might be darts rather than a single large arrow/bolt.

Fewer crew are needed to operate a ballista. We'd need someone responsible for the team and who likely aims it and possibly fires it. Only one person is needed to place a projectile onto it, which can be their dedicated job. A powder boy isn't needed. Since there's no recoil, no men are needed to keep repositioning the weapon. That leaves operation of a winch to wind it. A team of two, one on each side, seems ideal for speed, though for larger ballista, maybe there's more than one team. From this, we can determine how large our crew might be. Do we need to get into this sort of detail? Not really, though in a visual medium, we'll want to show a reasonable number of people doing realistic tasks.

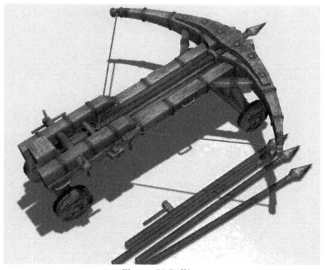

Figure 59 Ballista

How fast can a ballista fire? As fast as the winchmen can wind it, plus a few seconds for loading and aiming. Much of time between shots for a cannon is repositioning it and the number of actions needed to prepare a shot. Most of this is gone with a ballista. Aiming is also faster because the frame mounting allows for easy pivoting up,

274 | RANDY ELLEFSON

down, or side-to-side. We can surmise at least two to three
shots per minute, which is much faster than the two to
three shots in five minutes for a cannon.

On a smaller vessel with smaller cannons, we could
have crews of six per cannon. There might be a similar
number of men for a ballista. As a ship gets bigger, so do
the weapons. Bigger cannons require more men for repositioning it, but larger ballista don't. They don't scale the
same way. This means a first-rate ship-of-the-line wouldn't
need as many crew for the ballistae. During the Age of Sail,
few ships could afford enough men to staff the cannons on
both sides, requiring them to switch back and forth as
needed. We could decide our ships have enough men for
both sides, resulting in more crew after all.

SHIP PERSONNEL

It's beyond the scope of this book to describe all the personnel needed on a ship, but in a fantasy world, we have
new humanoid species and occupations that can be added
to the typical crew from Earth vessels. This can be true in
SF, too, but the crafts there are usually spaceships. Ships
often had livestock and even plants, mostly for consumption, which means our invented plants and animals can be
aboard, too.

WARRIORS

Many fighting ships have military on board for the
combat that might ensue when ships entangle (on purpose
or not). Any sailor can engage in the fighting, but trained
military are typically aboard during fleet actions. We can

have such people onboard any vessel as standard crew, their numbers depending on overall ship and crew size. Larger numbers of such warriors will need quarters set aside for them (they may not be berthed with the sailors), but we needn't go into such details unless desired.

CLOSE RANGE

Knights are an obvious choice for hand-to-hand combat. They weren't on ships during the Age of Sail for the reason of gunpowder: bullets, and by extension cannons, had rendered armor useless. If we lack this issue on our world, then knights might figure heavily in the military aboard. A single knight could be present to represent knightly values or a kingdom on formal terms, or a group could be there in expectation of combat at sea. They can be available for missions ashore. However, even in a world without guns, knights still sink rather handily once overboard. They also make fine targets for archers.

Pirates wouldn't have knights on their ships and might think twice about attacking such a ship, if knights are assumed to be aboard. Why would they assume this? British ships-of-the-line were known to have marines aboard, so a ship belonging to a country of our invention can, too. Raising the country's flag might warn off pirates.

Ninjas or other forms of martial artists could be highly prized, due to their superior rope climbing skills and balance on those yard arms. Imagine how quickly they can board an enemy ship at close range.

Aboard a ship, unless there's a duel of some kind, the fighting is in close quarters, so space constraints would render weapons such as a staff less effective. Consider the weapons used by your warrior class which is routinely assigned to a ship, and whether they're appropriate under these conditions.

LONG RANGE

If guns don't exist on our world, archery is the obvious long-range weaponry fired by one person at a time (as opposed to a cannon). This can happen before and after ships entangle. These can be long/short bows or crossbows that fire flaming arrows into rigging or the hull (or people). Consider where such individuals might be stationed as ships battle.

WIZARDS

Is there a ship's wizard? A practitioner of some other supernatural power? They could stir a wind for a becalmed vessel, navigate, find enemy ships, and control sea life or the waves. Assistance in battle would be appreciated. They could create something that replaces gunpowder, allowing cannons to exist. They could teleport themselves or others from ship to ship or to shore, to save crew the task of rowing a small boat, exposing themselves to risks from sea creatures or those ashore.

On Earth, sailors are famously superstitious, but that needn't be true on our invented world. But if they are, sailors from one region could be afraid of allowing wizards aboard, while others allow it. A wizard might expect a welcome but discover that the crew is from another kingdom and fears him.

SPECIES

We might have invented species that could be part of a ship's crew. What special skills do they have and how might they be of use? One that climbs well would be suited to the rigging. What if we have a humanoid species that flies? Think how much easier it would be for them to fly high while looking for ships or land, compared to the humanoids who can only climb into the rigging with a telescope. If the flying creature of one crew were killed, the opposing crew would have a tactical advantage. There are numerous stories of ships sailing into a fog and being unable to find each other. Might not a flying species assist such an issue? They could get lost, too, but in theory they could use sounds from the ship to find it again.

Water-dwelling humanoids can repair underwater damage to the hull or rudder, chart a course through hazards, and catch fish. They can perform the equivalent of missions for which we'd use scuba divers and submarines, such as recovery of sunken ships and materials. Conversely, they could be antipathetic to the ships, and do damage below the waterline or silently sneak aboard. They might have traditional enemies beneath the waves, whether animals or another humanoid species. Maybe they even look like one of those enemies and one can go overboard, be killed underwater, and replaced by the enemy, who might at least initially fool the crew. They could even summon sea creatures to do their bidding. Do they claim an area as their territory and attack anything that sails through?

WHERE TO START

Where to start depends on our goal. If trying to determine the travel time between two places, follow the steps outlined in "Ship Speeds." You'll need to decide on the distance first, then whether the trip is along a coast, the open ocean, or both. Then consider what sort of issues you'd like characters to face on the journey. You may need to slow them or accelerate their travel based on story needs. If trying to decide what weaponry or personnel ships have on your world, the sections on this will assist a decision. The section on ship types will help you determine the style of vessel you want, but when it comes to rated ships, it's largely immaterial which you choose unless you intend two or more ships to go to war with each other.

CHAPTER NINE

TRAVEL IN SPACE

The previous two chapters focused on how to determine travel times using the sort of locomotion available on Earth-like worlds. Space travel falls under two categories: existing technology from Earth and invented technology. As I'm not a rocket scientist, the former is best left for those in the know to explain. World builders tend to be focused on imagined technologies anyway, and there's no telling what detail you might want to know and utilize about real technologies. More to the point, the limits of real technology eliminate interstellar travel and therefore whatever we're hoping to achieve.

THE REALITIES OF SPACE

Writing fiction doesn't free us from the realities of space, such as the intense cold or lack of oxygen. Some will think gravity doesn't exist either, but gravity is everywhere and causes all rotation (i.e. orbits). The conceit of artificial gravity has long been accepted so that we only need to address it if we want to, such as designing a rotating ship.

The question we must address is whether to pretend certain realities are overcome by technology (or magic) or not. It's recommended to be consistent in a single product. For example, in the *Star Trek* universe, food replicators that make lunch appear from thin air is as unrealistic as the teleportation devices that move matter (including people) between places. Being equally unrealistic (or realistic) is wise and helps the audience accept the reality we're presenting; otherwise, incongruities creep in. Having food replicators and teleporters but no artificial gravity would be an example, as the gravity, or a simulacrum, would be easier to achieve from a technological standpoint.

When inventing technologies for space, creating a hierarchy of believability might be wise, if we'd like to have some things achieved while others are imaginary, even to our advanced inhabitants. Maybe we want them to have achieved artificial gravity (so actors have an easier time on screen) but still have the need to grow and cook food. At one time, the communication devices of *Star Trek* were considered fantastic but have been eclipsed by reality.

Generally, advanced communication is easier to achieve, as this often means little more than smaller devices with greater distance or computing power or capabilities, and sending of signals (not matter) long distances. Those signals can contain data just like here on Earth. This suggests that an advanced program, such as a hologram or A.I., could be sent vast distances, with the possibility of corruption in transit.

Any technology involving non-living matter is easier to create than something involving living creatures. This is especially true of transportation. Creating a new propulsion system using newly discovered elements from far flung solar systems is more believable than a technology that bends time and space and causes matter to just end up somewhere else in an instant. Such abilities are best seen as rare because making them commonplace implies the characters have other godlike abilities, too, and their lives become easy, which reduces conflict, the heart of stories.

PROPULSION

Engines fall into two basic categories: those designed for space travel and those designed for atmospheric conditions. Both kinds already exist, but it is mostly engines intended for space travel which get mentioned in our work. There appears to be a correlation between how often an engine's functionality is explained and how fictional it is; the more fictional, the more explanations are given. Writers have as little interest in learning and explaining actual technology as the audience, who typically understands it to some degree. But fictional tech? We're all ears.

AIR BREATHING ENGINES

Engines for atmospheric conditions are the sort currently in use by planes on Earth. We don't need to invent anything or get into details of whether it's a rocket or turbine engine unless we desire to. We should just be aware that characters may need to remark that they're switching to "so-and-so power" as they enter a planet's atmosphere because the space engines they were using might not be suitable. This minor touch adds realism. Slower-than-light (STL) engines might also be used here and it's up to us to decide a given ship can use such engines both in space and in an atmosphere. This is one way to distinguish between ship types: some vessels might have engines that can be used anywhere and be considered more advantageous than ships that must change propulsion.

SPACE ENGINES

Space engines can be divided into two categories: those that allow faster-than-light (FTL) speeds and those that do not. For STL engines, propulsion is similar to atmospheric engines in that matter is ejected, usually from the rear, to propel the ship forward through normal space. This is one reason slower-than-light engines could be used in an atmosphere. STL drives propelling a ship at high velocities can cause time dilation, which is when two observers experience a difference in how much time has passed. Some stories discuss a captain not letting the ship go too fast using those engines, generally, to avoid this problem.

Some FTL engines are discussed next and are all public domain ideas anyone can use.

JUMP DRIVE

As the name implies, a ship with jump drive essentially teleports between two locations in an instant. This may be safely called a "jump drive" or something else. The main problem with such technology is that it eliminates all conflict involving travel and not having enough time to reach a destination by an important date. Consider using this sparingly or placing severe limits on how often such a drive can be used, such as it uses too much power, relies on a rare fuel source, is expensive to manufacture, or is too large for ordinary ships. Ships equipped with jump drive do not experience time dilation.

HYPER DRIVE

A hyper drive moves a ship into hyperspace, a fictional, separate dimension adjacent to normal space. As a result, ships in hyperspace are often depicted as being unable to communicate with those in normal space. Normal physics, such as the barrier to FTL travel, may not exist in hyperspace, allowing the ship to traverse great distances quickly. It takes time to travel in hyperspace but those traveling this way experience time normally and experience no time dilation upon returning to normal space.

WARP DRIVE

Warp drive is a conceptual FTL drive that is public domain despite being associated with *Star Trek*. The idea includes multiple velocities of warp, such as warp one being slower than warp ten. Instantaneous travel is not possible. The ship suffers no time dilation and remains in normal space. Despite our use of the term "space", there are plenty of objects with which a ship could collide, which begs the question of how deadly such an impact would be. Without high-speed automated navigation systems and equally impressive shields, warp speed is unwise.

DISTANCE

To add realism to our space adventures, we should consider that all destinations are orbiting something. Moons orbit planets, planets orbit suns, and solar systems orbit their galaxy's center. If two objects are orbiting the same body, such as planets orbiting the same sun, the closer planet is orbiting faster. This means that the distance between two planets will change. They could be on the same side of the sun, opposite sides, or somewhere between.

This is different than fixed locations on a world's surface, and as a result, we have leeway when announcing how far apart two places are at a particular moment, and therefore how long the trip will take. Due partly to the considerable time such travel takes, a destination is chosen not because that's where the target is now, but because that's where it will be when the ship also gets there.

This sort of thing can cause believable problems for characters. What if they realize a critical event is taking place on another planet in a week, but due to the worlds' current locations, it will take longer than that to get there? Or maybe they only have enough fuel to reach the destination if the trip is short, but they need to go now and don't have funds to get more fuel. Now maybe they hatch a plan to earn some money. Such details make stories better than ones where everyone just gets on a ship and goes whatever distance they need without much comment or impact on their situation.

Should we decide how far apart our locations are first and then invent propulsion systems according to our story needs, or invent propulsion systems and then alter how far away locations are based on story needs? The latter seems sensible because locations in space aren't fixed. If we need two locations closer or farther apart for a story, this needs no explanation. Conversely, it makes little sense to devise propulsion systems to go between certain distances when those will change anyway or you haven't decided how far the characters need to travel.

TRAVEL TIME

The amount of time to travel between different objects in space has so much leeway that we don't need the same consistent precision that terrestrial travel may require. On land, we can fudge our numbers by writing, "Not drawn to scale" on a map. But in space, this isn't even needed. Nothing is in a fixed place except each planet's distance to the sun, and even that changes a bit depending on how circular its orbit is. And the technologies are imaginary, unlike the wooden ships from the previous chapter or the actual vehicles or animals from the chapter before that.

If you were hoping for a calculator like those in the previous chapters, there isn't one because most world builders will get along fine without worrying about this. It also involves a level of mathematics that is admittedly beyond me, and possibly you. And no one can come along and say that it would really take fifty-eight hours, not fifty, to travel between two invented planets in two imaginary solar systems, at a given time of the year (from the starting planet), at warp seven, especially since warp drives don't exist. This is one area where SF beats fantasy handily.

SHIP STRUCTURE

World builders in visual mediums will need to consider both internal and external ship structure, but authors may largely ignore this. Absent a schematic or picture, readers typically struggle to picture what we intend. This is true of other elements like the layout of a castle, for example. It's often better to not be overly specific about where each room lies in relation to another but rather focus on how long or difficult it is for characters to traverse locations within a certain time frame that matters to the scene we're writing. Still, even if we don't explain the structure, we should have an idea of it if for no other reason than consistency between scenes. We don't want characters to reach the engine room from the bridge in two minutes in one scene and in ten minutes during another.

EXTERNAL

There's a tendency to invent aerodynamic-looking ships used in space where air obviously doesn't exist. This is wise for two reasons: we expect such a design and are comfortable with it, and more importantly, it leaves open the option for the ship to enter a planet's atmosphere even if this is rare. Would ship builders make that nearly impossible with a non-aerodynamic exterior? Only if certain the vessel never leaves space. Since we've seen everything from aerodynamic ships to the Borg cube from *Star Trek*, we can get away with anything regarding aerodynamics.

What other considerations are there? One is the weaponry location, which determines which directions the vessel can fire in. Warships typically have this forward facing, with some ability to aim to the sides as well. Rear-facing weapons are for defense while fleeing. Some vessels have top or bottom mounted weaponry that can swivel and fire in all directions—except into itself, of course.

We might also consider where a ship can be boarded. Cargo is typically rear-loaded. People can be, too, or enter from the side, bottom, or even top hatches. Entering from the front is unusual. The decision can affect scenes where a ship has landed and a gunfight breaks out while characters are exiting or entering the vessel. The bottom-entrance seems problematic because if the ship crashes on its bottom, or the landing gear gives out, how does anyone get out? An emergency hatch elsewhere would be the answer. There's always a solution for these problems, so feel free to do as you please.

Figure 60 Rotating Space Station

The other obvious subject for external structure is the engine location, but this is typically rear-facing, especially for any vessel intended for atmospheric conditions. The engine doesn't have to be in the actual rear, as propeller planes make clear. Even jet engines can be like this. With laser-guided weapons that can easily target an engine, it makes sense to avoid engine locations that are vulnerable in this way.

From the previous section on propulsion, we should remember that there are fictional drives that don't operate on the principle of rear thrust; such engines could theoretically be located anywhere, preferably deep within a ship. What this means from a practical standpoint in war is that engines for STL travel might be rear-facing and vulnerable to attack, but FTL engines might be better protected and less vulnerable. Destroying those STL engines has a tactical advantage to inhibit maneuvering in the battle but won't stop the ship from going to warp to escape, for example. But if something volatile powers those FTL engines, then placing them deep in the ship might be unwise.

A ship that uses rotation to create artificial gravity will have this as the dominant feature of its exterior. The outside doesn't need to be round, however. It just needs to rotate. It's the inside that will be curved to some degree mostly because people and items will be pushed against those interior walls (that's the whole point), which act as the floor. Gravity increases the farther you are from the point of rotation. This is why we often see a configuration that looks like a spoke wheel; almost all of the living areas are far from the center.

INTERNAL

The internal structure of our ship is often important, unless it's so small as to have little more than a room or two. Characters need to move between locations such as the bridge, cargo, engine room, and quarters. We don't write about mundane scenes but active ones where the speed of transit is a factor in how the scene plays out. If it takes five minutes at a full run to reach the spot where aliens have breached the hull, and it will only take two minutes for the aliens to destroy the life support systems located there, we've got problems. Taking time to plan out our ship's structure (to some degree) is helpful for not only understanding such scenarios, but imagining them in the first place. No structure is foolproof, as organizing things to avoid one problem will likely cause another, so thinking about our story needs can help us build a vulnerability into our vessel.

Certain realities exist on many ships, such as living quarters being near dining areas. Crew typically have smaller quarters in poorer locations than passengers, except for captains and officers, who may still not enjoy great privilege. Most vessels will need propulsion located primarily in the rear, an area often reserved for dirty or less desirable conditions such as cargo holds, loading areas for both supplies and sometimes passengers and crew, and machinery to power everything. The bridge or command center is typically forward.

Vessels which travel on water load from lower decks, especially for cargo, so the ship does not become top heavy; cargo acts as ballast and should be lower anyway. Also, loading from above just means having to create buildings and ramps to lift potentially heavy items unnecessarily. In space, this consideration is gone, but a ship designed to enter an atmosphere must still be balanced internally, whether that's front to back or side to side. In a weightless environment, heavy items could theoretically be anywhere, but artificial gravity is seemingly never lessened in areas with heavy cargo. Regardless, one could presumably float cargo to its location with relative ease.

Consider the purpose of our invented vessel before creating its structure. Passenger, cargo, and war ships will share areas like a bridge, engine room, and crew quarters, but entertainment, storage, and weaponry will all differ in size, quantity, and placement. Ships that are intended to permanently remain in space do not need aerodynamics.

DO WE NEED TO INVENT STRUCTURE?

In video gaming, a ship's internal structure is crucial because the gamer will typically guide a character room by room through the ship. It should make sense even if the layout or the purpose of rooms is not explained or apparent to someone who's busy killing NPCs onscreen. World builders are advised to plan a detailed internal structure so that the graphics team can implement it.

But in books or movies/TV shows, the structure often seems irrelevant. Seldom do we follow a character from a room, down a hallway, and to another room; doing so wastes precious screen time. I've seen entire series runs of *Star Trek* and still had little to no idea where one section of the ship is in relation to another. Even so, if we'd like to be consistent for a ship we'll use often, decide which deck each major department you'll mention is on. This avoids indicating that engineering is on deck six in one book and on deck seven in another. We don't need to be more specific than which deck and whether fore, aft, port, or starboard, if we really don't want to. Having a sense of difficulty and/or speed of access from various other places on the vessel is more important. If creating internal structure helps us do that, then yes, make decisions.

WHAT TO INCLUDE

The level of detail we invent should be specific to our use. The list below will provide ideas on areas that can be included.

The Bridge. Consider calling the command center something else for variety, but this is obviously where the ship is commanded and flown from. For visual reasons, it is typically forward as on Earth vessels, even if there's less practical reason in space. Sensors, cameras, and auto-pilot are often assumed to be responsible for something like docking, but those can malfunction or be destroyed, leaving a physical window as the backup. However, we can ditch this and have the crew using a TV, essentially, with the bridge located somewhere other than forward. Farther inside the ship seems wise, particularly for war ships. A command center with a wall of TVs to provide 360-degree views (inside and out) also seems more useful than a single, forward-facing window.

Living quarters (for officers and non-officers). Passenger areas are typically more spacious than those for crew, and both living quarters and dining areas for passengers are located in areas that prevent them from seeing the ship's guts. An easy way to resolve this is different decks, as on a cruise ship. On such ships, the exterior rooms will be for wealthier or more important people (for windows). Even ships that seldom have passengers may have one or two rooms set aside for a guest, even if that room is used for storage when not needed for passengers.

Entertainment. Passengers might be on a vessel mostly for pleasure, in which case we'd likely have what cruise ships have: musicians, dancers, live shows, lessons (like dancing), gambling, gaming, sports (like ping-pong, mini golf, rock climbing, surfing), exercise gyms, and individual practitioners (like ice sculptors). We'd likely want alternatives to these specifics in SF. A more military ship will have fewer diversions but will have something to let crew mentally and even physically escape their duties.

Shops. Even on a military ship, crew need to buy supplies for themselves beyond the basics the military provides (and which they might seek to augment or not use at all). On a passenger or cruise ship, many more shops will exist, generally in a concentrated area.

Dining. The main dining areas should be adjacent to living quarters while smaller eateries may be scattered about the ship, depending on size, and typically located near major work areas. Consider something special near the bridge, for example. A pleasure ship may also have bars and restaurants.

Cargo. Place this near the working area of the vessel, such as near engineering. It's an unglamorous thing that no one wants to see. If the ship specializes in cargo transport, or carries valuable cargo, then consider a separate area for items that might be under heavy guard, whether that's armed people or technology.

The brig (aka jail). This is not somewhere pleasant, meaning the bowels of the ship, such as near engines or cargo. Our characters may have other ways of confining someone, using imagined technology that eliminates the need for an actual jail.

Medical. A central location seems ideal on a warship, as casualties can come from all places, though perhaps it's closer to the most important people on the bridge.

The engines. Unless designed for only operating in space, all ships will have rearward facing propulsion, hence an engine room in the rear. There may be a second room for other forms of propulsion, with both controlled from another location. In *Star Trek*, this area is called Engineering, but a different word, such as Propulsion, is advised to distinguish our work from something so well known.

Main and auxiliary power. A ship that expects violence will probably have power sources separated from each other so that an explosion destroys only one and not all power sources. On some ships, this is located with the engines, a logical choice that requires less cabling throughout a ship.

Escape pods. These are located in convenient places. This means most are near crew quarters while a smaller quantity will be near all critical areas such as the bridge, engine rooms, and weaponry.

Weaponry. While weapons on star ships can typically be fired from the bridge, those weapons must be located somewhere, with possible manual intervention. Some are physical projectiles while others are energy, for example, but even the latter must be generated from somewhere. On the one hand, near the ship's exterior seems wise so that an inadvertent explosion doesn't blow the ship apart, as would happen with weapons stored farther inside. On the other hand, the risk of weapons being detonated in an attack also rises. Plan where your weapons are located and controlled from, including which ones fire projectiles and from where these are loaded (if not by machinery).

TIME AND DISTANCE

We may want to decide how long it takes people to move between locations in a ship, but this only matters if our story benefits from it. It's a moot point in small vessels. In an episodic show like *Star Trek*, where one ship will be repeatedly used, consistency is crucial. In many episodes, characters from the bridge are ordered to another part of the ship to deal with an emergency and arrive seconds later in TV time. We could conclude that the show just skipped ahead a few minutes, but often, whatever emergency was occurring, like two characters fighting, hasn't progressed more than a couple seconds. The presumed reason shows do this is so that main characters, i.e. actors, are featured all the time, but it's not realistic. We accept it, however.

If you'd like to be more realistic, approximate how long it takes to walk or run between all locations on a ship and

294 | RANDY ELLEFSON

whether something like an elevator is required. How long does it take to climb or crawl through maintenance corridors like the Jefferies Tubes of *Star Trek*? Are there stairs or only ladders? We seldom see a stairway except in places like engineering (and even then it's usually ladders). Why is that? Surely if they can invent warp drive they can still see the value of stairs over ladders if the turbo lifts (i.e. elevators) stop working. Are there no stairs (or underwear) in space?

WHERE TO START

The first choice to make in planning a vessel is to determine if it needs to operate in atmospheric conditions, or even if it might expect to do so. This will determine whether rear-facing engines are required, but STL engines will also require this. We should also decide what sort of ship it is (cargo, war, passenger), as this determines the amount and type of quarters, and dining or entertainment possibilities for crew. Next we should decide how passengers and crew typically board or exit the vessel, where they stay, and what they do onboard. We can also determine the purpose of our ship, such as travel within a solar system or between stars. This will help determine what sort of additional engines it has. Lastly, we should decide the events we're intending to take place on this vessel so that we can decide what sorts of vulnerabilities it might provide us with and how characters and story might benefit from these; but we can also start with this subject. The best choice is to go with the subject that gives you ideas first, then return to less inspiring areas later.

CHAPTER TEN

CREATING TIME AND HISTORY

WHY CREATE HISTORY?

While an elaborate history isn't needed, a sense of the past can add realism to our work. How much history we'll need depends on how much we'd like it to inform the present. A short story needs little, but an epic trilogy of adventurers traveling across many lands requires it. The sovereign powers they traverse have history with each other, and some of that will be recent, such as a war or a new ruler who is crushing freedoms for the people or reducing restrictions. Even if we don't want to comment on this sort of thing much, characters will be aware of these new ramifications of entering another land. Traveling through similar places results in a flat narrative.

Science fiction often focuses on the future, given the presence of technologies that don't yet exist, but that future is far enough away that there's still past that's ahead of our current timeframe. In other words, a story set on Earth in 2500 AD has 500 years of history that hasn't happened yet. In settings not connected to Earth, we can create future history without worrying about how we get there.

A common fantasy trope is that ancient, and long-vanished, civilizations have left relics that characters discover and use. These can include magic items, forgotten spell books, powerful creatures, and ancient, long overgrown cities that harbor horrors that will one day reawaken. The characters responsible for the demise of these civilizations can become legendary figures, which is covered in "Creating World Figures" from *Creating Places*. We should have a high-level idea of what culture created these items and how that culture disappeared, but details included in the narrative can be sketchy because in a world with limited technology, the average person knows less history. This is true even in an advanced society such as our own, where most people aren't worried too much about the past; that said, we pick up little details from the news and entertainment, so we have a general sense of events without depth of knowledge.

The architecture of ancient civilizations can provide a sense of being alien and therefore unsettling, allowing us to characterize a scene with description and our characters' reaction to a location. To do this, we should decide what form of government this decrepit place had. There's a tendency toward the brutish, hulking, and threatening styles associated with authoritarian regimes (and the foreboding they produce), but we can also have an elegant place designed by an enlightened species, whose city has been destroyed by war or plague (resulting in a sense of nostalgic loss for visitors). Deciding on the reaction we want can help inform our decision.

Post-apocalypse works need a cataclysm that has created the present scenario. The cause can be technological, biological, supernatural, or somewhat ordinary (such as an asteroid strike). A world with gods might want a moral reason for the destruction, such as gods abandoning a wicked species. In *Dragonlance*, human pride caused the gods to stop answering prayers for hundreds of years. Such a scenario allows commentary on humanity's failings.

We might have multiple continents and therefore a whole world for which we're creating history. In this case, we might want to organize the history we create into smaller sections, possibly in different documents. World events, such as gods inventing a worldwide species, or a plague that spreads between continents, would go into one file. But we otherwise might want to organize our events by a continent or region.

SAMPLE ENTRIES

Think of each entry as a summary that only touches on the big issues. We don't need to know why a war was fought. Here are some examples of how to write logs.

HESSIAN 124—THE HORN OF KILLIAN LOST

Legendary necromancer Killian of the Lorfrost suffers an ignoble defeat at the hands of Lord Sinias of Kingdom Norin, when Sinias kills a spectral knight who is in the act of blowing the Horn of Killian. The resulting vortex pulls all the souls into the horn, including that of Killian, who briefly disappears from the world. By the time he returns weeks later, destroying Sinias, the horn has fallen into unknown hands.

HESSIAN 227—THE ORB OF STARAN CREATED

In the Hills of Asawan, the Wizard Obin creates the Orb of Staran in a black pool of molten ore. Its existence and properties are unknown to all but a trusted acolyte, who kills Obin, steals the Orb, and flees from the Hounds of Asawan to Kingdom Illiandor. He will go on to suffer the same fate in five years when he is killed for the orb.

HESSIAN 248—THE WAR OF BEASTS BEGINS

Driven by famine and drought, an army of monsters and animals begins its assault from the far eastern reaches of the continent. In their immediate path lies the Kingdom of Norin, which mounts a defense and wins the first battle in the War of Beasts.

HESSIAN 250—KINGDOM NORIN FALLS

In the War of Beasts, Kingdom Norin falls to the creatures from the untamed lands to the west, including the Hills of Asawan, the Sea of Serpents, and the Crags of Forever. The capital, Dokken, becomes a haunted ruin where the damned king is rumored to still walk with a ghostly retinue that can only be controlled with the Horn of Killian, which has long been considered lost.

HESSIAN 251—THE WAR OF BEASTS ENDS

With the warnings provided by the fallen Kingdom of Norin, neighboring kingdom Seva is better prepared for the onslaught. The king is aided by the rediscovered Horn of Killian, found by a farm boy who becomes the unlikely hero of the war when he enters the city of Dokken in Norin and summons the fallen King of Norin. The beasts are no match for the undead and living warriors of Seva, who destroy them.

HESSIAN 252—EXPEDITION INTO HILLS OF ASAWAN DISAPPEARS

Following rumors that an unknown wizard instigated the advance of the beasts from the Hills of Asawan, Kingdom Norin sends an expeditionary force into the hills. It is never seen again, the last signs of it being near the Tower of Sorin, halfway into the hills. No bodies are ever found, nor are weapons, horses, or anything else. A follow-up expedition reveals the tower is gone altogether.

The above examples were invented in a few minutes for this volume. It doesn't take long and can produce world figures, creatures, legendary missions, and artifacts, all of which we could have already thought of or just be making up on the spot, to be fleshed out later. This begins the process of shaping a world; start small, then build on that. I now have two magic items, an undead army, two kingdoms, a famous necromancer and a wizard, and a land of beasts. Not bad for ten minutes of goofing around.

What I'd do next is open my supernatural items file and create an entry for the tower, orb, and horn, then make up details. I'd also open the files on kingdoms Norin and Seva and add entries about the War of Beasts. For whatever continent that is, I'd open the file on land features and write an entry for the Hills of Asawan and the hounds within, deciding where that is on my map. My file on animals would get an entry for the hounds.

CREATION MYTHS

In fantasy worlds, most cultures have a creation myth of some kind to explain where the gods and the culture originated. In more advanced societies, there's less myth, so this might not figure in SF as much. In volume 1, *Creating Life*, we discussed creation myths in more detail. These events are the earliest ones to fill out in that history.

TIME

MEASURING TIME

How is time measured in our invented world? This is a subject we can ignore if everything is Earth-like and we're fine with the audience assuming time is similar, as they probably will unless we remark on it. Markedly different time measurement is an area of unnecessary exposition that is best avoided unless it matters for our work. Readers don't want to remember how many minutes there are in an hour, hours in a day, how long the week is, how many weeks there are per month, and how many months the year includes. Each time we mention that two characters will meet in an hour, but that's really two Earth hours, is an annoyance.

Should we create different time measurements? That depends.

MINUTES AND HOURS

I recommend leaving minutes and hour lengths alone. Changing them offers an audience confusion with no pay-off. There are better ways to make our world seem different. Even if we mention that an hour is ninety minutes, for example, but then we keep writing "hour" in our story, the reader will forget the different length. This is especially true if this alteration is arbitrary and has no rationale that makes it easier to remember. We can invent other words instead of "hour," but then those require explanations that must be remembered, too, doubling down on the encumbrance with which we've burdened the audience.

While it's true that time is likely measured differently on other planets, our audience is on Earth and needs to quickly understand time references in Earth terms. A workaround in SF that has characters from Earth is to have one mention "that's 1.5 Earth hours" to another person; the characters should likely go by Earth measurements for their comfort and that of the audience. In SF, a briefly visited planet is a good time to use different minute/hour measurements for a story impacted by this.

One reason to leave minutes and hours alone is that this unit of time measurement will be more frequently mentioned than days, weeks, or months. Story scenes take place in minutes, hours, and days. Having "minute" and "hour" be too different just messes with our audience's understanding of time. But scenes are less often separated by weeks or months, and once we're working in bigger units, does it really matter if "three months later" is one hundred days instead of ninety? Only a little.

As an example, on my world of Llurien, there are twelve months of twenty-eight days, resulting in 336 days. That's twenty-nine days, or a month, shorter than Earth. This means someone a year old on Llurien is eleven months old on Earth. But after ten years, a ten-year-old on Llurien would only be nine years old on Earth. While the gap has widened, the difference between a nine and ten year old isn't great. This is again true at 22 vs 20, and 33 vs 30. I don't need to ever point this out to my audience, but if I do, it doesn't matter unless characters from Llurien come to Earth (or vice versa).

On this note, it's important to figure out how long a year really is on an invented world. Once we've decided on all our measurements, do the math to figure out a scenario like the above.

We could name the hours of the day, but this can be another encumbrance that gains us little and requires exposition. Do so with a good reason that impacts your story or skip it. We can do these things and seldom mention them, however.

We can change the number of hours in a day, but it's recommended that day lengths be similar to Earth if we're building an Earth-like world. This means being off by a few hours at most, not having only twelve hour days unless we really mean for this to figure prominently. In SF, the life forms from a planet with different length days will have different sleep and eating cycles, but this will matter more when life forms from worlds with disparate cycles are brought together.

DAYS IN A WEEK

The number of days in a week is another area we can change. There are seven days on Earth due to ancient civilizations naming them after seven celestial bodies that were visible (this included the sun and moon, which are Sunday and Monday respectively). With planets named after gods like Thor (Thursday), we also acquired the names. We can do something similar on an invented world, using whatever rationalization we can make sensible. There could be eight moons that cause eight-day weeks. There could be six gods, each getting a day in a six-day week. We can depart from deities and decide the days are named after the six schools of magic in a world dominated by supernatural power. Or maybe there were six great heroes from long ago. Or six dragons. In SF, the days of the week are likely decided long before technological advances that could have days named after technology (or related scientists, explorers, etc.), but maybe a later empire forced change on everyone.

In the above examples from Earth, you'll note that Thor is spelled differently for Thursday. Most of the god names were altered in time from different cultures misspelling things, or just altering the spelling for their native language. We might want to do this, too, to make day names easier to say. For example, I could call a day Llurienday, but that's kind of a mouthful. Shortening it to Llurday or Rienday is a little better.

Regardless of our decision, we should take strides to minimize the use of day names in our writing because our audience will have no idea what we're talking about. This is true even if we explain it once. We can provide charts on a website, like a glossary, but skillfully handling this is the best approach. Our characters (as opposed to our narration) should be the ones most often using the day names, because they would. Take this example passage:

> *Kier asked, "When will the sword be ready?"*
> *"Next Rienday," the blacksmith replied.*
> *Kier nodded. A week and a day. Plenty of time to run it through his beloved's heart.*

If we change the number of days in a week, we might want to go with six or eight. The reason is that when we narrate "a week and a day" as above, this is still close to a week on Earth and the audience's sense of time passing is only slightly off. By contrast, if a week is twelve days, we throw the audience off quite a bit more and might have to keep reminding them of such a thing. In the above scenario, I would instead write, "Thirteen days. Plenty of time..."

WEEKS IN A MONTH

How many weeks do we want in a month? On Earth, this isn't set. Instead the number of days in a month is what determines how weeks are laid out. A month with thirty days could span four weeks one year and five the next, depending on what day of the week that month began. We might choose to standardize the weeks more, in which case the weeks might get names. On my Llurien world, every month has four weeks of seven days. Those weeks are associated with the four elements, resulting in Fireweek, for example. The fourteenth day is always the seventh day of the second week. No one needs a calendar to figure it out.

MONTHS IN A YEAR

How many months do we want in a year? Once again, and for the same reason, it's recommended to be off by one from Earth, meaning eleven or thirteen months in a year. Earth months are named and our invented world will need month names, too. Once again, our audience will have no idea what we're talking about, so they should be used sparingly and explained succinctly. Take this example passage:

Kier asked, "When will the dragon give birth?"

"In Dicerimon," the dragon keeper replied.

Kier nodded. Three months, just in time for the winter sacrifice.

In this passage, note the use of the suffix "mon" on the month name. On Earth, we have "uary" and "ber" to denote half of the months. We might want to choose a similar approach to indicate to our audience that we're referencing a month. A common prefix or suffix can assist their understanding. As with Earth, perfect uniformity may not happen or be advisable and can even look like too much planning on our part. Feel free to make exceptions.

When revealing the number of months, we can also work this into narration instead of writing exposition about it. See Kier's fate for guidance:

Kier asked, "When will I be executed for my crimes?"

"Two years from today," the judge replied. "One for your beloved. Another for the dragon."

Kier hung limp in the chains. Twenty-two months to agonize over his mistakes.

Universal Calendar

In our modern world, we're used to the Gregorian calendar being accepted worldwide. This wasn't always true and in some places it's not official and is only used when trying to correlate dates between different countries. We could invent a datebook for every kingdom, but that's a lot of work for little gain. A universal calendar, meaning one that's acknowledged across a planet, has both advantages and disadvantages.

Benefits

In stories, we might have little reason to mention the year, but this depends on our needs and the world's technological level. A fantasy setting might be less concerned with information in general, not to mention date, but some SF frequently mentions this, such as the well-known "star date" for a captain's log entry in *Star Trek*. What's important is that, whether we mention dates or not, we need a universal calendar for our notes even if not used by our characters. Otherwise, we can't reconcile two differing calendars and understand when events occurred. There's no way to tell that year 734 D.C. in Kingdom X is thirty years later than year 343 O.E. in Kingdom Y.

Each power may have its own time measurement. Year one will be an important event, such as the kingdom's founding or the life and death of someone important. There could be a technology that shapes life, or a supernatural event or discovery. It should be something that resonates with society or which the power wants to champion, such as the first ruler in a dynasty. While we're free to invent these internal calendars, we need a universal one.

Whether our universal calendar is recognized on the planet is another matter. For this to happen, there must be a globally accepted event. On Earth, we use the birth of Christ, with years before that counting down like a timer and the years after counting up. However, this scheme wasn't recognized for hundreds of years and didn't become standard for hundreds more. Christianity slowly spread, and with it, the calendar. For an invented world, we might need something like the birth of magic or a new technology to occur and slowly spread, too. A swifter way is a cataclysm, which is especially viable in post-apocalyptic fiction and which will quickly dominate minds and ways of life. A mass exodus from a planet might be, too. We need an event that most people in the world will think is a big deal.

If we want our story to be directly impacted by the event, by which I mean the characters and world are still recovering from it, the event should be recent, within the last few hundred years. Otherwise, place the event farther in the past. The invention of a technology might impact modern life, but the moment of that invention doesn't have to be recent.

Deciding no universal calendar exists is also fine, but be sure to choose one for your private notes if you're building a world intended to be used a long time, and which has multiple sovereign powers with differing calendars. If you can't decide, then go with a believed creation date rather than the timespan required by evolution. It took millions of years for life to evolve on Earth, but according to some religions, God put us here less than ten thousand years ago. We can also decide that the first civilization is a marker, as that might've been much closer; years longer than five digits (10,000) can seem unwieldy.

When it comes to the initials like A.D. and B.C., whether for a universal calendar or not, we'll want a naming convention of some sense, such as B.M. and A.M., as in

308 | RANDY ELLEFSON

"Before Magic" and "After Magic." We don't need to use this style. Terms such as Heisei 12 in Japan means it's the twelfth year of the current emperor, named Heisei. People might want a positive spin on the years, but in a dystopian setting, a negative sounding term can be accepted.

CHALLENGES

If we're inventing a world for long term use or might use both hemispheres, there are some issues to consider for calendar names. On Earth, January is a winter month to some and a summer month to others, and since the word "January" has nothing to do with a season, we're okay. But what if it was called "Snowtime" instead? That would only make sense to areas which receive snow in January. Tropical climates may never get snow regardless of hemisphere, polar areas always have snow, and some areas have no seasons.

If we want to do it anyway, regional terms can add dimension. A character from such a place can express how different things are back home, now that they're away. On Earth, there's no shortage of people from the northern hemisphere saying how weird it is to celebrate Christmas in summer while south of the equator. Some holidays, like Christmas, have nothing to with a season but have become associated with it.

It's tempting to decide the year starts with spring, but this is once again only true for certain areas. For others, it would be the first day of winter or not associated with any specific season. How likely is it that everyone north of the equator likes that spring idea and everyone south of it likes the winter idea? Not very. The likely result is a different calendar, which might be local in focus.

So what do we start the year with? An event that has nothing to do with weather, climate, or seasons. In this chapter, the "Historical Event Categories" section may provide ideas.

CREATING AGES

Time periods are sometimes given names like the Stone Age or Bronze Age here on Earth. In fantasy, we can see an Age of Swords or maybe an Elven Age, for a time dominated by elves, possibly because their talents gave rise to their prominence. In SF, we might have a Terrestrial Age, meaning before space flight became possible, or an Interstellar Age. While the present age might not have a name, all past ages will get a name if we choose to do this at all; otherwise there's a gap with no name. At worst, we can all an age the "Pre" age, such as "Pre-Interstellar Age" when the following era is the Interstellar Age. A current age can lack a name because names are typically applied after the fact.

Ages are typically thousands of years but could be less. When creating events within that time period, be aware of the time frame's implications. If those of Earth begin space exploration more akin to *Star Trek*, that can be the start of an Interstellar Age. Events from our current time frame can either be fit into that age or the previous one. It's our decision how to group events as leading to a revolution and being in the previous age, or being part of the next age they trigger.

USES FOR HISTORY

Inventing history can have uses beyond world building. The main use is to make our present and future stories more believable and detailed. We might also invent world figures, artifacts, and mysteries we can utilize. These can offer twists and turns to our work. We could connect new ideas to previously created ones. Maybe we have a supernatural creature with an origin we haven't worked out yet, and we like the world finding this mysterious and creepy. Then we later invent an item that has some side effects. One day we bring them together and decide the item caused the creature. We can decide no one knows this until our characters discover it. With only two examples, this seems obvious, but in a world with dozens of inventions, an intricate layering becomes possible.

We can also write stories using the best incidents we conjure, so don't be afraid to let your imagination run wild, even if you create a bunch of stuff you don't think you can use at first. We can turn them into short stories that we send to loyal readers in our newsletter, as bonus materials. Or it can be on our website, or published.

HISTORICAL EVENT CATEGORIES

There are different types of entries with which we can fill an imagined history. This list isn't exhaustive but can provide inspiration.

THE GODS

In some story worlds, the gods keep to themselves, but in others they interfere with life and cause events. This could be fathering children with members of mortal species, resulting in monsters or demi-gods. They might have sacred places that are built or destroyed. Perhaps most fun is that gods sometimes have very powerful magic items that fall into the wrong hands, causing events with long-term consequences. This can include the invention of new species or monsters that proliferate. A god can even be killed or otherwise inhibited (imprisoned) due to some event, whether they acted badly and were punished by the gods, or because a mortal somehow did something to them. Maybe some of these incidents are celebrated or otherwise noted, like an anniversary, by the species.

TECHNOLOGICAL EVENTS

Many technological events are possible, especially in SF. These include failed or successful missions, rocket/satellite/ship launches, explosions, discoveries, weapons tests, and first contact with other aliens/species. The latter is especially important; the longer the history between two species, the greater the odds of conflict and familiarity breeding contempt. Or those who've been hostile can learn the other isn't so bad, possibly due to help needed against a mutual threat. Disasters of technology, like America's space shuttle tragedies, often spur innovation and memorial; a main character can be a descendant of someone lost in one. Classes of vessels might also be invented, used, and then retired. Another event is the discovery of special ore needed by ship engines or to forge metal in fantasy, or even the creation of famous items. Ships, fleets, and items can also disappear, be destroyed, or be captured.

SUPERNATURAL EVENTS

For fantasy worlds and some SF, no history is complete without the supernatural. Phenomena must start or be discovered, and possibly wreak havoc, and then be neutralized. We might have famous expeditions to deal with somewhere or something. Magic (in general or specific spells) can be discovered, expanded, and proliferate or be squashed in one region or sovereign power. Famous practitioners or victims will come and go. This is true of items, whether armor, weapons, scrolls, potions, or jewelry. Perhaps a useful material is discovered or exploited into nonexistence (or restricted by law). Monsters might result from events, too. Did something of the gods fall into mortal hands? Celestial events like a conjunction, eclipse, or comet can be assigned supernatural significance.

THE RISE AND FALL OF SOVEREIGN POWERS

No sovereign power lasts forever or retains the same government. The bigger events, such as the power signs an important treaty, or collapses can be noted here, but most internally relevant events can be kept in that power's file. How a kingdom came to be doesn't really require an explanation in our world history, and few will question this. However, its demise benefits from an explanation (see Chapter 5, "Creating a Sovereign Power"); these include being conquered, revolution, and a coup. Its fall will impact neighbors, but we might not need to comment on this unless an empire has fallen, as other powers that fell under its control will enter a period of instability.

WARS

A world without war isn't realistic. We can invent these while conjuring a world history or while working in sovereign power's file. Doing this requires some idea of the governments existing in those powers and their locations; otherwise it's hard to know why the war is being fought, not to mention where, or what impact it has on the powers or anyone caught in the conflict. It helps to understand technological or supernatural level of the combatants.

Is there a goal we hope this war will achieve? Perhaps we want simmering resentments between characters of today. Maybe we want a disaster to result as the logical conclusion of animosities we've set in motion. Is a resource under contention? Is that place a danger that one power wants to secure but which another wants to utilize?

Remember that former enemies can become allies later, sometimes through government upheaval, defeat, or just the passing of time. We've seen this on Earth, where in as little as a few generations, animosities have given way to mutual aid and reconciliation. Don't be afraid to decide two friendly nations today weren't enemies as little as decades ago. The speed of change may depend on technology and information; worlds with less, as in fantasy, might harbor animosity for far longer.

"Ethnic cleansing", one group trying to eradicate another, has caused some of the worst wars; this sort of animosity won't quickly disappear. A power might try to unite ethnic groups that have become split across nations. For example, Russia recently invaded Ukraine with one justification being that the Ukraine has regions with mostly ethnic Russians, who want to be part of Russia. There were also natural resources at stake.

Pride is yet another reason for war, as a new dictator must make a show of power. Or the dictator feels pride in their nation and heritage and feel they and their people have been oppressed or wrongly scaled back in a previous war. Starting a new war to right wrongs from a previous war is a classic. Leaders may have a grand vision of superiority or desire a fate different from, and better than, their current reality, for themselves or their kingdom, and the stress of this simmers for years before leading to war.

Taking back territory, resources, or something else believed to rightly belong to a kingdom is another reason for war. Sometimes these are perpetual disputes—until an empire absorbs both opponents.

GROUPS FORMING

We might want to indicate when a special military group was formed. Use this for famous knight orders or naval/space forces, even dragon riders, spectral groups, elite guards, horsemen, archers, or whichever groups you've created. If there's a wizard or warrior order, like monks of a certain region, note their formation date, or when a powerful leader rose, influenced, disappeared, or fell. Did this group or someone from it accomplish something? Is there a force for good or evil, like the Justice League from comics? *Cultures and Beyond* goes into more details about groups we can create.

ARTIFACTS DISCOVERED/INVENTED

Creating magic items is one of the fun things about writing fantasy. For SF, legendary devices or ships are equally fun, particularly when they disappear, creating mystery, intrigue, and excitement when they show up in a story. These can fall under the protection of a sovereign power or individual and be contested. They can be feared or admired. They can come with a prophecy about the sort of person who might wield them one day, causing dreams and struggles. Each time you create an important item, add its invention date to the history, though lesser objects don't need an origin date.

MISSIONS UNDERTAKEN

Missions to explore, rescue, kill or kidnap someone/something, or investigate strange phenomena can be listed in our history. Be sure to indicate the outcome, whether this is known to characters or not. This history is for your files, so it's okay to drop the truth here and only reveal that to an audience in a story. Those who undertook a mission might be famous, giving us world figures. They might have also triggered an event, such as a war or new phenomenon, or discovered a new item or material.

WHERE TO START

History can be created at random, though at times we'll want to create multiple events regarding a subject at once. Entries needn't be related, making this ideal for piecemeal invention. For any subject, such as a sovereign power or group, we can either start inventing the past in our history file or do it in the file for that power or group. The biggest items should go on the world history with minimal redundancy across files. The event categories above should provide ideas on what might need to be created before a history, but we want to work on history after inventing the thing for which we're creating that past. Otherwise, follow your heart and feel free to let creativity run free.

CHAPTER ELEVEN

CREATING PLACES OF INTEREST

Noteworthy locations provide our characters somewhere to stumble upon, avoid, or seek out on missions. They can cause interesting items or life forms to exist, possess, or flee from. World builders can place these in almost random locations, reducing the burden of logic needed to explain origins. Some phenomena simply exist where they do or are the result of natural geological forces (such as volcanoes or meteor strikes), while events such as explosions, battles, or experiments gone awry can cause others. Used in small doses, they can add complexity, interest, and variety to a setting.

ORDINARY PLACES

Not every location needs to be spectacular. Anything unusual can do and should not be overlooked.

CATACOMBS AND HIDDEN PASSAGES

Catacombs, bomb shelters, sewer lines, tunnels, and subway lines, especially beneath a settlement, can provide somewhere to hide people, creatures, or possessions, and be used for stealthy maneuvering. We can decide they are known to all or a select few who are using them for nefarious purposes. Even if known, the extent of them seldom is; much of the fun lies in the mystery. When inventing these, decide why they exist. They might have been designed for covert work, such as in military locations. Royalty could have decided they wanted ways to move about without being noticed (or for their spies). Excessive heat in tropical locations might have led to these cooler places to dwell at times, or store things like wine or munitions. Perhaps there are secret training facilities.

In a world with dwarves, perhaps they just enjoy such locations as a reminder of home and have tunneled deep, with or without permissions. They might no longer live here, leaving abandoned tunnels that are partly in use by those with both good and bad intentions. Sometimes these locations aren't known because a civilization or population from a thousand years ago might have left it. The current settlement could even have been built atop such a place with no one realizing it.

STEP WELLS

For most of us, a water well might not sound interesting, but if you Google "step wells in India," the pictures will change your mind. These are elaborate pits in the ground with flights of stairs leading down to the water. The steps appear akin to an amphitheater, being wide and often on all four sides in a square or rectangular shape. Platforms can exist in these, and with some imagination, we might decorate them with carvings and statues. Some structures have cave-like openings into a cliff face and buildings that are carved from within. If we have a species which dwells in fresh water, they may swim up underground rivers to emerge from these wells.

Figure 61 Step Well

MONUMENTS

Monuments can be buildings, monoliths, or statues. Some could be spectacular and qualify as famous locations. This can be due to size, complexity, or the individual or occasion being memorialized. Having world figures helps us decide on the latter. We should also determine the condition such monuments are in. Those in abandoned places might be in disrepair or have been vandalized, even destroyed utterly, whether this is known or discovered by characters in a story. Visiting such a place to acquire power or an item can therefore throw characters off their intended quest. Monuments located amid existing civilization might be prone to thievery attempts and desecration.

On Earth, we have Egypt's great pyramids, the Great Wall of China, or Stonehenge. The ancient world included the Seven Wonders, which included a temple, two statues, the pyramids, a mausoleum, gardens, and a lighthouse. These seven were chosen because there were, at the time, seven bodies in the heavens: the sun, moon, and five discovered planets. An invented world might benefit from a similar explanation if monuments are being counted. The lists can be longer, and different lists have existed over time. The original seven don't sound impressive until one considers the unusual size, adornment, or subject (often a god) of most. Many of these wonders were destroyed by earthquakes or floods.

GRAVES

While most cemeteries won't be of much interest, other burial sites may be. One possibility is a system of catacombs, where skulls and bones have been stacked. Mausoleums can be enormous, uniquely decorated, or house famous people; these may contain items, such as treasure, which others plunder. These would require guards of ordinary or extraordinary kind, such as ferocious animals/monsters, or humanoids with demonic, technological, or magical powers. Graveyards could also have unique layouts where different classes of people are interred separately. Rituals might also be done at regular intervals. A day of the dead festival might exist, the macabre scene fitting for a story. Lone grave sites in the wilderness might achieve significance for location or features.

EXTRAORDINARY PLACES

UNDERWATER SETTLEMENTS

While extraordinary to us, an underwater settlement might be commonplace, if a water dwelling species exists to construct them. Are there dry areas or air pockets allowing land species to reside there safely? Or be imprisoned because there's no way to reach the surface? Perhaps magic or technological portals allow people to enter or leave such a city. Think about what sort of industry and skills a water dwelling species might acquire if they not only have water-filled areas but dry ones, assuming they can move on land. Might they craft a large enough space to practice with weapons they'd need skills for on land?

FLOATING SETTLEMENTS

We've seen cities in *Star Wars*, and rock formations in *Avatar*, both suspended in the air. We can use magic, technology, or unexplained physics to do the same. Aside from this floating aspect, these settlements otherwise differ little from more ordinary communities. However, we should think about what opportunities are afforded. A flying species might be prone to inventing such places or find them very attractive. There might be few predators except the flying kind, making life safe. While no city walls will exist, what kind of aerial fortifications might be needed? Trade might be quite difficult without ships, large flying animals, or other means to transport resources. It may also be at extraordinary risk of crashing to the ground, which seems an obvious sabotage focus for enemies. How does this place protect itself from hurricanes, tornados, or strong storms? The obvious answer is that it's only built somewhere that doesn't experience these.

On Earth, we have Venice, which is built largely on stilts, but the impression is still of floating on water. This does not require magic or advanced technology, but we can invent a place that genuinely floats on the sea. A water dwelling species might find this accommodating and even be the ones to invent it. The setting can be a place where land and water species can interact more easily. This must occur where significant waves are rare if not unheard of, so look for a lagoon or otherwise protected inlet in waterways like bays or sounds. If there are large sea monsters that could easily wreck the place, then it won't exist, but if there's a new sea monster never considered before, we can have fun destroying the settlement in a story.

OTHER UNUSUAL HOMES

A species might build homes inside hills like the Hobbits of *The Lord of the Rings*. Elaborate mountain homes are a staple of fantasy dwarves. A flying species could build small homes inside enormous trees, but with no way to reach the ground so that predators, including other species, can't access them.

PHENOMENA

Strange phenomena are staples of fantasy and SF, especially when the latter involves explorations of the cosmos. Space offers nebulas, radiation, and alien planet environments. We can invent all manner of experiences that have no real explanation or at best, pseudoscience to impart believability or specific effects on characters and their environment, such as an interstellar ship. Space phenomena have a great advantage in that their location is flexible; we can place them wherever we feel like it and invent them on the fly.

By contrast, singularities on a planet or other body (moon, asteroid, etc.) are typically associated with a given location. They often benefit from at least speculation as to their causes. Technological or magical disasters, resulting from experiments or battle, offer easy rationalizations and even suggest world figures or famous items that might've been involved. Monsters or creatures can be a result, too. Does this phenomenon influence only things that come in contact with it or can it affect nearby objects? Maybe it can compel people to approach.

We can also create seemingly unrelated phenomena in different locations but which bear some similarities, but later associate them with each other. We might also have phenomena that begat other phenomena, with no one knowing this until characters stumble upon the truth. This sort of layering adds depth while fascinating audiences as oddities they've experienced before are revealed to have new significance.

There might be places where magic or technology doesn't work, is unpredictable, or is supercharged. Animals could go wild, which is a cliché, or become docile if we want a new impact. There can be locations allowing extraordinary travel, whether actual doorways, random spots, or the former built on the latter. These gateways can lead to other physical locations, supernatural ones, or an alternate reality or timeline. These methods may be predictable, controllable, or neither. Can only certain people or devices activate them? Or we can have a portal open constantly because no one knows how to close it. Beings could be summoned through them.

On Earth, we have places where strange behavior is believed to occur, like the Bermuda Triangle or crop circles. Then there's Area 51, a rumored place for storing unusual items. The origins of places like Stonehenge or Easter Island have been debated, but we can invent similar locations and attribute fantastic reasons for their existence.

RUINS

Abandoned places are ripe for death by misadventure. Monsters, treasure, and items can all lure people to investigate and figure out what's there or what went wrong. To that end, dropping clues is vital to intriguing an audience. Some of these places will be legendary while others are previously unknown. Both have their merits.

These can range from simple caves or tunnels, like a monster lair or dwarven home, to entire cities or even planets; if we want to be extreme, we can include solar systems or entire galaxies. The scale of abandonment suggests the scale of calamity that caused that abandonment, so choose accordingly. Danger is often assumed to lurk in such places, whether that danger is the new inhabitant, nature having taken over, or the remnants of the reason abandonment took place. Valuables are often assumed to have been left behind, attracting thieves and opportunists who might interfere with a band of characters going there.

Ruins are fun for audiences to watch people discover and explore. We can create mystery about what's happening there now and what led to its demise. Clues and rumors should evoke curiosity and maybe feelings of dread, foreboding, wonder, and excitement. The more suggestive these are, the better, but it pays to have a reveal that goes beyond audience expectations regarding how cool the truth is, surpassing it. The trick to this is being coy about the truth, and inventing plausible variants on that truth, each one compelling but not as cool as the actuality.

But not everywhere needs a wonderful story. Disease, drought, climate change, natural disasters, and destruction in war are simple explanations that are the most likely culprits. Some places vanish for commercial reasons, such as over-exploitation of the resource (as in mining) or because a better commercial location usurped it, leaving a ghost town, which may have some residents after all.

Bear in mind how overgrown the location is. A rainforest or swamp quickly consumes a place so that it's nearly impossible to find and less likely to be known; roads to it will disappear, too. More exposed locations will endure wind erosion and may become buried by sediment. An underground place won't suffer much erosion but will instead lose structural cohesion from earthquakes, the toll of which we can tailor to our intended desire. Similarly, a mountain settlement might suffer rock falls. Sometimes people wonder why more dust doesn't accumulate in abandoned places, but dust is partly particles from people, so no people means no more dust accumulation or the tracking in of other contaminants.

The durability of buildings is greatly impacted by their material. In less advanced settings, the roof is often the first part of a structure to disintegrate, allowing more rain and animals inside and speeding interior erosion. Stone structures could last centuries despite deterioration, but remember that locals might steal these materials for their own uses. With the advanced technology in SF, a location could last far longer, unaffected by erosion except for becoming overgrown and buried. Then again, maybe automated machines are keeping it pristine long after life has departed.

Magical or technological items are among the best ones left behind, whether by accident or on purpose. They are begging to be found by heroes, villains, or some random fool. Depending on the item, this could empower someone who shouldn't have such power, raising them to king or overlord among their kind, such as goblins. Think of a weapon, armor, information found in books or scrolls, or a space ship or other tech, depending on your story. The object found might also be cursed. It doesn't have to be the item responsible for the ruin existing. We might want to create a group of people who see it as their job to find, neutralize, and store these items to prevent such events.

SHIPWRECKS

Wooden shipwrecks aren't always completely submerged, but if so, they become more useful if we have a water-dwelling species that can plunder them, whether that's items, coins, gems or something else worthwhile. The species can be benevolent or nefarious, and the items found can be dangerous or benign. We can empower sea-dwelling life in some way that makes them more formidable to landlubbers, possibly upsetting the balance of power. They can also become a threat to ships. Perhaps a good species rescues people or performs salvage missions in cooperation with land species. They might even raise a ship back to the surface, or use it as a home. They might claim that everything below the waves is in their domain and therefore theirs, causing conflict.

In SF, shipwrecks may be more accessible, whether in space or on the surface of a planet, moon, asteroid, or space station; they could also be underwater. The technology available on one could be a boon or threat to those who discover it. The most obvious reason for abandoned spacecraft are crashes, partial destruction, or abandoned ship. Wars in space can leave a huge field of debris in orbit, whether around a planet, moon, or a sun; such a ship graveyard must be navigated carefully and might even be named. When creating one, decide the reason for the battle, how many ships were involved, who won, and what kinds of craft were involved. Was it a fight between war craft? Or was this a peaceful convoy that someone attacked? This will likely be part of a larger conflict between sovereign powers across the same or different worlds.

We should decide what happened to the crew. The easy answer is that everyone's dead, but other options are more entertaining. Capture and being marooned offer chances for survivors to have new lives quite different than their previous ones.

SOURCE OF FAME

When creating a shipwreck, there must be a reason people remember it. It could be in a remote place that makes recovery hard. Or it could be in the mouth of a crucial river or outside a noteworthy settlement, or scene of battle. It could be on an asteroid or orbiting a unique body.

The ship could have been famous before crashing/sinking, whether for its attributes or missions it undertook, including the one causing its demise. Did it have a special engine, new A.I., or experimental weapons or defenses, some of which could be the reason it met its doom? Someone could have tried to destroy or capture it. Maybe it just had an appearance or configuration that struck fear into people's hearts. It could be famous for its captain or crew; the former allows us to create a world figure (see *Creating Life (The Art of World Building, #1)*).

The reason for a ship's demise can also be famous. This can include a mutiny, striking a rock, reef, or iceberg, or a storm strong enough to overturn the ship. For spaceships, we often use technology to rupture hulls or propulsion systems, but they can also strike space debris, whether that's other manmade objects or leftovers from the solar system's formation (rock and ice). A disabled ship can become unable to maneuver away from an impending collision, but the disabling incident should be interesting. The event which damaged the ship may leave the wreck dangerous, such as with radiation or supernatural residue tainting it; maybe this causes monsters (see *Creating Life*).

A sea or space monster could have caused damage. We should decide who attacked whom; perhaps the way in which the crew brought demise upon itself rendered their fate famous. War is an easy way to destroy vessels, but since it's mundane, we might need to make the battle famous or assign another attribute to this ship to make its wreck renowned.

Cargo is an easy way to make a shipwreck famous. We can place anything we've invented in the hold, provided that transporting it between two locations makes sense. If this form of transportation is rare, that makes the wreck rare, too. We end up with a "lost" item. The question then becomes whether this has been recovered or not. Stories to acquire lost treasure suggest themselves.

A creature inhabiting the ship now could be the source of infamy, especially if that creature can pilot the vessel. A ship that's fallen into the wrong hands provides opportunities for mayhem whether it remains disabled from travel or not. A stationary ship, if equipped with the right technology, could still be a great danger to anyone who comes near.

Combining two reasons for a ship's fame makes it more intriguing, but don't go overboard with justifications for its fame; no more than two, generally.

EVENT SITES

Any interesting event can cause a location to acquire significance—a famous battle, if a high body count occurred, or if the tide of war turned there, or a species massacred. Religious sites abound, whether a martyr died there, a prophet revealed something, or a sighting of a deity took place. A shrine, church, or other monument may mark a site. A first (or last) instance of anything can make a site known, such as the first execution of a king, the place where a species was invented, or if it's the first place a weapon was used. The location of natural phenomena can also acquire significance, such as geysers, sinkholes, or the aurora borealis. Solitary mountains or volcanoes have also inspired people, not just when they erupt, but as a place where deities may dwell. The trick to creating these is the story associated with them. Otherwise, they're only slightly more interesting than your average tree, for example.

330 | RANDY ELLEFSON

METEORS

Meteor impacts leave craters that might leave less technologically advanced people wondering what's occurred. Myths might result. Meteors are sometimes believed to be carrying life that can now inhabit the world. These are often of a viral nature, but may be sentient, and capable of inhabiting and controlling people. Either way, the site can be a place of interest, one that might be worshipped. The sighting of meteors, comets, and eclipses can also herald important events in a fantasy world. In SF, a meteor still in space can be a destination if it possesses rare minerals.

WHERE TO START

Places of interest can crop up anywhere we need them. They can be created long after we're already using our world. But if we have wars or battles in mind, we can start with these as sources of phenomena. Any fight involving titanic forces, like great magical or technological power, can be the instigator. Decide where you'd like this place to be, such as in a remote location or a central one that impacts life all around it, probably via avoidance; the latter will be a major factor in stories taking place near the location—remote locations give us leeway to invent places of lesser impact. If we have a goal in mind, such as wanting a point of origin for a monster, inventing the creature first can give us ideas on where and what caused it. If we've already invented several places, we can invent a different type of place, in a different location.

DRAWING MAPS

Whether we're an artist or not, creating maps has advantages. They help us visualize a location and think about what lies where. This can be anything from land features on continent or region maps, to buildings and public areas in settlement maps, cells and escape routes in dungeon maps, stations or ships (whether those vessels are wooden or space-faring), and even planets, moons, asteroids and suns on star maps. Seeing empty spaces to fill on our map can inspire invention that leads to more creativity, realism, and realization about what's feasible or even likely, given our design. Impossible scenarios can be avoided. A map also helps us remember what we visualized, should we be absent from our story world for an extended time.

Some of us are good enough artists to include our map in published works, but even if we can't draw, there are programs that can greatly assist us. They don't require drawing skill; rather, the ability to place pre-existing objects, like a city or mountain icon, is all that's needed. Then we just repeat this as often as needed or desired until we're done. And maps can be created piecemeal. Even if we don't use such a program, we might want to hire someone to depict a location for us, and even squiggles on a page are helpful in telling an artist what to create.

CONTINENTAL MAPS

Whether it's a continent map or just a region of one, we should consider the merits of creating a map and how to do so. We can create one ourselves or hire artists for a few hundred dollars, which is comparable to the cost of book covers but which can be used repeatedly.

SHOULD YOU DRAW ONE?

For a world that an author will only use for a short story or one book, a map may not be needed or worth the time, but worlds we'll use often (across a series or not) will benefit from maps. The more the characters travel through the wilderness, the more likely this need is. Even stories that take place primarily in cities might need a regional map if the audience must follow two or more storylines that are concurrently happening in different locations that the audience struggles to understand; *Games of Thrones* comes to mind. A city-centric tale has little use for continent maps unless referencing nearby locations, whereupon a regional map is helpful. Game designers may need one for the same reasons, even outside of digital gaming, where it is often mandatory.

If we want to calculate travel times, a map can help us measure with accuracy, even if we decide our map isn't drawn to scale. We can discover problems with intended time frames in our story and find adjustments that might be creative. If a journey will happen too fast, we can cause calamity to slow our travelers. We might use magic, steeds, or technology to increase travel rates. Or we can change our story. If we'd like to cite specific distances, like "it is one hundred kilometers to Illiandor by horse and it will take two days riding hard," we can make such statements with greater confidence.

Drawing maps can be fun and may provide ideas for both stories and setting. Chapter 1 on "Case Studies" provides examples. But if we don't want to draw one, there's a good way around this: base locations on Earth ones. We might use England, France, and Spain as our respective countries, calling them something else. In our notes, we can just write that "Illiandor is England," for example, and even use its geography. Readers will never know unless we provide a map with a familiar shape. We can do this on a smaller scale as well, such as using the provinces of Canada as different countries, even while changing the latitude to something balmier near the equator.

HOW TO CREATE ONE

We should decide on our initial goal: are we intending to draw a continent or the region around where our story takes places?

CONTINENT FIRST

For a continent, we can base the overall size on an existing Earth one or just a region, like a country (or several). A smaller area, like a U.S. state or province like those in Canada can also be used but might be designated an island. In all cases, we'll just surround it with water instead of

334 | RANDY ELLEFSON

other land masses. This analogue can help our sense of scale, distance, and travel times.

With this decided, we can begin drawing a shape for our coastline. Nature doesn't create straight lines, typically, so the inability to draw one is not a disadvantage. We can once again base part of this on Earth analogues. Just don't use an entire coastline for even one side of a continent. We can take the west edge of Spain, the south edge of Britain, the region between North Carolina and Florida for the east, and the northern coastline of South America. We can also draw all of these on the "wrong" coastline. Stealing continent edges this way takes the difficulty out of this, and if you miss draw it, so much the better. We could also trace these.

We should have a general sense of what climates we want. This will determine how far from the equator the continent is. A broad, inclusive climate range means a land mass that runs thousands of miles north to south, if the planet is at all Earth-like in size. Make this decision early because it determines which direction the prevailing winds are. And as we learned in Chapter 2, "Creating a Planet," this predicts where rain shadows from mountain ranges develop. This affects the amount of vegetation, causing everything from dense forest to arid deserts.

But first, we'll want to decide where those mountain ranges are, using what we learned from Chapter 3, "Creating a Continent." Nature often places one range along the edge of a continent, with deep water (and possibly sea monsters) just offshore. Find a place you'd like this, the best culprits being on the eastern or western shores; a northern or southern range means a single climate (cold or hot) takes place in that mountain range, which provides less variety.

For a second range that's somewhat parallel, choose a different length and starting point rather than starting at the same latitude or longitude and traversing the same distance. With a range that's more perpendicular to existing ones, try not to form right angles like an upper case "L." Placing empty space between two such ranges helps prevent this. Remember that there are different kinds of mountain ranges and that we can place solitary peaks, or a few in a row, virtually anywhere. We don't have to create every mountain range at once, being able to work on one region of our map at a time, but it can be helpful to do so if we have ideas.

With this decided, and with our knowing which way prevailing winds blow at the latitude where this mountain range stands, we can determine where rain shadows and therefore deserts exist. If there's a significant gap between two ranges that are north and south of each other, for example, moisture may get through there and cause a forest near that gap. Also, remember that smaller mountain ranges cause less of a rain shadow. Knowing these things allows us some flexibility to justify having a forest where a desert might actually lie if the peaks were taller. Using Google maps, we can look at satellite images of continents and figure out what typically happens; these show ranges, vegetation, and deserts.

We'll want to draw rivers that flow toward the sea, possibly stopping at a large lake. And this fresh water is where our settlements will be, as humans cannot consume salt water without becoming sick (but we can invent a species that can). When creating a continent map, we don't need to draw every lake; in fact, doing so would be impractical, just as every river would be. This is one justification for putting a settlement somewhere that water doesn't appear on the map, but do this on purpose, not by accident.

Vegetation will grow around rivers and lakes, but it will also grow on the opposite side of a mountain range from the desert that a rain shadow causes. Generally, we'll want a forest on one side, a desert on the other. However, if the prevailing winds are east to west (or vice versa), and the mountains also run that way, then the winds aren't blocked by the peaks; the winds are parallel. This makes forest on each side likely, but desert on either side unlikely.

LOCAL REGION FIRST

If we're creating a map for a specific story, we might only need a regional drawing that focuses on the area where our story occurs. This requires knowing our story's requirements regarding land features that impact storytelling and whether weather plays a role. First decide about what you need for each. Weather determines latitude, as does the need for a rain forest or frozen tundra. If only one is needed, we could move our continent north or south (depending on which hemisphere it's in). If both cold and hot are needed, a more temperate zone or longer continent (north to south) might be needed. With this decision made, we can choose latitude, basing this on an Earth continent or country if needed for better understanding.

With latitude and hemisphere decided, we can understand which direction the prevailing winds blow. We might not be drawing the whole continent, but if we decide to place mountains along a north-south trajectory, then wind direction will determine rain shadows and vegetation locations. For example, if the winds blow east and we place a north-south range on the eastern edge, then a forest will be between the ocean and range, and a desert will be to the range's west. If we don't want a desert, then put the mountain range somewhere else, such as on the western edge or more east-to-west.

With such information, we can decide what land features surrounded the settlement or region where the story takes place. While our focus might be on that area, approaching development from the continental mindset helps us be realistic. We don't need to ever draw the rest of the land mass. It does help to have some idea how much land is in either direction, however. A region at the coast has an ocean or sea available to it, and therefore shipping and trade options unavailable to a landlocked area. The number of potential allies and enemies in every direction also matters to overall mindset, but these are less mapping issues than world building ones.

MY PROCESS

I use Campaign Cartographer 3 (CC3) to draw my continent maps, which I also use for region maps by zooming in. There's an add-on called Fractal Terrains, which can be used to generate continent shapes with the click of a button. It actually creates entire planets but I've typically looked for a continent that I like the look of. Mountains, hills, vegetation, and even lakes or bays, etc., are also depicted. If I don't like what I see, another click and I get another planet. There are changeable parameters to generate more or fewer land masses, for example.

I take a screen shot of one I like, crop it to size in an image program like Windows Paint, and save it. In some cases, I take two different continents and overlay them atop each other to create a composite shape that I like. I then import the image into CC3 using their instructions for doing so. Then I use CC3's tools to trace the continent outline. I sometimes change little features I don't want to include, or add them.

I'll have already decided the continent's latitude, hemisphere, and which direction it lies from any existing continents I have. For the latter, the reason is that on Earth, tectonic activity sometimes separates one large continent into two smaller ones that appear to fit together like a jigsaw puzzle; see the western edge of Africa and the eastern edge of South America for an example. I might want to imply such a relationship between two continents.

In CC3, I use the hill and mountain tools to drop these icons over the Fractal Terrains image, though I'm free to ignore or add features that weren't present. For a mountain range, it's best to drop the foothill icons first because these will be farther out from the range's center. Then I drop the mountain icons on top of the foothills, starting at the top of the range and going down. The reasons for this would be apparent if you did it in reverse yourself. Basically anything you add will cover what's already on there, so the southernmost mountain should be fully visible but partly covering the mountain icon to its north. To achieve this, just start at the top and move down. Top to bottom is generally the way to work.

Once I have outlined the continent and mountains/hills that were depicted on the Fractal Terrains image, I no longer need the latter and hide it in CC3. I add some major rivers and lakes. There are tools to draw rain forests, shrub land, deciduous and coniferous trees, and more. I start at the top of my continent and work my way down, adding items as I deem appropriate, with an eye for the information in this volume and with what little artistic sense I have. I add cities and towns at fresh water locations and by the ocean. I tend to use the rivers as country boundaries.

For each settlement, I give it some farmland, maybe a bridge over the rivers, and roads/trails to the neighboring settlements. Then I start filling in clear areas predominantly with trees, unless I have reason to believe rainfall is limited, in which case I give it grasslands or shrub lands. On the windward side of mountains, I put thick forest due to the rainfall. Desert goes on the leeward side, then maybe grasslands farther from the mountains as moisture is picked up in the atmosphere again. I just repeat this process as I work my way around the map, dropping icons for whatever I need.

CC3 comes with different color icons for settlements, with some blue, gold, red, etc. To help readers (and myself) understand the country boundaries, I tend to stick with one style of icon for a given country, such as the gold ones for one country and the blue ones for a neighbor. If you're zoomed in enough, you can tell just by looking at the map what areas are in a territory. The results are good and publishable with my manuscripts, and yet I can't draw to save my life. You can see the resulting maps at http://www.llurien.com/Antaria and
http://www.llurien.com/Llorus.

DRAWING THE WORLD

Creating a map of the entire world we've invented can be a challenge. As mentioned in the section above, the Fractal Terrains add-on to CC3 can create an entire planet with the click of a button. However, while it will have continents, oceans, bodies of water, mountains, and vegetation, that's all it will have. If you happen to like the entire planet and need one, you can follow my process to incorporate the result into CC3 and then re-draw each land mass with the missing features, like settlements. This can give us the best of both worlds: a globe that looks like a Google map photo without data, and smaller, more detailed areas.

Another option is to create continents, and then manually place an image of each continent on a blue background which simulates the ocean. This can give us a world map. If we have a program like Photoshop, we can paste high quality images of our continents to make a giant, detailed map.

SETTLEMENT MAPS

SHOULD YOU DRAW ONE?

For game designers who'll have characters roaming within a settlement, the map is essential for knowing where everyone, and the dangers they'll face, are located, but few if any books include maps of cities or towns, so one isn't expected with stories. A map may even interfere with a reader's ability to form their own mental picture as the story progresses. There comes a point where an audience doesn't care where we said something is; what matters is their impression. Referring to a map at the beginning of a book is optional but might jar them. Placing the map toward the book's rear is less advisable because they'll have their own ideas by then. Including it within the text, when the layout is described, is the best option.

If our settlement's layout is distinctive enough to impact story events, then a map is more important, whether we share this with an audience or not. One reason to create it is that we may forget this layout in time if we need it again. However, these issues can be solved without a map, just by notating locations in a file.

The existence of a map does not free us from the succinctly describing our location, in ways which are easy to visualize. It can be best to say that a church stands at one end of the town and a mayor's hall is at the opposite, rather than that one is east and the other west unless the compass points matter in some way. For example, if the sun sets on the mayor's house and we like foreshadowing his demise, we could try that. Including specific details which are irrelevant to the story implies those specifics matter when they don't, overwhelming our readers. Unsure what to remember, they may remember nothing.

A settlement map can make us think about locations we haven't considered, such as segregation of the wealthy and poor, or crime-ridden areas. The wealthy will likely live near rivers or a treasured location like a shrine or park, the latter being more important in urban areas because so much land might be paved or occupied by buildings. In larger settlements, the poor will inhabit the areas that are heavily trafficked or polluted, and the wealthy will be upstream of this, if on a river, or in a separate area of a lake.

Urban planning is a subject few of us know about, but zones are often created to improve the quality of life. Factories are not typically near homes. Commercial locations can be almost anywhere. Homes are often grouped into neighborhoods. Infrastructure like roads, sewage, and power are carefully planned. It's a massive subject deserving of its own book, and yet few of us will ever need to know where these locations are unless trying to draw a map, because our audience will assume these things are somewhere logical without us being specific. The depth of this subject is one reason not to draw a map, but that depends on how many details we intend to include. Sometimes being vague has advantages.

One way to avoid drawing is to use Google Maps and find a place of similar size to the one you imagine. For fantasy writers, we might want to choose an older location like those in Europe. Then we can zoom in on a town and make a screen capture or print out. From this, we can write names of places on it (and just use this for our personal files, not publishing it). Either that, or we can still draw it ourselves using this as inspiration.

HOW TO CREATE ONE

Decide what the settlement's water supplies are (lake, river, wells?) and draw this on a map, whether with pencil and paper or a program like City Designer 3 from Pro Fantasy. Then choose an area as "old town," which is where the settlement began before spreading out. There's probably an original set of buildings, possibly surrounded by a small, dilapidated wall. Here lie crowded streets and possibly thieves and the poor. An original mayor's hall could be here. Sometimes these old towns are preserved but other times they might be demolished due to the space being needed for something better. There's likely to be some industry near the river, too, including anything that produces waste.

Upriver from here, if applicable, create the wealthy area, which can be one of several. We might have another location that qualifies, too, such as higher land or a castle or other fortification. There's likely to be a port, and related commercial industry near the river but not fully occupying the territory. We don't need to be specific about the latter, just that factories and the like are there.

Remember that while a small village might be on level ground, larger places seldom are due to expansion and variable surfaces. Higher areas are often used for the wealthy, fortifications, or important buildings like a shrine or mayor's residence. Lower areas might flood, especially along the river, lake, or ocean. If this happens or the tide causes extreme fluctuations in water level, consider how this might affect structures along the shore (such as being built on stilts).

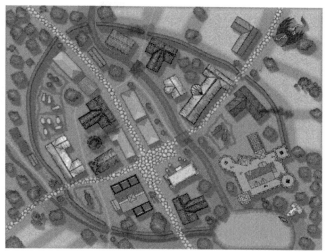

Figure 62 Village Map

If you have multiple species living here, decide if they have their own sections of town and where those areas are. A water dwelling species is by the water source, most likely, unless they're salt water creatures, and their ability to come upon land will impact their influence. Elves might be near a forested area, but if there isn't one, then is there a town gate with a road that leads toward the nearest forest, and which provides a better view of it? The same holds true of other species like dwarves wanting a view of hills or mountains, but there's no reason they can't live all the way across town, too. The question is where is a concentrated group of them dwelling?

Now that we've chosen a few locations for "old town," the wealthy, species quarters, and important buildings, we can begin filling in housing, commercial, and industrial locations. We can include spaces for parks, a stadium, cemeteries, and public gatherings. An array of other specifics could be included, such as the prison, but these are only worth noting if we intend to use them.

Before depicting any, decide which kind of neighborhood each is. The reason is that if we want a crime-ridden, poor area, we probably want more industry there, too, and fewer parks; parks may exist, but they will be poorly maintained (a detail we can ignore). What we're after is the knowledge of what reputation each section of town has. We then want to create our neighborhoods with that in mind. Think about where you live; somewhere is considered nice while another is run down, while a third might be downright dangerous. Naming neighborhoods can be as simple as compass points: southeast is unsafe while northwest is wealthy. I'd probably say that northwest is therefore up on a big hill, has more parks, and a great shrine to a cherished god. Southeast might be near the river, industry, and a place of frequent muggings, unrest, and dissent, with close, crowded streets and smaller, old homes.

We'll need to leave space for roads. Consider leaving a wide avenue in wealthier areas or from the castle to a major gate. We should also determine where a garrison is, if it exists, and what the likeliest point of attack is, as that's where the castle goes (on a hill). We should also form an idea of where the main city wall is; does it surround the entire community or has further development taken place since its construction so that some buildings are now outside the wall?

This should be enough to get world builders started on map creation. Once you're working, you'll have ideas on how to proceed.

DUNGEON & SHIP MAPS

SHOULD YOU DRAW ONE?

If relative locations matter, creating a map is a good idea, even if it's just for your reference and never published. We seldom see a map of ships, lairs, or dungeons in stories, suggesting authors might avoid this without complaint from an audience. Gamers and game designers might benefit from such maps, as the audience's characters will need to navigate through the locations. For readers, a map could be quite beneficial. My own experience in reading about someone's journey through a dungeon, castle, or similar labyrinth is that I have little to no understanding of where they are. Maybe the characters don't either, being lost, but these scenes often lack orientation.

Even if we don't show a map to the audience, it's crucial to accurately convey the layout we've envisioned. Otherwise we can describe a series of twists and turns that doesn't make sense to readers with a strong sense of direction. This can be one reason to be slightly vague. Rather than writing that a hallway turned left twice and then right once, we can say it turned to one side twice and then the other, but to some people, that's worse.

One reason for a map is to determine what rooms exist and what's in them. This can be problematic; few of us understand how a dungeon is laid out, assuming there's a standard way, and we might have trouble assigning a purpose to rooms. Some room examples are cells, guard stations, weapons rooms, torture chambers, latrines, pantries, mess halls, and visiting areas. Depending on the setting, some might have a library, laundry area, kitchen, a mini-hospital, anti-magic zones or cells for wizards, bullet-proof rooms, or areas where prisoners are forced to do hard labor (of various kinds). Think of modern prisons for ideas on rooms and layouts, including security zones for different levels of dangerous prisoners. All of this matters because of the tradition of adventurers exploring such a place and finding monsters and valuables in various rooms, with some sketchy justification for these things existing where they do. Some thought can raise our dungeon above the competition, and having a map can give us ideas.

In SF, maps of a ship could be invaluable as a reader because explanations can be difficult to visualize, though it may not matter for your story. When I watch TV, I seldom understand where parts of a ship are in relation to each other, but characters typically solve this for me with explanations like, "We have to crawl through this tube and up two decks to reach engineering." To write things like this, we'll need to remember our layout, but that may not require a map. We could just jot down what deck everything is on and whether it's fore, aft, port, or starboard. For example, engineering might be aft, port side, deck 5 of 20.

HOW TO CREATE ONE

For dungeon maps, we can use lined graph paper to draw hallways, doors, and rooms, each with a width determined by the scale we've chosen, such as a square on the grid being five feet. We need to decide where the entrance is but may freely arrange areas such as those named in the previous section. A dungeon is often below another structure like a castle, meaning foundation walls, pillars, and other supports will be incorporated into the design.

For space ships, we should determine a list of areas we need. This can be based partly on something like a cruise or cargo ship or actual military vessels on which people live. In addition to places like the bridge, engineering, and propulsion, living areas are needed, including dining, recreation, sleeping quarters, general stores, and more. An interstellar ship could keep travelers on it for a very long time and need to satisfy their needs. See the next section for software that can help create a spaceship map.

For wooden vessels, we'll want to find a resource (possibly online) that shows us typical configurations, such as this one: http://www.artofworldbuilding.com/warship. We can model our design on this, removing decks in smaller vessels. This might take some drawing skill, but the point is that we don't need to invent internal layouts so much as understand how these ships are already structured. We can print such an image and trace it, or hire an artist to do it, or suggest readers refer to a link included in an author's note at the start of a tale.

For wooden ship layouts, most people don't understand existing ones and aren't bored with them, so we should research what's commonplace on Earth and use something similar. Creating a layout might be beneficial for readers, in order to clarify little-understood nautical terms like port, starboard, orlop, bow, stern. We may point readers of an eBook to an online resource, but print books lack this capability. Including an existing image requires gaining the copyright, but we can hire an artist to create one similar or attempt to draw it ourselves, using a program like Cosmographer 3.

Map Generation Software

There are programs available which require no drawing experience to create maps. I recommend checking out

ProFantasy. Campaign Cartographer, which is excellent for creating continent and region overland maps, has optional add-on programs. One is City Designer, which allows us to create villages, towns, and cities using everything from fantasy-looking buildings to futuristic ones. Dungeon Designer can do the same for dungeons. Cosmographer can create star maps and space ships. With some ingenuity, we might be able to create deck plans for wooden ships, too.

These products produce professional-looking results that can be included on our websites or within the pages of our books. Game designers can use them for campaigns. Hobbyists can have endless fun inventing places.

A quick internet search will turn up other options for drawing maps, or you can follow this link http://www.artofworldbuilding.com/mapprograms to a list of programs.

CONCLUSION

While this volume focuses on creating places, world building doesn't need to start with the planet itself, or anywhere on it. We could start with inventing species, plants, animals, gods and other beings as described in *Creating Life (The Art of World Building, #1)*. More often than not, we'll crisscross between subjects as we refine our ideas. Everything is optional, but if you're stuck on deciding what to do first, follow your heart. Start with what matters most to you so that you don't burn out on creating things you care about less. It's also vital to remember your goals: create what you need for your story or career but don't invent anything you can't or won't use. The templates will help you stay organized and might even inspire more invention. And if you ever get frustrated or overwhelmed, take a break.

Remember, world building is fun!

SOLAR SYSTEM TEMPLATE

SOLAR SYSTEM NAME

STAR

What type of star is it (yellow, red dwarf) and does it have a name? Are there two stars?

PLANETS COUNT

How many planets are in the system?

GALAXY

In what galaxy is this solar system found?

NAME

TYPE

Is this a spiral galaxy?

PLANET 1 NAME

PLANET TYPE

Rocky, ice, or gas? Does it have an atmosphere and breathable by humans or another species? How far from the star is it? Is it in the habitable zone? What is the temperature range? What species live here?

ENVIRONMENT

What is the axial tilt (23.5 degrees like Earth)? Does it orbit counterclockwise or clockwise? Is it tidally locked to the sun? How long does it take, in days, to orbit the sun?

SATELLITES

Does it have a ring system and if so, what is it made of? Ice, gas, stone? is it visible from other planets with the naked eye?

MOONS

How many moons does it have?

MOON 1 NAME

Is it tidally locked? Is it the nearest moon or not? Is the orbit circular, elliptical, retrograde? Is it habitable?

SOVEREIGN POWER TEMPLATE

POWER NAME

GOVERNMENT TYPE

Your sovereign power's government is an important factor to decide because it will impact most other items in this template. That said, government can change in the course of history. Decide what type it is in your "current" time period. You can create a different historical version later if you want.

Example text: Since 510 AE, Nivera has been a federal republic of fifteen provinces governed by a constitution, congress and elected president who is both head of state and government. The president's official residence is in the capitol and called the "The Spired Dome" for its iconic dome, which is also the national symbol.

WHO RULES

Your government type will determine who is head of state and head of government. Now name someone who is currently in those roles, such as: "King Huma is a ceremonial head of state with limited powers. Prime Minister Olina is head of government. The two are often at odds with each other privately but publicly pretend they aren't—a poorly kept secret."

WHO REALLY RULES

Sometimes other groups have power or affect things considerably. For example, in the United States, powerful lobbyists and special interest groups are often thought to be buying influence. Who in your realm is doing such things? It can be the wealthy, land holders, or even clandestine groups or an evil wizard who has the head of government (or legislature) in their power. The public can also be in power by voting people out of office, or applying pressure to get their way.

HISTORY

If you want to, create previous versions of your power. Examples suggested below. I wrote these in chronological order (oldest first) because it's easier.

ABSOLUTE MONARCHY (1-150 AE)

Nivera was an absolute monarchy for many years, with the king claiming the divine right of kings gave him authority to do as he pleased. His abuses, and those of his descendants, slowly eroded confidence in the monarchy and led to demands for more freedom. These rebellions were crushed brutally, heretics being burned at the stake, earn-ing Nivera a bad reputation for harshness. During this time, many castles of the realm were built.

CONSTITUTIONAL MONARCHY (150-340 AE)

After the War of Whatever with Kingdom Nemon, the King of Nivera was forced by the people to sign the Treaty of Whatcamacallit, ceding much power to a newly forming parliament. The king became an increasingly ceremonial head of state while the prime minister ran the government. Prosperity for the common people increased due to their voting power to elect members to parliament, which enacted laws to grant more personal liberty.

DICTATORSHIP (341-388 AE)

When Kingdom Sumor conquered Nivera in the Ten Years War, a power vacuum remained because the conquering kingdom didn't have the men to hold Nivera, whose remaining forces regrouped and expelled their conquerors. The military general seized control and ruled Nivera as a dictator.

FEDERAL REPUBLIC OF THE EMPIRE OF FAIN (388-510 AE)

Nivera became a state of the Empire of Fain, which defeated the dictatorship that had previously existed, annexing Nivera in the process and installing a republican government so Nivera could manage its own affairs. With the collapse of the empire, it remained a federal republic.

IDENTIFIERS

FAMOUS FOR

Think of any country on Earth—what comes to mind?
Add something for your power. Products, wars, rulers,
heroes, villains, and influence are good choices.

SYMBOL OR BANNER

Before deciding on one, it helps to know what sort of
government exists. Make it simple and memorable.

SLOGAN

Does your power have a slogan?

COLORS

Most powers have two to three colors associated with
them. The colors don't need to symbolize anything but it's
often better if they do.

LOCATION

What continent is it on, and in what general region
(north, west)? Use land features to specify its borders

where possible, and use the names of other powers for this later when you've established them.

SETTING

Name the land and sea features found here and how the population feels about them. Are some foreboding? Just dangerous? A source of pride and wonder? Are some coveted by other sovereign powers? Has the land feature changed hands at times?

CLIMATES

Is your power large enough to have territory in more than one climate, or differing elevations, which may themselves have different climates?

SETTLEMENTS

List the major settlements found in your sovereign power and how they relate to the power. Details on each will be in their own file, but a few comments here can help shape your power. For example, "Valendria is the wealthiest city in Nivera and home to many spectacles that bring visitors from all over the kingdom and other lands. Most in Nivera aspire to visit Valendria one day."

UNIQUE PLACES

Are there any places which have acquired significance due to supernatural phenomena, or a field of famous battles? How well known are they?

RELATIONSHIPS

ORGANIZATIONS

Discuss groups that live in your power and whether they're supported or the power tries to curtail their activities.

SOVEREIGN POWERS

Explain relationships with other powers.

POWER 1

Example: "Nivera has long been allies with Kingdom Fain due to their mutually threatening neighbor, the authoritative state Iruna."

POWER 2

Example: "A long history of aggression from Iruna has made Nivera a traditional enemy, with multiple major battles going back centuries. The strife is largely ideological in nature, but Nivera also controls access to the valuable ore found in the Nivera Mountains."

SPECIFIC ACCOMPLISHMENTS

INVENTIONS AND DISCOVERIES

Has anyone from the power invented or discovered something special? It could be weapons no one else has, such as those made here but nowhere else. Maybe there's an important plant only found within its borders. Or a supernatural phenomenon.

PLACES BUILT

Has the power built any place like specific buildings, infrastructure (like damns or aquafers), or even entire settlements that were formed on purpose (for a reason you'll want to cite) after the power came to be?

WORLD VIEW

LANGUAGES

Is there an official language and if so, what's it called? Naming it after the sovereign power is easiest. What other languages are widely spoken here? It might be dependent upon region. If you have species, which of their languages are spoken here? Read and written? Is a language forbidden? You'll need a reason for that one, such as elven being forbidden because war with elven lands nearby has occurred frequently and those speaking it are thought to be elven sympathizers who can't be trusted.

SOCIETY

Your society will be greatly affected by the current government, and to some extent, previous governments. What's the work week like here (number of days and hours)? How much freedom do people have in personal lives? Are they mostly content and complaining about trivial things, or do basic needs of food, shelter, and health occupy their times? Are public places well kept?

CUSTOMS

THE INHABITANTS

POPULATION

You don't need to know how many people there are, as figuring this out can be rather difficult. It may be more helpful, and less restrictive to you, to decide on population percentages. How many are human or elven, for example? Moreover, how do they get along? Are some concentrated in certain areas more? What about ethnicity?

Sample text: "The overall population is considered to include all of the good species, humans, and elves within its borders. Any evil species like ogres are not considered part of the population despite numbers in the hundreds of thousands."

HUMANS

Humans make up the majority of the population, at 45%. They dominate the legislature and are usually chosen as prime minister.

ELVES

The elves are 30% of the population, including half-elves, which are estimated at 1% of the elven total.

DWARVES

Dwarves are believed to be 25% of the population, most living in the mountain strongholds so that less than 5% are regularly seen elsewhere. The result is that they appear to be less of the population than they actually are.

ARMED FORCES

You might have knights, elven archers, or more in your sovereign power's army, or as part of the royal court, or just in the land as independent warriors. Decide who's around and what they're used for. How much prestige do they have? Are they feared or respected or both? Are some of these guys the sort who could become dictator should your power become weak?

IMPORTANT CHARACTERS

Who is important in this country aside from the obvious government people? Any wizards? Knights? Heroes?

Villains? You can invent some individuals without worrying too much about them as characters—that's a storytelling issue for another time.

PUBLIC PLACES AND OCCASIONS

NOTABLE FESTIVALS AND HOLIDAYS

On the anniversary of your power's formation, there's probably a public holiday. Just pick a date. It doesn't have to mean anything prior to that. While you're at it, decide on other important ones, such as when a dictator fell from power, or a hero was born or saved "the world." You can just make up some stuff, spreading these out in the year. Hopefully you'll have a chance to use or mention that in your work. A new year's celebration is almost universal.

NOTABLE BUILDINGS, ESTABLISHMENTS, AND GUILDS

SETTLEMENT TEMPLATE

SETTLEMENT NAME

GENERAL

ALLIANCES

Is this an independent city or part of a kingdom? Who are its allies? Note how many smaller settlements are nearby and in which directions; if this is a city, then is there one town ten miles to the north and a dozen villages on the other sides, or is one area devoid of settlements for some reason?

IDENTIFICATION

Symbol and Banner:
City Colors:
Slogans:

FAMOUS FOR

What comes to mind when people think of this place?

LOCATION

What continent, and where on it (northeastern, south)? Nearby land features? How accessible?

SETTING

What is the terrain (forests, mountainous, desert, plain, sea/river port?) Climate?

RELATIONS WITH OTHER SETTLEMENTS AND PLACES

TOWN 1

ELVEN FOREST 1

IMPORTANT FEATURES IN TOWN

Is there a distinctive land feature? City layout?

NOTABLE RELIGIOUS OR MAGIC/ TECHNOLOGICAL SITES

OTHER SPECIAL SITES

FORTIFICATIONS

WALLS/GATES

Is there a wall around it? How many gates? Well-guarded? Has it ever been breached?

CASTLE

Where is it and what condition is it in? Ruined or intact? What's it made of? How many towers? Ever been destroyed?

LOCAL LORE

Any legends or mysteries about the place?

PRODUCTS

This depends on geography. State why this is a product, such as having wood or fish from nearby land features.

HISTORY

What events are important in the formation of this settlement?

YEAR FOUNDED

WARS

BATTLES

Outcome? Who attacked them? Or did they attack?

THE INHABITANTS

What is their attitude toward magic, technology, gods, the supernatural, the species, and strangers?

LEADERS

What sort of government is here and who is currently running it? What type of mayor is here and what is his relationship with the council?

INFLUENCERS

Is some organization or individual really in control of the city?

POPULATION

What is the overall population count and which species live here? How do they get along? Are they segregated? What are they afraid/proud of?

HUMANS

RACE 1

RELIGION

What religions are taught/tolerated/shunned here?

ARMED FORCES

Is there an army? Garrison? Just local guards? Militia? Knights? Star fighters?

THE LOCAL GUARDS

How many? Well trained? Well equipped? Who's in charge?

KNIGHTS

IMPORTANT PEOPLE

PRIESTS

WIZARDS

Are they in town or nearby in a tower? Is magic tolerated? Feared? Can wizards cast spells in public or only in secret? Are they a rare/common sight?

HEROES

VILLAINS

NEARBY MONSTERS/CREATURES

Which ones are near and how many? What is the effect on the inhabitants and fortifications?

PUBLIC PLACES AND OCCASIONS

RELIGIOUS TEMPLES AND SITES

FESTIVALS AND HOLIDAYS

TAVERNS AND INNS

Are there any? Are they in a designated area or just anywhere? How friendly or suspicious of strangers are they? Are they safe or might you wake up dead?

GUILDS

Equipment Shops

What kinds of items are available for purchase or trade here? Is this place famous for making anything? Two-handed swords? Full plate armor? Silk tunics? Strong ropes? Devices?

Weapons

Armor

Clothing

General Gear

Special Considerations

Supernatural Phenomenon

Unknown

Are there are any secrets about this place, whether known to a few or not?

ABOUT THE AUTHOR

Randy Ellefson has written fantasy fiction since his teens and is an avid world builder, having spent three decades creating Llurien, which has its own website. He has a Bachelor of Music in classical guitar but has always been more of a rocker, having released several albums and earned endorsements from music companies. He's a professional software developer and runs a consulting firm in the Washington D.C. suburbs. He loves spending time with his son and daughter when not writing, making music, or playing golf.

Connect with me online

http://www.RandyEllefson.com
http://twitter.com/RandyEllefson
http://facebook.com/RandyEllefsonAuthor

If you like this book, please help others enjoy it.

Lend it. Please share this book with others.
Recommend it. Please recommend it to friends, family, reader groups, and discussion boards
Review it. Please review the book at Goodreads and the vendor where you bought it.

JOIN THE RANDY ELLEFSON NEWSLETTER!

Subscribers receive discounts, exclusive bonus scenes, and the latest promotions and updates! A FREE eBook of *The Ever Fiend (Talon Stormbringer)* is immediately sent to new subscribers!

www.ficiton.randyellefson.com/newsletter

Randy Ellefson Books

Talon Stormbringer

Talon is a sword-wielding adventurer who has been a thief, pirate, knight, king, and more in his far-ranging life.

The Ever Fiend
The Screaming Moragul

www.fiction.randyellefson.com/talonstormbringer

The Dragon Gate Series

Four unqualified Earth friends are magically summoned to complete quests on other worlds, unless they break the cycle – or die trying.

The Dragon Gate

www.fiction.randyellefson.com/dragon-gate-series/

The Art of World Building

This is a multi-volume guide for authors, screenwriters, gamers, and hobbyists to build more immersive, believable worlds fans will love.

Volume 1: Creating Life
Volume 2: Creating Places
Volume 3: Cultures and Beyond
Volume 4: Creating Life: The Podcast Transcripts

Volume 5: Creating Places: The Podcast Transcripts
Volume 6: Cultures and Beyond: The Podcast Transcripts
185 Tips on World Building
The Complete Art of World Building

Visit www.artofworldbuilding.com for details.

RANDY ELLEFSON
MUSIC

INSTRUMENTAL GUITAR

Randy has released three albums of hard rock/metal instrumentals, one classical guitar album, and an all-acoustic album. Visit http://www.music.randyellefson.com for more information, streaming media, videos, and free mp3s.

2004: The Firebard
2007: Some Things Are Better Left Unsaid
2010: Serenade of Strings
2010: The Lost Art
2013: Now Weaponized!
2014: The Firebard (re-release)

BIBLIOGRAPHY

"Angular Speed Formula." *SoftSchools.com*, SoftSchools.com. Retrieved 03 OCT 2017

Barnes, Rory, ed. *Formation and Evolution of Exoplanets*, John Wiley & Sons 2010

Barak A. *The Judge in a Democracy*, Princeton University Press 2006

Bouvier, John; Gleason, Daniel A. (1999). *Institutes of American Law*. The Lawbook Exchange, Ltd. p. 7.

Budge, Ian. "Direct democracy". In Clarke, Paul A.B. & Foweraker, Joe. *Encyclopedia of Political Thought*. Taylor & Francis 2001

Casson, Lionel. "Speed Under Sail of Ancient Ships." *Transactions of the American Philological Association*. New York University 1951

Choi, Charles. "How Many Planets Can Fit Inside a Star's Habitable Zone?" *Space.com*, Space.com. 31 OCT 2016, Retrieved 03 OCT 2017

Culver, Henry B., *The Book of Old Ships: From Egyptian Galleys to Clipper Ships*, 2nd edition, New York: Dover, 1992

Diamond, Larry. *In Search of Democracy.* London: Routledge 2015

Diamond, Larry. "Timeline: Democracy in Recession". *The New York Times.* 15 September 2015 Retrieved 25 JAN 2016.

Gaballa, Nervana (2006). "Speed of a River." *The Physics Factbook.* Retrieved 03 OCT 2017

Hénaff, Marcel; Strong, Tracy B. *Public Space and Democracy.* University of Minnesota Press 2001

Her Majesty's Nautical Almanac Office and United States Naval Observatory (2012). "Conjunction". *Glossary, The Astronomical Almanac Online.* Retrieved 08 JUL 2012

Israel, Robert (2017). "Two moons Orbiting at Different Speeds. Formula for When They Coincide." *Math.StackExchange.com,* Math.StackExchange.com. 4 JAN 2017, Retrieved 03 OCT 2017

Jane Burbank and Frederick Cooper, *Empires in World History: Power and the Politics of Difference,* (Princeton & Oxford, Princeton University Press, 2010

Kricher JC. *A neotropical companion: an introduction to the animals, plants, and ecosystems of the New World tropics,* 2nd Edition. New Jersey: Princeton University Press. 1997

Lambeck, K. "Tidal Dissipation in the Oceans: Astronomical, Geophysical and Oceanographic Consequences". *Philosophical Transactions of the Royal Society* 1977

Lavery, Brian. *Nelson's Navy: The Ships, Men and Organisation* 1793—1815. Annapolis: Naval Institute Press 1989

Linacre   Edward   and   Geerts   Bart,HYPERLINK "https://books.google.com/books?id=10lElCT7v5wC&pg=PA363&dq=%22Behaviour+of+teleost+fishes%22+%22%22 Functions+of+shoaling+behaviour+in+teleosts%22%22& num=50&ei=JzYKSpyWM42GkQSM992bBA" *Climates and Weather Explained*. Routledge 1997

Lutwyche, Jayne (2013). "Why are there seven days in a week?" *BBC Religion and Ethics*. bbc.co.uk/religion. Retrieved 03 OCT 2017

"LZ-129 Hindenburg," *Airships.net*, Airships.net. Retrieved 2017-10-03

Krasner, Professor Stephen D. *Problematic Sovereignty: Contested Rules and Political Possibilities*. Columbia University Press 2001

Malanczuk, Peter. *Akehurst's Modern Introduction to International Law*. International politics/Public international law. Routledge 1997

Murray, C.D.; Dermott, Stanley F. *Solar System Dynamics*. Cambridge University Press 1999

National Oceanic and Atmospheric Administration, "Climate." Retrieved 03 OCT 2017

Núñez, Jorge Emilio. "About the Impossibility of Absolute State Sovereignty". *International Journal for the Semiotics of Law*. 24 OCT 2013, Retrieved 03 OCT 2017

O'Brian, Patrick, *Men-Of-War: Life in Nelson's Navy* 1st edition, New York: Norton, 1974

O'Callaghan, Jonathan. "Five Amazing Facts About Interstellar Space." *Space Answers*, SpaceAnswers.com, 13 SEP 2013, Retrieved 03 OCT 2017

O'Callaghan, Jonathan. "What Would Happen If We Blew up The Moon." *Space Answers*, SpaceAnswers.com, 11 MAR 2013, Retrieved 03 OCT 2017

O'Neil, Patrick H. *Essentials of Comparative Politics*. 3rd ED. W. W. Norton 2010.

Ossian, Rob. "Complete List of Sailing Vessels." The Pirate King. *ThePirateKing.com*, Retrieved 03 OCT 2017

Riemers, Bill. "Are a planet's moons and/or rings all in the same plane as the planet's orbit?" *Quora.com*. Quora.com. 26 AUG 2015, Retrieved 03 OCT 2017

Rodger, Nicholas. *The Command of the Ocean: A Naval History of Britain 1649-1815*. W. W. Norton & Company 2005

Scharringhausen, Britt. *Ask an Astronomer*. Curios.astro.cornell.edu. "Is the Moon Moving Away From The Earth? When Was This Discovered?" 18 JUL 2015, Retrieved 03 OCT 2017

Skyship Services. "FAQ." *Sky Ship Services*, SkyShipServices.com. Retrieved 03 OCT 2017

"Sloop." *The Way of the Pirates.* TheWayOfThePirates.com. Retrieved 03 OCT 2017

Touma, Jihad; Wisdom, Jack. "Evolution of the Earth-Moon system". *The Astronomical Journal* 1994

"Trigonometry." (2000) *Physics Laboratory,* Clemson Education. Retrieved 03 OCT 2017

"Types of Wetlands and Their Roles in the Watershed." *North Carolina State University,* Water.NCSU.edu. Retrieved 03 OCT 2017

Webster's Encyclopedic Unabridged Dictionary of the English Language, Portland House, New York 1989

Whipple, Addison. *Storm.* Time Life Books 1982

Whiteman, C. David. *Mountain Meteorology: Fundamentals and Applications.* Oxford University Press 2000

Wolford, Rider, Scott, Toby. "War, Peace, and Internal Sovereignty." Retrieved 19 JUN 2011.

Made in the USA
Middletown, DE
05 June 2020